W9-ABG-195

THE INDIANS AND ESKIMOS

of North America: A Bibliography
of Books in Print through 1972

by
Jack W. Marken, Ph.D.
South Dakota State University

WITHDRAWN

Dakota Press
1973

University of South Dakota, Vermillion, S.D. 57069

KVCC KALAMAZOO VALLEY
COMMUNITY COLLEGE
LIBRARY

41431

Copyright, © 1973, University of South Dakota
Library of Congress Catalog Card Number: 73-78384

ISBN 0-88249-016-8
Printed in the United States of America

To
Marty
and
Janice and Jack, Roger and Niki
and Hal and Jami

PREFACE

Except for the short list of books compiled by Arlene Hirschfelder for the Association on Indian Affairs and one or two mimeographed checklists locally compiled and generally unavailable, no handy modern bibliography of the American Indian exists. Hirschfelder's list is almost exclusively books by Indian authors as she, perhaps wisely, makes no attempt to include other works, except a few anthologies. I have attempted in my list to include all books by and about the American and Canadian Indian and the Eskimo in print in 1972. Included are a few books not in print, but these are likely to be reprinted in the near future as the accelerated activity of American presses brings out new Indian books and reprints at an amazing rate.

The bibliography consists of books on Eskimos and Indians of North America only, except that books by American Indians on other areas are included. The price and number of pages for most books are given, and books published in paperback edition are marked with an asterisk. Books for children are designated by the grades in the American schools for which they are appropriate, following the usage of *Books in Print*. Most fictional works on the American Indian are omitted except a rather large list for school children and a representative group of the twentieth century novels from Lafarge's early *Laughing Boy*, a novel understandably unsatisfactory to the American Indian, to Momaday's *House Made of Dawn*, an outstanding novel which has deserved the honors bestowed on it.

The bibliography is divided into several sections. Perhaps the most useful for quick reference is the alphabetical "Selected Subject Index." In this section every subject containing three or more references within the bibliography is listed so that the reader may find almost all the books on that subject quickly. I say almost because many general works will contain major sections, including whole chapters and separate articles in edited books, on these subjects, and this information is not indicated in this index. Even within this major section such a subject as "Kwakiutl" might be included under "Canadian Indian," but is not. Also "Chippewa" and "Ojibwa" and "Osceola" and "Seminole" might have been separated into four distinct areas rather than two. Some readers might place some entries under "Art" within "Culture"; in such general subjects it is difficult to make specific distinctions, and the subject lists are intended to be useful in a general way rather than to offer definitions of subject areas.

For the convenience of readers, I have listed some books twice. These are books which might occur to readers under title rather than author, or are generally known by title rather than author. But such distinctions may be more in the compiler's mind than the readers, and I have kept duplication to a minimum. I have also noted most of the reprints in the University of California *Publications in American Archaeology and Ethnology*, Nos. 4001-4050, by giving authors only in the text. As the list is printed separately, readers can refer to these important publications easily.

Where I know that the author is Indian or of Indian descent, I have indicated that in the entry, and this is perhaps the most controversial aspect of the bibliography. I do not wish to enter into a definition of Indian, but I am sure that many readers want to know which authors are Indian. I am certain that I have omitted some Indian authors and hope that the omission will be considered to be inadvertent. Corrections of this and other elements within the bibliography will be accepted with sincere gratitude.

This bibliography will be useful to students, teachers, and scholars. Teachers who order books for school libraries will find the list useful because most of the books are available, and scholars will find that the list provides a supplement to even the best library holdings, containing, as it does, books on almost any subject associated with the Indian and Eskimo.

For her expert typing and aiding in the editorial work on this bibliography, I owe thanks to Mrs. Cathy Tritle, which this short statement can partially acknowledge.

Jack W. Marken
English Department
South Dakota State University
Brookings, South Dakota 57006

Contents

SELECTED SUBJECT INDEX

1411, 1463, 1464, 1497, 1522, 1524, 1528, 1568, 1687, 1727,
1742, 1743, 1766, 1772, 1780, 1782-84, 1831, 1872, 1873,
1908, 2003, 2005, 2007, 2015, 2065, 2140-42, 2174-77, 2200,
2201, 2232, 2318, 2392, 2407-12, 2415, 2436, 2440, 2474,
2504, 2570, 2571, 2594, 2622, 2762, 2800, 2814, 2817, 2860,
2876, 2948, 3031-34

Nez Perce: 210, 211, 329, 429, 583, 640, 694, 783, 879, 1133, 1139,
1328, 1442, 1589, 1590, 1593, 1722, 1777, 1895, 2113, 2347,
2657, 2889,

Osceola (Seminole): 685, 700, 789, 916, 1059, 1195, 1446, 1942,
1943, 2059, 2068, 2659, 2963

Pima: 449, 575, 867, 895, 2472

Pocahantas: 618, 1006, 1261, 1856, 1974, 2438, 2554, 2555, 3020

Pomo: 515, 625, 788

Pueblo: 473, 480, 508, 567, 606, 698, 816, 830, 843, 883, 884, 899,
912, 941, 977, 1016, 1121, 1122, 1168, 1176, 1189, 1207, 1264,
1291, 1296, 1429, 1431, 1481, 1521, 1710, 1715, 1770, 1841,
1911, 1972, 2083, 2084, 2252, 2296, 2489, 2585, 2613, 2650,
2711, 2822, 2827, 2867-69, 2888, 2917, 2920, 2955-57, 2965

Sacajawea: 686, 1182, 1293, 1494, 1588, 2546, 2879

Seneca: 620, 1153, 1320, 1476, 2276, 2277, 2281, 2895

Sioux (Dakota): 116, 117, 152, 162-70, 187, 191, 192, 203, 206,
258, 282, 293, 304, 305, 361, 364, 367, 373, 391, 402, 430, 433,
478, 486, 487, 544, 565, 566, 574, 581, 582, 682, 701, 719, 776,
777, 779, 794-96, 801, 823, 824, 851, 863, 885, 887, 892, 893,
896, 897, 908-11, 913, 950, 972, 985, 1038-42, 1044, 1081,
1109, 1135, 1143, 1146, 1184, 1188, 1190, 1252, 1267, 1330,
1332, 1366, 1390, 1412, 1434, 1451, 1455, 1465, 1483, 1509,
1536, 1558, 1632-34, 1651, 1654, 1740, 1833, 1848, 1868,
1878, 1912, 1916, 1920, 1921, 1931, 1949-51, 2014, 2023,
2039, 2041, 2092, 2095, 2101, 2104-06, 2125, 2170, 2182-84,
2224, 2239, 2242, 2245, 2268, 2292, 2325, 2333, 2361, 2378,
2404, 2421, 2431, 2432, 2439, 2463, 2494, 2497, 2618, 2619,
2658, 2664, 2838-40, 2863, 3022

Sitting Bull: 539, 1332, 2230, 2685, 2862, 2983

Tecumseh: 954, 982, 1124, 2017, 2259, 2687, 2802

Tewa: 454, 1118, 2297

Yuma: 868, 1275, 1278

Zuni: 261-63, 289, 424, 425, 464, 817, 941, 990-92, 1053, 1874,
2205, 2207, 2549, 2614, 2688, 2689, 3038

BIBLIOGRAPHIES

101. *An Annotated Bibliography of Young People's Fiction on American Indians.* Curriculum Bulletin No. 11. Office of Education Programs. U.S. Bureau of Indian Affairs. Washington, D.C., 1972. Books listed by tribe. 55 pp. Approximately 100 books annotated.

102. Barrow, Mark V., et al. *The Health and Diseases of American Indians North of Mexico. A Bibliography, 1800-1969.* Gainesville: University of Florida Press, 1970.

103. * Bell, Robert E. *Oklahoma Archaeology: An Annotated Bibliography.* A Stovall Museum Publication. Norman: University of Oklahoma Press, 1971. $1.95.

104. * Ceremonial Indian Book Service. *1970-1971 Inter-Tribal Indian Book List.* Gallup, New Mexico. 58 pp. Lists approximately 3,000 books on the Indian in print in 1970-71. $1.00. A sale catalog.

105. DePuy, Henry F. *A Bibliography of the English Colonial Treaties with the American Indians.* 1917; rpt. New York: AMS Press, 1970. $10.00. Also: St. Clair Shores, Michigan: Scholarly Press, 1970. $8.50.

106. * Dockstader, Frederick J. *Books About Indians.* 2nd ed. Rev. New York: Museum of the American Indian, 1972. $ .50.

107. * *Economic Development of American Indians and Eskimos, 1937-1967, A Bibliography.* 1968. Washington, D.C.: Government Printing Office, 1969. 263 pp. $2.00

108. Field, Thomas W. *Essay Toward an Indian Bibliography.* 1873; rpt. Detroit: Gale Research Publications, 1967. $12.50.

109. Freeman, John, and Murphy D. Smith. *A Guide to Manuscripts Relating to the American Indian in the Library of the American Philosophical Society.* Philadelphia: APS, 1966. 491 pp.

110. Harding, Anne D., and Patricia Bolling, eds. *Bibliography of Articles and Papers on North American Indian Art.* 1938; rpt. New York: Kraus Reprint Co., 1971. $15.00.

111. Hargrett, Lester. *Bibliography of the Constitutions and Laws of the American Indians.* 1947; rpt. New York: Kraus Reprint Co., 1971. 124 pp. $9.50.

---

* Indicates paperback

112. Haywood, Charles. *Bibliography of North American Folklore and Folksong.* 2 vols. New York: Dover Publications, Inc., 1961. $10.00 each.
113. * Hirschfelder, Arlene B. *American Indian Authors. A Representative Bibliography.* New York: Association on American Indian Affairs, Inc., 1970. 45pp. $1.00. Books by Indian authors only.
114. Klein, Bernard, and Daniel Icolari. *Reference Encyclopedia of the American Indian.* 2nd ed. Rev. Rye, New York: Klein Co., 1970. 536 pp. $15.00. Includes tribal offices, various kinds of information relating to Indian tribes.
115. Kluckhohn, Clyde, and Katharine Spencer. *A Bibliography of the Navaho Indians.* 1940; rpt. New York: AMS Press, 1970. $7.50.
116. McMullen, John, O.S.B. *A Guide to the Christian Indians of Upper Plains.* (An Annotated, Selective Bibliography.). Blue Cloud Abbey, 1969. 56 pp. Contains list of churches, Indian organizations, etc. Not all entries are annotated. Mimeographed.
117. * The Minnesota Historical Society. *Chippewa and Dakota Indians.* A Subject Catalog of Books, Pamphlets, Periodical Articles, and Manuscripts in the Minnesota Historical Society, A-Z, 1969. St. Paul: Minnesota Historical Society, 1969. 131 pp. $7.50. Approximately 2,100 entries.
118. Murdock, George P. *Ethnographic Bibliography of North America.* New Haven: Yale University Press. Regularly updated; it is the "bible," listing books and monographs by tribe and culture area.
119. Newberry Library. *Dictionary Catalog of the Edward E. Ayer Collection of Americana and American Indians.* 16 vols. Boston: G. K. Hall and Co., 1961. $820.00. See also No. 2197.
120. * Pearce, T. M., and Mabel Major. *Southwest Heritage: A Literary History with Bibliography.* 3rd ed. rev. Albuquerque: University of New Mexico Press, 1972. $10.00. In paper: $4.95.
121. Pilling, James C. *Bibliography of the Chinookan Languages.* 1893; rpt. Seattle: Shorey Publications, 1970. $6.00.
122. ——. *Bibliography of the Eskimo Language.* 1887; rpt. Seattle: Shorey Publications, 1971. $7.50.
123. ——. *Bibliographies of the Languages of the North American Indians.* 1887-1894; rpt. 9 parts in 3 vols. New York: AMS Press, Inc., 1970. $67.50.
124. Ullom, Judith C. *Folklore of the North American Indians.* An Annotated Bibliography. Washington, S.D.: Government Printing Office, 1969. Also listed under Folklore. 126 pp. $2.25.

HANDBOOKS

130. Boas, Franz. *Handbook of American Indian Languages.* 2 Parts. Smithsonian Institution Bureau of American Ethnology Bulletin 40. 1911; rpt. New York: Humanities Press, Inc., 1969. $65.00.

131. ——. *Introduction to the Handbook of American Indian Languages.* 1911; rpt. Seattle: Shorey Publications, 1970. $5.00.

132. ——. *Introduction to Handbook of American Languages.* Ed. Preston Holder, and J. W. Powell. *Indian Linguistic Families of America North of Mexico.* Gloucester, Mass.: Peter Smith, 1971. $4.25.

133. Cohen, Felix S. *Handbook of American Indian Law.* 1941; rpt. Albuquerque: University of New Mexico Press, 1970. Facsimile Edition. 700 pp. $25.00. Classical work on Indian law.

134. Cohen, Felix S. *Handbook of Federal Indian Law.* Washington, D.C.: Government Printing Office, 1946. Not an exact reprint of the preceding book. Reptd. New York: AMS Press, 1971. $20.00

135. * Heizer, Robert F. *The Languages, Territories, and Names of the California Indian Tribes.* Berkeley: University of California Press, 1966. 62 pp. $4.00.

136. * Heizer, Robert, F., and M. A. Whipple. *The California Indians.* A Source Book. Berkeley: University of California Press, 1951. 492 pp. $12.95. In paper: 1971. $3.95. See also Nos. 4040, 4042, 4044, and 4047.

137. Henry, Jeanette. *The American Indian in American History.* Indian Handbook Series No. 1. San Francisco: The Indian Historian Press, 1970. 84 pp. Author is Cherokee.

138. Hodge, Frederick W., ed. *Handbook of American Indians North of Mexico.* In Two Parts. Smithsonian Institution: Bureau of American Ethnology. Bulletin 30. Washington: Government Printing Office, 1907. Rpt. New York: Rowman and Littlefield, 1970. St. Clair Shores, Michigan: Scholarly Press; and Westport, Connecticut: Greenwood Press, Inc., 1971. $82.50.

139. Hodge, Frederick W. *Handbook of Indians of Canada.* Reprinted From *Handbook of American Indians North of Mexico.* Bulletin 30, Bureau of American Ethnology. Sessional Paper No. 21A. Ottawa, 1913; rpt. New York: Kraus Reprint Company, 1969. 632 pp. $25.00.

140. * Holder, Preston, ed. *An Introduction to the Handbook of American Indian Languages.* With Franz Boas' *Indian Linguistic*

3

Families of America North of Mexico. Lincoln: University of Nebraska Press, 1966. $1.85.

141. Holmes, William H. *Handbook of Aboriginal American Antiquities*. Part I. 1919, rpt. New York: Burt Franklin, Pub., 1969. $22.50. Also: Nashville, Tenn.: The Blue and Gray Press, 1971. 380 pp. $12.50.

142. Kroeber, Alfred L. *A Handbook of the Indians of California*. 1925; rpt. St. Clair Shores, Michigan: Scholarly Press, 1972. 995 pp. $49.50. Also: Berkeley: California Book Company, Inc., 1970. $17.50. See also: Nos. 4002-4047, many of which contain studies by Kroeber.

143. Owen, Roger C., James J. F. Deetz, and Anthony D. Fisher, eds. *The North American Indians: A Sourcebook*. New York: Macmillan, 1967. 752 pp. $10.95.

144. Robbins, Maurice, and Mary B. Irving. *The Amateur Archaeologist's Handbook*. New York: Thomas Y. Crowell Company, 1966. $6.95.

145. Rogers, Hugh C. *Indian Relics and Their Story: A Handbook for Collectors*. Fort Smith, Arkansas: Yoes Printing and Lithographing Co., 1962. 134 pp.

146. Schoolcraft, Henry R. *Historical and Statistical Information Respecting the History, Condition and Prospects of the Indian Tribes of the United States*. 7 vols. Ed. Francis S. Nichols. 1851-57; rpt. New York: AMS Press, 1969. $1500.00.

147. Suhm, Dee, and Edward B. Jelks, eds. *A Handbook of Texas Archaeology: Type Descriptions*. Ann Arbor, Michigan: University Microfilms, 1968. $9.00.

148. Wiley, G. R., General Ed. *Handbook of Middle American Indians*. 9 vols. Austin: University of Texas Press, 1964-69. $15.00.

AUTOBIOGRAPHIES

150. Barrett, Steven, M., ed. *Geronimo's Story of His Life*. American Biography Series. 1906; rpt. New York: Garrett Press, Inc., 1969. $11.95. See also Geronimo.

151. Bennett, Kay. *Kaibah: Recollections of a Navajo Girlhood*. Los Angeles: Western Lore Press, 1964. 253 pp. $7.50.

152. * Black Elk, (Nicholas). *Black Elk Speaks: Being the Life Story of a Holy Man of the Oglala Sioux*. As Told to John G. Neihardt. 1932; rpt. Lincoln, Nebraska: University of Nebraska Press, 1961. 280 pp. $1.50. Also: New York: Pocket Books, 1972. 238 pp. $1.50. Also: Gloucester, Mass.: Peter Smith, 1970. $3.75.

153. * Black Hawk. *Autobiography of Black Hawk*. As Dictated by Himself to Antoine Le Clair, 1833. Historical Society of Iowa. 1932; rpt. Ed. Donald Jackson. Champaign: University of Illinois Press, 1964. $1.75.

154. Buffalo Child Long Lance. *Long Lance*. New York: Cosmopolitan Book Corp., 1928. 278 pp.

155. Buffalo Child Long Lance, Chief. *Redman Echoes. Comprising the Writings of Chief Buffalo Child Long Lance and Biographical Sketches by His Friends*. Los Angeles: Dept of Printing, Frank Wiggins Trade School, 1933. 219 pp.

156. Chona, Maria. *Autobiography of a Papago Woman*. Ed. Ruth Underhill. Memoirs of the American Anthropological Association. Vol. 46. Menasha, Wisconsin, 1936. 64 pp. Author was Papago.

157. Chris. *Apache Odyssey: A Journey Between Two Worlds*. New York: Holt, Rinehart, Winston, 1969. 301 pp.

158. * Cochise, Ciyé "Nino". *The First Hundred Years of Nino Cochise*. The Untold story of an Apache Indian Chief. As Told to A. Kinney Griffith. New York: Pyramid Communications, Inc., 1972. 416 pp. $1.50.

159. * Crashing Thunder. *Crashing Thunder: The Autobiography of a Winnebago*. Ed. Paul Radin. 1926; rpt. New York: Dover Publications, 1963. 91 pp. $1.25. Also: Gloucester, Mass.: Peter Smith, 1972. $3.25.

160. Crook, George. *General George Crook: His Autobiography*. New edition. Ed. Martin F. Schmitt. Norman: University of Oklahoma Press, 1960. $6.95.

161. Cuero, Delphina. *The Autobiography of Delphina Cuero: A Diegueno Indian.* As told to Florence C. Shipek. Los Angeles: Dawson's Book Shope, 1968. 67 pp.

162. Custer, Elizabeth C. *Boots and Saddles: Or Life in Dakota with General Custer.* Western Frontier Library, No. 17. Rpt. Norman: University of Oklahoma Press, 1968. $2.95. Also: 1885; rpt. New York: Harper-Row, 1970. $4.95.

163. * ——. *Following the Guidon.* Rpt. Norman: University of Oklahoma Press, 1966. $2.95.

164. ——. *Tenting on the Plains.* Rpt. Western Frontier Library, Vols. 46, 47, 48. Norman: University of Oklahoma Press, 1970. $8.85.

165. * Custer, George A. *My Life on the Plains, or Personal Experiences with the Indians.* Rpt. Norman: University of Oklahoma Press, 1968. $7.95. Also: Gloucester, Mass.: Peter Smith, 1970. In paper: Ed. Milo M. Quaife. Lincoln: University of Nebraska Press, 1966. $2.25.

166. Eastman, Charles A. (Ohiyesa). *From the Deep Woods to Civilization: Chapters in the Autobiography of an Indian.* Boston: Little, Brown, 1916. 205 pp. Author was Sioux.

167. * Eastman, Charles A. (Ohiyesa). *Indian Boyhood.* 1902; rpt. Rapid City, S.D.: Fenwyn Press Books, 1970. 289 pp. $2.95. Also: New York: Dover Publications, 1970. $2.00. Also: Gloucester, Mass.: Peter Smith, 1972. $5.00.

168. ——. *Indian Today: The Past and Future of the First American.* 1915; rpt. Detroit: Gale Research Co., 1971.

169. ——. *Old Indian Days.* 1907; rpt. Rapid City, S.D.: Fenwyn Press Books, 1970. 279 pp. $2.95.

170. Fire, John (Lame Deer), and Richard Erdoes. *Lame Deer Seeker of Visions.* New York: Simon and Shuster, 1972. 288 pp. $7.95.

171. * Geronimo: His Own Story. As Told to Steven M. Barrett. 1906. Newly Edited with Introduction and Notes by Frederick W. Turner III. New York: Ballantine Books, Inc., 1971. 207 pp. $1.25. Hardbound: New York: E. P. Dutton Co., 1970. $6.95.

172. *Goodbird the Indian. His Story.* Told by himself to Gilbert L. Wilson. Illustrated by Frederick N. Wilson. New York: Fleming H. Revell Co., 1914.

173. Greene, Alma (Gah-wonh-nos-doh). *Forbidden Voice: Reflections of a Mohawk Indian.* London: Hamlyn, [1971]. 157 pp.

174. Griffis, Joseph K. (Chief Tahan). *Tahan: Out of Savagery into Civilization.* New York: George B. Doran Co., 1915. 263 pp.

175. *Howling Wolf: A Cheyenne Warrior's Graphic Interpretation of His People.* Ed. with Text by Karen D. Petersen. Palo Alto, California: American West Publishing Co., 1968. 64 pp.

176. * Jackson, Donald, ed. See Black Hawk, Number 153.

177. * Left Handed. *Son of Old Man Hat: A Navaho Autobiography.* As Told to Walter Dyk. 1938; rpt. Lincoln, Nebraska: University of Nebraska Press, 1967. 378 pp. $4.50.

178. * Linderman, Frank B. *Plenty-Coups: Chief of the Crows.* The Life Story of a Great Indian. London: Faber and Faber, Ltd., 1930; rpt. Lincoln: University of Nebraska Press, 1962. 324 pp. $1.80. Original title was *American, The Life Story of a Great Indian, Plenty-Coups, Chief of the Crows.* Also: Rpt. Gloucester, Mass.: Peter Smith, 1971. $4.00.

179. * Lone Dog, Louise. *Strange Journey: The Vision Life of A Psychic Indian Woman.* Ed. Vinson Brown. Healdsburg, California: Naturegraph Publishers, 1964. 68 pp. $1.50.

180. Long, James Larpenteur (First Boy). *The Assiniboines From the Accounts of the Old Ones Told to First Boy.* Ed. Michael S. Kennedy. Norman, Oklahoma: University of Oklahoma Press, 1961. 209 pp.

181. Chief Longlance Buffalo Child. *Autobiography.* New York: Cosmopolitan Book Corp., 1928.

182. * Lurie, Nancy O., ed. *Mountain Wolf Woman: Sister of Crashing Thunder.* The Autobiography of a Winnebago Indian. Ann Arbor Paperbacks. Ann Arbor: The University of Michigan Press, 1961. 142 pp. $4.95. In paper: $1.75.

183. Mitchell, Emerson Blackhorse. *Miracle Hill: The Story of a Navajo Boy.* Told to T. D. Allen. Norman: University of Oklahoma Press, 1967. 230 pp. $5.95.

184. Moises, Rosalio, Jane Holden Kelley, and William Lurry Holden. *The Tall Candle. The Personal Chronicle of a Yaqui Indian.* Lincoln: University of Nebraska Press, 1971. 251 pp.

185. * Momaday, N. Scott. *The Way to Rainy Mountain.* Albuquerque: University of New Mexico Press, 1969. $4.95. In paper: Ballantine Walden Editions. New York: Ballantine Books, 1970. $1.25. See also No. 2110.

186. *Old Mexican, A Navajo Autobiography.* As Told to Walter Dyk. New York: Viking Fund Publications in Anthropology. No. 8. 1947; rpt. New York: Johnson Reprint Corp., 1970. 218 pp.

187. * Red Fox, Chief William. *The Memoirs of Chief Red Fox.* With an Introduction by Cash Asher. New York: McGraw-Hill Book Co., 1971. 208 pp. $6.95. In paper: Greenwich, Conn.: Fawcett Crest Book, 1972. Largely spurious.

188. Sekaquaptewa, Helen. *Me and Mine: The Life Story of Helen Sekaquaptewa.* As told to Louis Udall. Tucson: University of Arizona Press, 1969. 262 pp. $3.95. Author is Hopi.

7

189. Senungetuk, Joseph. *Give or Take a Century: The Story of an Eskimo Family.* San Francisco: The Indian Historian Press, 1970. 120 pp. $12.00. Author is Eskimo.

190. *Sewid, James. *Guests Never Leave Hungry: The Autobiography of James Sewid, a Kwakiutl Indian.* Ed. James P. Spradley. New Haven: Yale University Press, 1969. 310 pp. $10.00. In paper: Montreal: McGill-Queens University Press, 1972. $3.95.

191. Standing Bear, Luther. *My Indian Boyhood.* Boston: Houghton Mifflin, 1928. 288 pp.

192. ———. *My People, The Sioux.* Ed. E. A. Brininstool. New York, 1931. 189 pp.

193. *Stands in Timber, John, and Margot Liberty. With assistance of Robert M. Utley. *Cheyenne Memories.* New Haven: Yale University Press, 1967. 330 pp. $10.00. In paper: Lincoln: University of Nebraksa Press, 1972. 330 pp. $2.25.

194. Steward, Julian H. *Two Paiute Autobiographies.* University of California Publications in American Archaeology and Ethnology. Vol. 33, Part 5. Berkeley: University of California Press, 1934. See also Nos. 4024, 4029, 4033, and 4034 below.

195. Sun Bear. *At Home in the Wilderness.* Sparks, Nevada: Western Printing and Publishing Co., 1969. Author is Chippewa.

196. *Sun Bear. *Buffalo Hearts.* A Native American's View of Indian Culture, Religion and History. Healdsburg, California: Naturegraph Publishers, 1970. 124 pp. Author is Chippewa.

197. Sweezy, Carl. *The Arapaho Way: A Memoir of An Indian Boyhood.* As told to Althea Bass. New York: Clarkson N. Potter, Inc., 1966. 80 pp. Author was an Arapaho.

198. *Talayesva, Don C. *Sun Chief: The Autobiography of a Hopi Indian.* Ed. Leo W. Simmons. 1942; rpt. Yale Western Americana Paperbound. New Haven, Conn.: Yale University Press, 1970. 460 pp. $3.75.

199. *TwoLeggings: The Making of a Crow Warrior.* Ed. Peter Nabokov. New York: Thomas Y. Crowell, 1967. 226 pp. $6.95. In paper: New York: Appollo Editions, Inc., 1970. $2.25.

200. *Underhill, Ruth M., ed. *The Autobiography of a Papago Woman.* 1936; rpt. New York: Kraus Reprint Co., 1971. $3.00.

201. Webb, George. *A Pima Remembers.* Tucson, Arizona: University of Arizona Press, 1959. 126 pp. $3.00. Author is a Pima Indian.

202. White, Elizabeth (Polingaysi Qoyawayma). *No Turning Back.* As told to Vada F. Carlson. Albuquerque: University of New Mexico Press, 1964. 180 pp.

203. White Bull, Joseph. *The Warrior Who Killed Custer: The Personal Narrative of Chief Joseph White Bull*. Ed. James H. Howard. Lincoln: University of Nebraska Press, 1968. 84 pp. See also: Parks, Jack, and Vestal, Stanley.

204. * *Jim Whitewolf: The Life of a Kiowa Apache Indian*. Ed. with an Introduction and Epilogue by Charles S. Brant. New York: Dover Publications, Inc., 1969. 141 pp. $1.75.

205. Winnie, Lucille (Sah-Gan-De-Oh). *Sah-gan-de-oh, The Chief's Daughter*. New York: Vantage Press, 1968. 190 pp. $3.95. Autobiography of a Seneca-Cayuga woman.

206. * *Wooden Leg: A Warrior Who Fought Custer*. Interpreted by Thomas B. Marquis. Minneapolis, Minnesota: The Midwest Co., 1931; rpt. Lincoln: University of Nebraska Press, 1962. 384 pp. In paper: Lincoln: University of Nebraska Press, 1962. 389 pp. $1.90.

207. Worthylake, Mary M. *Children of the Seed Gatherers*. Chicago: Melmont Publishers, Inc., 1964. (Grades 2-4) $2.75.

208. ——. *Nika Illahee: My Homeland*. Chicago: Melmont Publishers, Inc., 1962. (Grades 2-5) $2.75.

209. Yellow Robe. *An Album of the American Indian*. New York: Franklin Watts, Inc., 1969. 96 pp. Author is Sioux.

210. *Yellow-Wolf: His Own Story*. Ed. Lucullus V. McWhorter. Caldwell, Idaho: The Caxton Printers, 1940. 324 pp.

211. * Young, Joseph. *Chief Joseph's Own Story*. 1879; rpt. Fairfield, Washington: Ye Galleon Press, 1972. $2.00.

9

MYTHS AND LEGENDS

220. Adamson, Thelma E., ed. *Folk-Tales of the Coast Salish.* American Folklore Memoirs Series, 1934; rpt. New York: Kraus Reprint Co., 1970. $18.00.
221. Alexander, Hartley B. *L'Art et La Philosophie Des Indians de L'Amerique du Nord.* Paris: Editions Ernest Leroux, 1926.
222. ———. *North American Mythology.* Mythology of All Races Series, Vol. 10. 1916; rpt. New York: Cooper Square Publishers, Inc., 1964. $13.00.
223. * Alexander, Hartley B. *The World's Rim: Great Mysteries of the North American Indians.* A Bison Book. Lincoln, Nebraska: University of Nebraska Press, 1967. 259 pp. $1.95.
224. *American Indian Fairy Tales.* Retold by W. T. Larned. Illustrated by John Rae. 9th ed. New York: P. F. Volland Co., 1921. Stories are adapted from the Legends of Henry R. Schoolcraft. Unpaged children's book.
225. *American Indian Poetry.* See Cronyn, George W.
226. Anderson, Bernice G. *Indian Sleep-Man Tales.* New York: Bramhall House, 1940. 145 pp. $2.50. Children's book.
227. Applegate, Frank G. *Indian Stories from the Pueblos.* 1929; rpt. Glorietta, New Mexico: Rio Grande Press, Inc., 1971. $8.00.
228. * Astrov, Margot, ed. *American Indian Prose and Poetry.* New York: Capricorn Books, 1962. (1946) Originally published in 1946 as *The Winged Serpent.* 366 pp. $2.45. Also: New York: John Day Co., 1972. $7.95.
229. Bagley, Clarence B. *Indian Myths of the Northwest.* 1930; rpt. Seattle, Washington: Shorey Publications, 1970. $8.50.
230. Bailey, Carolyn S. *Stories From An Indian Cave: The Cherokee Cave Builders.* Chicago, Ill.: Albert Whitman and Co., 1935. A Junior Press Book. (Told for children.) 217 pp. 25 stories, adopted from Cherokee legends.
231. Barrett, Samuel A., ed. *Pomo Myths.* 1933; rpt. New York: Johnson Reprint Co., 1971. $25.00. See also Nos. 4012 and 4016.
232. Beauchamp, William M. *Iroquois Folklore Gathered from the Six Nations of New York.* Empire State Historical Publications Series, No. 31. 1922; rpt. Port Washington, N. Y.: Ira J. Friedman, Inc., 1970. $7.50.
233. Beckwith, Martha W. *Manden-Hidatsa Myths and Ceremonies.* 1937; rpt. New York: Kraus Reprint Co., 1969. 320 pp. $14.00.

234. Belting, Natalia M. *The Earth is on a Fish's Back: Tales of Beginnings*. New York: Holt, Rinehart and Winston, 1965. $3.27. Grades 4-6.

235. ———. *The Long-Tailed Bear and Other Indian Legends*. Eau Claire, Wisconsin: E. M. Hale and Co., 1961. (Grades 4-6) Also: Indianapolis: Bobbs-Merrill Corp., 1961. $3.25.

236. Benedict, Ruth F. *Tales of the Cochiti Indians*. Bureau of American Ethnology. Bulletin 98. Washington, D.C., 1931.

237. ———. *Zuni Mythology. Columbia University Contributions to Anthropology*, Vol. 21. New York: Columbia University Press, 1935; rpt. 2 vols. New York: AMS Press, 1969. $47.50; $25.00 each.

238. Bennett, Kay, and Russ Bennett. *A Navajo Saga*. San Antonio, Tex.: Naylor Co., 1969. Grades 8 up. $6.95.

239. Bierhorst, John, and Henry R. Schoolcraft, eds. *Fire Plume Legends of the American Indians*. New York: Dial Press, Inc., 1969. (Grades 2-7). 90 pp. $4.50.

240. Bierhorst, John, ed. *In the Trail of the Wind: American Indian Poems and Ritual Orations*. New York: Farrar, Straus and Giroux, Inc., 1971. (Grades 7 up). 200 pp. $4.95.

241. ———.*The Ring in the Prairie: A Shawnee Legend*. New York: Dial Press, 1970. (Grades 1-4) 36 pp. $4.95.

242. Boas, Franz. *Bella Bella Tales*. 1932; rpt. New York: Kraus Reprint Co., 1970. $7.50. See also: No. 4020.

243. ———. *Bella Bella Texts*. Columbia University Contributions to Anthropology Series, Vol. 5. 1928; rpt. New York: AMS Press, 1969. $15.00.

244. ———. *Folk Tales of Salishan and Sahaptin Tribes*. Lancaster, Pa.: American Folk-Lore Society, 1917; rpt. New York: Kraus Reprint Co., 1971. $9.00.

245. Boas, Franz. *Kwakiutl Culture as Reflected in Mythology*. 1935; rpt. New York: Kraus Reprint Co., 1970. $9.00.

246. ———. *Kwakiutl Tales*. Columbia University Contributions to Anthropology Series, Vol.2. 2 vols. 1910; rpt. New York: AMS Press, 1969. $34.00; $18.00 each.

247. ———. *Tsimshian Mythology. Based on Texts Recorded by Henry W. Tate*. 1916; rpt. New York: Johnson Reprint Corp., 1970. $35.00.

248. Boatright, Moody C., ed. *The Sky is My Tipi*. Dallas: Southern Methodist University Press, 1949. $5.95.

249. Brinton, Daniel G. *American Hero-Myths: A Study in the Native Religions of the Western Continent*. Series in American Studies Series. Rpt. New York: Johnson Reprint Corp., 1970. $9.00.

250. ——. *Ancient Nahuatl Poetry. Library of American Aboriginal Literature.* Vol. 7. 1890; rpt. New York: AMS Press, 1971. $8.00.

251. ——. *Annals of the Cakchiquels.* 1885; rpt. New York: AMS Press, 1970. $8.00.

252. ——. *The Lenape and their Legends. Library of Aboriginal American Literature Series*, No. 5. 1884; rpt. New York: AMS Press, 1971. $8.00.

253. ——. *The Library of Aboriginal American Literature.* 8 vols. 1882-90; rpt. New York: AMS Press, 1970. $60.00; $8.00 each.

254. ——. *The Maya Chronicles. Library of Aboriginal American Literature Series*, No. 1. 1882; rpt. New York: AMS Press, 1971. $8.00.

255. ——. *Myths of the New World: A Treatise on the Symbolism and Mythology of the Red Race of America.* Americana Series, No. 37. 1876; rpt. New York: Haskell House Publishers, Inc., 1969. 360 pp. $12.95. Also: 2nd ed. Westport, Conn.: Greenwood Press, Inc., 1962. $13.25.

256. ——. *The Religions of Primitive Peoples.* 1897; rpt. Westport, Conn.: Negro Universities Press, 1970. $10.50.

257. ——. *Rig Veda Americanus. Library of Aboriginal American Literature Series*, No. 8. 1890; rpt. New York: AMS Press, 1971. $8.00.

258. * Brown, Joseph Epes. *The Sacred Pipe.* Black Elk's Account of the Seven Rites of the Oglala Sioux. Norman: University of Oklahoma Press, 1953. 144 pp. $3.75. In paper: Baltimore: Penguin Books, Inc., 1971. $1.75.

259. * Brown, Lisette. *Tales of Sea Foam.* Healdsburg, California: Naturegraph Publishers, 1971. (Grades 6 up) $3.75. In paper: $1.75.

260. Budd, Lillian. *Full Moons: Indian Legends of the Seasons.* New York: Rand McNally and Co., 1971. (Grades 4-6) $4.95.

261. Bunzel, Ruth. *Introduction to Zuni Ceremonialism.* 47th Annual Report of the Bureau of American Ethnology. Washington, 1939, pp. 469-544.

262. ——. *Zuni Ritual Poetry.* 47th Annual Report of the Bureau of American Ethnology. Washington, D.C., 1932, pp. 613-835.

263. ——. *Zuni Texts.* Publications of the American Ethnological Society. Vol. 15. New York: Stechert, 1933.

264. Burland, Cottie. *North American Indian Mythology.* London: Paul Hamlyn, 1965. 141 pp. Included also in *Mythology of the Americas.* New York: Hamlyn, 1970. 407 pp. $17.95. Bound together in this book are: Burland, *North American Indian Mythology*, Irene Nicholson, *Mexican and Central American Mythology*, and Harold Osborne, *South American Mythology*.

12

265. Canfield, William W. *Legends of the Iroquois.* Empire State Historical Publications Series. 1902; rpt. Port Washington, N. Y.: Kennikat Press, Inc., 1970. $7.50.

266. Chafetz, Henry. *Thunderbirds and Other Stories.* New York: Pantheon Books, 1964. (Grades 3-5) $4.59.

267. Chalmers, Harvey, II. *Tales of the Mohawk: Stories of Old New York State from Colonial Times to the Age of Homespun.* Empire State Historical Publications Series. Rpt. Port Washington, N. Y.: Ira J. Friedman, Inc., 1968. $6.50.

268. * Clark, Ann. *Navajo Life Stories.* Illustrated by Hoke Denetsosie. Lawrence, Kansas: Haskell Press, 1940. $2.00.

269. Clark, Cora, and Texa B. Williams, eds. *Pomo Indian Myths and Some of their Sacred Meanings.* Deer Park, N. Y.: Brown Book Co., 1970. $3.00.

270. Clark, Ella E. *Indian Legends from the Northern Rockies.* Civilization of the American Indian Series. No. 82. Norman: University of Oklahoma Press, 1966. 350 pp. $6.95.

271. * ——. *Indian Legends of the Pacific Northwest.* Berkeley: University of California Press, 1953. 225 pp. In paper: 1969. $1.95.

272. * Coffin, Tristram P., ed. *Indian Tales of North America: An Anthology for the Adult Reader.* American Folklore Society Bibliographical and Special Series, Vol. 13. Austin: University of Texas Press, 1961. $4.00.

273. Coleman, Sr. Bernard, et al. *Ojibwa Myths and Legends.* Minneapolis: Ross and Haines, 1970. 135 pp. $4.95.

274. Compton, Margaret, and Lorence F. Bjoklund. *American Indian Fairy Tales.* New York: Dodd, Mead and Co., 1971. (Grades 5 up) 159 pp. $3.95.

275. Cornplanter, Jesse J. *Legends of the Longhouse.* Empire State Historical Publications Series, No. 24. 1938; rpt. Port Washington, N.Y.: Ira J. Friedman, Inc., 1963. 218 pp. $6.75. Author was Seneca.

276. * Costello, Joseph A. *Siwash: Their Life, Legends and Tales.* 1895; rpt. Facsimile ed. Seattle, Wash.: Shorey Publications, 1970. $10.00

277. * Courlander, Harold. *Fourth World of the Hopi.* New York: Crown Publishers, Inc., 1970. $6.95. Also: In paper: New York: Fawcett World Library, 1972.

278. ——. *People of the Short Blue Corn: Tales and Legends of the Hopi Indians.* New York: Harcourt, Brace, Jovanovich, 1970. (Grades 2-6) $5.95.

279. Cowles, Julia Darrow. *Indian Nature Myths.* With illustrations by Dorothy Dulin. Chicago: A. Flanagan Company, 1934. 128 pp.

280. Crane, Warren. *Totem Tales*. 1932; rpt. Facsimile ed. Seattle, Washington: Shorey Publications, 1970. $4.00.

281. * Cronyn, George W., ed. *American Indian Poetry*. An Anthology of Songs and Chants. New York: Liveright, 1962. (Originally titled *The Path on the Rainbow*, 1918.) 360 pp. In paper: $2.75.

282. Cropp, Richard. *Dacotah Tales*. Mitchell, S.D.: Mitchell Printing Co., 1968(?) 38 pp.

283. Crowell, Ann. *Shadow on the Pueblo: A Yaqui Indian Legend*. American Folktales Series. Champaign, Illinois: Garrard Publishing Company, 1972. (Grades 2-5) $2.95.

284. Curry, Jane L. *Down From the Lonely Mountain: California Indian Tales*. New York: Harcourt, Brace, Jovanovich, 1965. (Grades 4-6) 128 pp. $3.50.

285. Curtin, Jeremiah. *Creation Myths of Primitive America*. 1898; rpt. New York: Benjamin Bolm, Inc., 1969. 532 pp. $12.50.

286. ———. *Myths of the Modocs: Indian Legends of the Northwest*. 1912; rpt. New York: Benjamin Blom, 1972. 401 pp. $12.50.

287. ———. *Seneca Indian Myths*. Rpt. Bowling Green Station: N.Y.: Gordon Pr., 1972. $11.50.

288. * Curtis, Natalie. *The Indian's Book: An Offering by the American Indians of Indian Lore, Musical and Narrative, to form a Record of the Songs and Legends of their Race*. New York: Dover Publications, 1968. Unabridged and unaltered republication of second edition of Harper & Bros. in 1923. 584 pp. $4.00.

289. Cushing, Frank. *Outlines of Zuni Creation Myths*. 13th Report of the Bureau of American Ethnology. Washington, 1896, pp. 321-447.

290. Dangberg, Grace. *Washo Texts*. See No. 4022.

291. * Day, A. Grove. *The Sky Clears: Poetry of the American Indians*. 1951; rpt. Lincoln: University of Nebraska Press, 1964. 204 pp. $1.75.

292. * DeAngelo, Jaime. *Indian Tales*. New York: Hill and Wang, 1953. 246 pp. $4.50. Delightful story of the Bear family and friends in their travels with Grandfather Coyote, and others. Not legends, but in the spirit of Indian stories.

293. Deloria, Ella C. *Dakota Texts*. Publications of the American Ethnological Society. Vol. 14. New York: Stechert, 1932. 279 pp.

294. Demetracopoulou, D. *Wintu Myths*. See No. 4028, and DuBois, Constance, No. 302.

295. Dolch, Edward W., and M. P. Dolch. *Lodge Stories*. Basic Vocabulary Series. Champaign, Illinois: Garrard Publishing Company, 1957. (Grades 1-6) $3.95.

296. ——. *Navaho Stories.* Basic Vocabulary Series. Champaign, Illinois: Garrard Publishing Company, 1957. (Grades 1-6) $2.69.

297. ——. *Pueblo Stories.* Basic Vocabulary Series. Champaign, Illinois: Garrard Publishing Company, 1956. (Grades 1-6) 160 pp. $2.69.

298. ——. *Tepee Stories.* Basic Vocabulary Series. Champaign, Illinois: Garrard Publishing Company, 1956. (Grades 1-6) 165 pp. $2.69.

299. ——. *Wigwam Stories.* Basic Vocabulary Series. Champaign, Illinois: Garrard Publishing Company, 1956. (Grades 1-6) 165 pp. $2.69.

300. Dorsey, George A. *The Cheyenne Indians: The Sun Dance, Wyoming.* Rpt. Glorieta, New Mexico: Rio Grande Press, 1972. $20.00.

301. ——. *The Pawnee Mythology.* Washington, D.C.: Carnegie Institution of Washington, 1906.

302. * DuBois, Constance, and D. Demetracopoulou. *Wintu Myths.* University of California Publications in American Archaeology and Ethnology. Vol. 28, No. 5. Berkeley, California: University of California Press, 1931. See also No. 4028 below, a reprint of the original. See also No. 4036.

303. Dyson, Verne. *Heather Flower and Other Indian Stories of Long Island.* Empire State Historical Publications Series, No. 52. Fort Washington, New York: Ira J. Friedman, Inc., 1968. $4.75.

304. Eastman, Charles A. (Ohiyesa). *Red Hunters and the Animal People.* New York: Harper and Brothers, 1904. 249 pp.

305. Eastman, Mary. *Dahcotah; or, Life and Legends of the Sioux Around Fort Snelling.* 1849; rpt. Minneapolis, Minnesota: Ross and Haines, Inc., 1962. 268 pp. $8.75.

306. Emerson, Ellen R. *Indian Myths or Legends, Traditions, and Symbols of the Aborigines of America Compared with those of Other Countries Including Hindostan, Egypt, Persia, Assyria, and China.* 1884. Rpt. Minneapolis, Minnesota: Ross and Haines, Inc., 1965. 677 pp. Also: Gardoner, 1972. $11.00.

307. * Feldman, Susan. *The Story Telling Stone: Myths and Tales of the American Indians.* New York: Dell Publishing Company, 1971. 271 pp. In paper: $ .75.

308. Fisher, Anne B. *Stories California Indians Told.* Berkeley, California: Parnasus Press, 1957. (Grades 3-7) $3.50.

309. Fletcher, Alice C. *Indian Story and Song from North America.* 1900;rpt. New York: AMS Press, 1970. $7.50 Also: New York: Johnson Reprint Corp., 1970. $5.50.

310. *Folklore of the North American Indians.* An Annotated Bibliography. See Ullom, Judith C., No. 124.

311. Frachtenberg, Leo J. *Coos Texts*. Columbia University Contributions to Anthropology Series, Vol. 1. Rpt. New York: AMS Press, 1969. $11.25.

312. ———. *Lower Umpqua Texts and Notes on the Kusan Dialects*. Columbia University Contributions to Anthropology Series, Vol. 4. 1914; rpt. New York: AMS Press, 1969. $10.00.

313. Gatschet, Albert S. *A Migration Legend of the Creek Indians, with a Linguistic, Historic and Ethnographic Introduction*. 2 vols., 1884 and 1888; rpt. in one volume. New York: Kraus Reprint Co., 1969. 251 pp. and 207 pp. $17.50. Also: *A Migration Legend*. 1884; rpt. New York: AMS Press, 1972. $8.00.

314. Gayton, Anna, and Stanley S. Newman. *Yokuts and Western Mono Myths*. Anthropological Records of the University of California. Vol. 5, No. 1. Berkeley: University of California Press, 1940. See also Nos. 4021, 4024, and 4028 below.

315. * Giddings, Ruth W. *Yaqui Myths and Legends*. Tucson: University of Arizona Press, 1959. $3.95. In paper: $1.50.

316. Gilman, Benjamin I. *Hopi Songs*. Journal of American Ethnology and Archaeology. V (1908), 1-235.

317. Gilmore, Melvin R. (PAHOK). *Prairie Smoke*. New York: Columbia University Press, 1929; rpt. New York: AMS Press, 1970. $9.00.

318. Glass, Paul. *Songs and Stories of the North American Indians*. New York: Grossett and Dunlap, 1968. (Grades 3-5) $2.99.

319. Goddard, Pliny E. *Navajo Texts*. Anthropological Papers of the American Museum of Natural History. Vol. 34. New York, 1933.

320. Goodwin, Grenville, ed. *Myths and Tales of the White Mountain Apache*. 1939; rpt. New York: Kraus Reprint Co., 1969. 223 pp. $10.00.

321. Grey, Herman. *Tales From the Mohaves*. Civilization of the American Indian Series, No. 107. Norman: University of Oklahoma Press, 1970. 87 pp. $4.95.

322. Gridley, Marion E. *Indian Legends of American Scenes*. Chicago: M. A. Donohue and Company, 1970. $3.50.

323. Griffis, Joseph K. (Chief Tahan). *Indian Story Circle Stories*. Burlington, Vermont: Free Press Printing Company, 1928. 138 pp. Author was Osage.

324. * Gringhuis, Dirk. *Lore of the Great Turtle: Indian Legends of Mackinac Retold*. Mackinac Island, Michigan: Mackinac Island State Park Commission, 1970. $1.00.

325. * Grinnell, George B. *Blackfoot Lodge Tales*. 1890; rpt. Lincoln: University of Nebraska Press, 1962. 310 pp. Bison Book, BB 129. $2.25.

326. * ——. *Pawnee Hero Stories and Folk-Tales*. 1889; rpt. Lincoln: University of Nebraska Press, 1961. 417 pp. In paper: Bison Book, BB 116. $2.25.

327. * ——. *By Cheyenne Campfires*. Lincoln: University of Nebraska Press, 1971. 305 pp. $2.25. Folk-tales of the Cheyenne.

328. Haile, Father Berard. *Origin Legend of the Navaho Enemy Way*. Yale University Publications in Anthropology. New Haven: Yale University Press, 1938. 320 pp.

329. Heady, Eleanor B. *Tales of the Nimipoo: From the Land of the Nez Perce Indians*. New York: World Publishing Company, 1970. (Grades 7 up) $4.50.

330. Henry, Will. *Maheo's Children: The Legend of Little Dried River*. Philadelphia: Chilton Book Company, 1968. (Grades 8 up) $4.50.

331. Herman, James, and Others. *Kashaya Texts*. Ed. Robert L. Oswalt. University of California Publications in Linguistics. Vol. 36. Berkeley: University of California Press, 1964. 340. pp.

332. Hill, Kay. *Badger, the Mischief Maker*. New York: Dodd, Mead, and Co., 1965. (Grades 4 up) 95 pp. $3.25.

333. ——. *Glooscap and His Magic: Legends of the Wabanaki Indians*. New York: Dodd, Mead, and Co., 1963. (Grades 3 up) 192 pp. $3.50.

334. ——. *More Glooscap Stories*. New York: Dodd, Mead and Co., 1970. 160 pp. $4.50.

335. Hogner, Dorothy C. *Navajo Winter Nights: Folk Tales and Myths of the Navajo People*. New York: E. M. Hale and Company, 1938. (This is a special edition. The regular edition was published by Thomas Nelson and Sons.) 180 pp. Intended for children.

336. Hoijer, Harry. *Chiricahua and Mescalero Apache Texts*. With Ethnological Notes by M. E. Opler. The University of Chicago Publications in Anthropology. Linguistics Series. Chicago: University of Chicago Press, 1938.

337. Hood, Flora, ed. *The Turquoise Horse: Prose and Poetry of the American Indian*. Pictures by Marylou Reifsnyder. New York: G. P. Putnam's Sons, 1972. $4.69.

338. Hooke, Hilda M. *Thunder in the Mountains: Legends of Canada*. New York: Oxford University Press, 1947. $4.50.

339. Houston, James A. *Eagle Mask: A West Coast Indian Tale*. New York: Harcourt Brace Jovanovich, 1966. (Grades 2-6) $3.25.

340. ——. *Songs of the Dream People: Chants and Images from the Indians and Eskimos of North America*. New York: Atheneum Publishers, 1972. (Grades 4 up) $5.95.

341. ——. *Tikta 'liktak: An Eskimo Legend*. New York: Harcourt Brace Jovanovich, 1965. (Grades 2-4) $3.30.

342. ——. *White Archer: An Eskimo Legend*. New York: Harcourt Brace Jovanovich, 1970. (Grades 4-6) $3.50.

343. Howard, Victoria. *Clackamas Chinook Texts*. Ed. Melville Jacobs. 2 vols. Indiana University Research Center in Anthropology, Folklore, and Linguistics. Bloomington: Indiana University Press, 1958. Author is Clackamas Chinook.

344. Hudson, John B. *Kalapuya Texts*. Part I: Santiam Kalapuya Ethnologic Texts. Part II: Santiam Kalapuya Texts. Ed. Melville Jacobs. University of Washington Publications in Anthropology. Vol. XI. Seattle: University of Washington Press, 1945. 142 pp. Author is Kalapuyan.

345. Hulpach, Vladimir. *American Indian Tales and Legends*. London: Paul Hamlyn, 1965. 237 pp. Also: New York: Tudor Publishing Company, 1972. $3.95.

346. Hum-Ishu-Ma (Mourning Dove). *Coyote Stories*. Ed. D. G. Heister Caldwell, Idaho: Caxton Printers, Ltd., 1933. 228 pp.

347. * Hunt, Joe. *Northwest Sahaptin Texts*. Ed. Melville Jacobs. University of Washington Publications in Anthropology. Vol. II, No. 6. Seattle: University of Washington Press, 1929. 77 pp. Author is Klikitat.

348. Hunter, Milton R. *Utah Indian Stories*. Salt Lake City, Utah: Deseret Book Company, 1970. $1.95.

349. * *Indian Stories and Legends*. Fairfield, Washington: Ye Galleon Press, 1972. $2.50.

350. * Jacobs, Elizabeth D., and Melville Jacobs. *Nehalem Tillamook Tales*. Eugene: University of Oregon Press, 1959. $3.00.

351. Jacobs, Melville. *Content and Style of an Oral Literature: Clackamas Chinook Myths and Tales*. Chicago: University of Chicago Press, 1959. $5.00. See also No. 1658.

352. * ——. *Coos Narrative and Ethnologic Texts*. Publications in Anthropology. Seattle: University of Washington Press, 1939. $3.50.

353. * ——. *Northwest Sahaptin Text, One*. Publications in Anthropology. Seattle: University of Washington Press, 1929. $2.50.

354. ——. *Northwest Sahaptin Texts*, 2 Pts. Columbia University Contributions to Anthropology Series, Vol. 19. 1934; rpt. New York: AMS Press, 1969. $32.50; $17.50 each.

355. * ——, et al. *Kalapuya Texts*. Publications in Anthropology. Seattle: University of Washington Press, 1945. $7.50.

356. Jones, Hettie, ed. *Longhouse Winter*. Stories adapted from Iroquois Transformation Tales. New York: Holt, Rinehart, and Winston, 1972. $4.95.

357. Jones, Hettie, ed. *The Trees Stand Shining*. Poetry of the North American Indians. Paintings by Robert A. Parker. New York: Dial Press, 1971. Unpaged. Approximately 50 pp. Poem on verso; painting on recto. $4.95.

358. Jones, James A. *Traditions of the North American Indians*. 3 vols. 1830; rpt. Upper Saddle River, New Jersey: Literature House / The Gregg Press, 1970. $37.50. One of the most important sources of Indian legends.

359. Jorgensen, Joseph G. *The Sun Dance Religion: Power for the Powerless*. Chicago: University of Chicago Press, 1972. $22.00.

360. Judd, Mary C. *Wigwam Stories Told by North American Indians*. 1901; rpt. Boston, Mass.: Ginn and Company, 1925. (Stories from various tribes told for children.) 278 pp.

361. Judson, Katherine B. *Myths and Legends of the Great Plains*. Chicago: A. C. McClurg and Company, 1913. 205 pp.

362. ———. *Myths and Legends of the Pacific Northwest*. 1910; rpt. Facsimile ed. Seattle: Shorey Publications, 1970. $7.50.

363. * Kroeber, Theodora. *Inland Whale: Nine Stories Retold from California Indian Legends*. Gloucester, Mass.: Peter Smith, 1970. In paper: Berkeley: University of California Press, 1959. 2.45.

364. * La Pointe, James. *Legends of the Lakota*. San Francisco: Indian Historian Press, 1971. $7.00. In paper: $4.00.

365. * Laski, Vera. *Seeking Life*. Memoirs of the American Folklore Society, Vol. 50. Austin: University of Texas Press, 1959. $6.00. In paper: $3.50.

366. Leekley, Thomas B. *World of Manabozho: Tales of the Chippewa Indians*. New York: Vanguard Press, Inc., 1964. (Grades 4-7) 128 pp. $3.50.

367. * *Legends of the Mighty Sioux*. Compiled by Workers of the South Dakota Writers Project Work Projects Administration. Chicago: Albert Whitman and Company, 1941. In paper: Sioux Falls, S.D.: Fantab, Inc. [1970]. 158 pp. $2.25.

368. Leland, Charles G. *Algonquin Legends of New England*. 1884; rpt. Detroit, Michigan: Gale Research Company, 1968. A Singing Tree Press Book. $12.50.

369. Linderman, Frank B. *Indian Why Stories: Sparks from War Eagle's Lodge-Fire*. Illustrated by Charles M. Russell. New York: Charles Scribner's Sons, 1915. 233 pp.

370. * Lotz, M. Marvin, and Douglas Monahan. *Twenty Tepee Tales*. New York: Association Press, 1950. $1.25.

371. * Lowie, Robert H. *Primitive Religion*. Rev. ed. 1947; rpt. New York: Liveright, 1970. $6.95. In paper: $2.95.

372. ———. *The Religion of the Crow Indians*. Anthropological Papers of the American Museum of Natural History. Vol. 25. New York, 1922.

373. ——. *Studies in Plains Indian Folklore.* University of California Publications in American Archaeology and Ethnology. Vol. 40, No. 1. Berkeley, California: University of California Press, 1932. See No. 4040.

374. Lowry, Annie. *Karnee: A Paiute Narrative.* Ed. Lalla Scott. Reno, Nevada: University of Nevada Press, 1966. 149 pp. Author is Paiute.

375. Ludewig, H. E. *The Literature of American Aboriginal Languages.* 1858; rpt. Ed. Nicholas Trubner. New York: Kraus Reprint Co., 1970. $13.00.

376. Macfarlan, Allan A., ed. *The Heritage Book of American Indian Legends.* New York: Heritage Press, 1970. $8.50.

377. Maher, Ramona. *Blind Boy and the Loon: A Collection of Eskimo Myths.* New York: John Day Company, 1969. (Grades 5 up) $4.29.

378. Manning-Sanders, Ruth. *Red Indian Folk and Fairy Tales.* New York: Roy Publishers, Inc., 1970. (Grades 4-8) $4.75.

379. Markoosie. *Harpoon of the Hunter.* McGill-Queens University Press, 1970. $4.95.

380. * Marriott, Alice. *Saynday's People: The Kiowa Indians and the Stories They Told.* 1947; rpt. Lincoln: University of Nebraska Press, 1963. Also contains *Indians on Horseback*, bound with it. 222 pp. In paper: Rpt. Bison Book, 1963. $1.75.

381. ——. *The Ten Grandmothers.* Civilization of American Indian Series, No. 26. 1945; rpt. Norman: University of Oklahoma Press, 1968. 306 pp. $6.95.

382. ——. *Winter Telling Stories.* New York: T. Y. Crowell, Company, 1969. (Grades 4-7) 82 pp. $3.95.

383. * Marriott, Alice, and Carol Rachlin. *American Indian Mythology.* New York: Thomas Y. Crowell, 1968. 211 pp. In paper: New York: New American Library, 1972. $1.25.

384. Mason, Bernard S. *Dances and Stories of the American Indian.* New York: Ronald Press Company, 1944. 269 pp. $7.00.

385. * Masson, Marcelle. *Bag of Bones.* Healdsburg, California: Naturegraph Pub., 1966. $4.25. Wintu legends told by Grant Towendolly. In paper: $2.25.

386. Mathews, Cornelius, ed. *Enchanted Moccasins and Other Legends of the American Indians.* 1877; rpt. New York: AMS Press, 1972. $9.50.

387. Matson, Emerson. *Legends of the Great Chiefs.* Camden, New Jersey: Thomas Nelson, 1972. (Grades 5-8) $4.95.

388. ——. *Longhouse Legends.* Camden, New Jersey: Thomas Nelson, Inc., 1968. (Grades 3-7) 128 pp. $3.95.

389. Matthews, Washington, ed. *Navaho Legends.* 1897; rpt. New York: Kraus Reprint Co., 1969. 299 pp. $12.00. See also No. 4005.

390. Mayol, Lurline. *Talking Totem Pole.* Portland Oregon: Binfords and Mort, Publishers, 1943. (Grades 5-6) $3.00.

391. McLaughlin, Marie L. *Myths and Legends of the Sioux.* Bismarck, North Dakota: Bismarck Tribune Company, 1916. 198 pp.

392. McClintock, Walter. *The Blackfoot Tipi.* Los Angeles: Southwest Museum, 1936.

393. * ——. *The Old North Trail of Life, Legends and Religion of the Blackfeet Indians.* London: Macmillan, 1910; rpt. Lincoln: University of Nebraska Press, 1968. 539 pp. $2.95. Bison Book, BB 379.

394. * ——. *Old Indian Trail.* 1923; rpt. Gloucester, Mass.: Peter Smith, 1972. $6.00. In paper: $2.95.

395. McNickel, D'Arcy. *Runner in the Sun.* Land of the Free Series. New York: Holt, Rinehart, and Winston, 1954. (Grades 7-9) $3.27.

396. ——. *The Surrounded.* New York: Dodd, Mead, and Company, 1936. 297 pp.

397. ——. *They Came Here First.* The Epic of the American Indian. Philadelphia, Pa.: J. B. Lippincott Company, 1949. 352 pp.

398. * Melancon, Claude. *Legendes Indiennes du Canada.* New York: International Scholastic Book Service, 1971. $4.00.

399. Melzack, Ronald. *The Day Tuk Became a Hunter and Other Eskimo Stories.* New York: Dodd, Mead, and Company, 1968. 92 pp. $3.95.

400. ——. *Raven: Creator of the World.* Boston: Little, Brown and Company, 1971. (Grades 3-7) $4.95.

401. Moon, Sheila. *Magic Dwells: A Poetic and Psychological Study of the Navaho Emergence Myth.* Middletown, Connecticut: Wesleyan University Press, 1970. 206 pp. $7.95.

402. * Mooney, James. *The Ghost-Dance Religion and the Sioux Outbreak of 1890.* Ed. and abridged by F. C. Wallace. Chicago: The University of Chicago Press, 1965. (Reprinted from original ed. published as Part 2 of the *Fourteenth Annual Report of the Bureau of Ethnology to the Secretary of the Smithsonian Institution, 1892-1893.* Washington, D.C.: Government Printing Office, 1896.) 331 pp. In paper: $2.95. Also: Glorieta, New Mexico: Rio Grande Press, 1971. $20.00.

403. ——. *Myths of the Cherokee.* 1900; rpt. St. Clair Shores, Michigan: Scholarly Press, 1970. $19.00. Also: New York: Johnson Reprint Corp., 1970.

404. ——. *Sacred Formulas of the Cherokees.* 7th Annual Report of the Bureau of American Ethnology. Washington, D.C., 1891.

405. * Morgan, William, et al. *Coyote Tales.* Navajo Series. Lawrence, Kansas: Haskell Press, 1970. $ .35. English and Navajo Text.

406. *My Indian Tale Library.* 8 books. Boxed. Bronx, New York: Platt and Munk Company, 1970. (Grades 1-5) $1.50.

407. *Navaho Indian Poems.* Translation from the Navajo, and Other Poems. As Told to Hilda Faunce Wetherill. New York: Vantage Press, 1952.

408. Nequatewa, Edmund. *Truth of a Hopi: Stories Relating to the Origin, Myths, and Clan Histories of the Hopi.* 1936. Rpt. Museum of Northern Arizona Bulletin, No. 8. Flagstaff, Arizona: Northland Press, 1967. 136 pp. Author was Hopi.

409. Newcomb, Franc J. *Navajo Bird Tales.* Told by Hosteen Clah. Ed. Lillian Harvey. Wheaton, Illinois: Theosophical Publishing House, 1970. (Grades 3-9) $3.95.

410. ——. *Navaho Folk Tales.* Sante Fe Museum of Navaho Ceremonial Art, Inc., 1967. 203 pp.

411. Newell, Edythe W. *The Rescue of the Sun and Other Tales from the Far North.* Chicago: Albert Whitman and Company, 1970. 142 pp. $3.50.

412. Nye, Wilbur S. *Bad Medicine and Good Tales of the Kiowas.* Norman: University of Oklahoma Press, 1962. 291 pp. $7.95.

413. Opler, Morris E. *Dirty Boy: A Jicarilla Tale of Raid and War.* 1938; rpt. New York: Kraus Reprint Co., 1970. $3.00.

414. ——, ed. *Myths and Legends of the Lipan Apache Indians.* 1940; rpt. New York: Kraus Reprint Co., 1971. $10.00.

415. ——, ed. *Myths and Tales of the Chiricahua Apache Indians.* 1942; rpt. New York: Kraus Reprint Co., 1970. $7.50.

416. ——. *Myths and Tales of the Jicarilla Apache Indians.* American Folklore Society Memoirs Series. 1938; rpt. New York: Kraus Reprint Co., 1971. $18.00.

417. * Ortiz, Alfonso. *The Tewa World: Space, Time, Being and Becoming in a Pueblo Society.* Chicago, Illnois: University of Chicago Press, 1969. 197 pp. $8.00. In paper: $2.45.

418. * Oswalt, R. L. *Kashaya Texts.* University of California Publications in Linguistics Series, Vol. 36. Berkeley: University of California Press, 1964.

419. Owl, Mrs. Samson, and others. *Catawba Texts.* Ed. Frank G. Speck. Columbia University Contributions to Anthropology. Vol. XXIV. New York: Columbia University Press, 1934. 91 pp. Authors or narrators were Catawba.

420. Parker, Arthur C. *Seneca Myths and Folk Tales.* Buffalo Historical Society Publications. Vol. 27. Buffalo, New York: Buffalo Historical Society, 1923. 465 pp. Rpt. Ann Arbor, Mich., Finch Press, 1972. $15.00.

421. ———. *Skunny Wundy Indian Tales.* Chicago: Albert Whitman and Company, 1970. (Grades 3 up) $3.95.

422. * Parsons, Elsie C. *Hopi and Zuni Ceremonialism.* 1933; rpt. New York: Kraus Reprint Co., 1970. $5.00. See also No. 4017 below.

423. ———. *Kiowa Tales.* 1929; rpt. New York: Kraus Reprint Co., 1969. 152 pp.

424. * ———. *Notes on the Zuni.* 2 vols. 1917; rpt. New York: Kraus Reprint Co., 1971. $10.00.

425. * ———. *The Scalp Ceremonial of the Zuni.* 1924; rpt. New York: Kraus Reprint Co., 1970. $3.50.

426. ——— ed. *Taos Tales.* 1940; rpt. New York: Kraus Reprint Co., 1971. $9.00.

427. ———, ed. *Tewa Tales.* 1926; rpt. New York: Kraus Reprint Co., 1971. $12.00.

428. Phillips, W. S. (El Comancho). *Indian Tales for Little Folks.* New York: The Platt and Munk Company, Inc., 1914. (A children's book) 80 pp.

429. Phinney, Archie. *Nez Perce Texts.* Columbia University Contributions to Anthropology. Vol. XXV. New York: Columbia University Press, 1934. 497 pp. Author is Nez Perce.

430. Pond, Samuel W. *Legends of the Dakotas and Other Selections from the Poetical Works.* Minneapolis, Minnesota: K. Holter Pub. Co., 1911.

431. * Porter, C. Fayne. *The Battle of the Thousand Slain and Other Stories of the First Americans.* Starline Books. New York: Scholastic Book Series, 1969. (Grades 7 up) $ .60.

432. Powell, Peter J. *Sweet Medicine: The Continuing Role of the Sacred Arrows, the Sun Dance, and the Sacred Buffalo in Northern Cheyenne History.* 2 vols. Civilization of the American Indian Series, Vol. 100. Norman: University of Oklahoma Press, 1969. $25.00.

433. Price, S. Goodale. *Black Hills: The Land of Legend.* Los Angeles: De Vorss and Company, 1935. 50 pp.

434. * Radin, Paul. *The Trickster: A Study in American Indian Mythology.* with commentaries by C. G. Jung and Karl Kerenyi. New York: Philosophical Library, 1956. 211 pp. $9.50. See also No. 4019. Rpt. Westport, Connecticut: Greenwood Press, Inc., 1971. $9.50. In paper: New York: Schocken Books, 1972. $2.95.

435. Rand, Silas T. *Legends of the Micmacs.* 1894; rpt. New York: Johnson Reprint Corp., 1970. $22.50.

436. Raskin, Joseph, and Edith Raskin. *Indian Tales*. New York: Random House, 1969. (Grades 3-5) 63 pp. $3.50.

437. Reed, Earl H. *The Silver Arrow and Other Indian Romances of the Dune Country*. Chicago: Reilly and Lee, 1926; rpt. Ann Arbor, Michigan: University Microfilms, 1968. $10.00.

438. Reichard, Gladys A. *An Analysis of Coeur D'Alene Indian Myths*. 1947; rpt. New York: Kraus Reprint Company, 1969. 218 pp. $10.00.

439. Reid, Dorothy N. *Tales of Nanabozho*. New York: Henry Z. Walck, 1963. (Grades 4-6) $4.75.

440. Roberts, Helen M. *Mission Tales: Stories of the Historic California Missions*. 7 vols. Palo Alto, California: Pacific Books, Publishers, 1962. $19.25.

441. * Roberts, Helen M., and Morris H. Swadesh. *The Songs of the Nootka Indians of Western Vancouver Island*. Philadelphia: American Philosophical Society, 1955. $2.00.

442. * Rothenberg, Jerome, ed. *Shaking the Pumpkin: Traditional Poetry of the Indian North Americas*. New York: Doubleday, 1972. 475 pp. $8.95. In paper: $3.95.

443. Scheer, George F., ed. *Cherokee Animal Tales*. New York: Holiday House, Inc., 1968. (Grades 3-5) 79 pp. $3.95.

444. Schoolcraft, Henry R. *The Myth of Hiawatha and Other Oral Legends, Mythologic and Allegoric, of the North American Indians*. 1856; rpt. New York: Kraus Reprint Co., 1970. $14.50.

445. ———. *Schoolcraft's Indian Legends*. Ed. Mentor L. Williams. East Lansing: Michigan State University Press, 1956. $7.50.

446. Scott, Lalla. *Karnee: A Paiute Narrative*. Tucson: University of Nevada Press, 1966. 149 pp. $5.25.

447. * Seiler, H., ed. *Cahuilla Texts*. Language Science Monographs. The Hague: Mouton Publishers, 1970. 204 pp. $8.30.

448. Seton, Julia M. *Indian Creation Stories*. Sante Fe, New Mexico: Seton Village, 1952. 161 pp. $2.50.

449. * Shaw, Anna Moore. *Pima Indian Legends*. Tucson: University of Arizona Press, 1968. 111 pp. $2.50.

450. Skinner, Charles M. *Myths and Legends Beyond Our Borders*. Philadelphia: J. B. Lippincott and Company, 1899; rpt. 2 vols. Detroit, Michigan: Singing Tree Press, 1969. 319 pp. $15.00.

451. Smithson, Carma L., and Robert C. Euler. *Havasupai Religion and Mythology*. 1964; rpt. New York: Johnson Reprint Corp., 1972. $10.00.

452. Speck, Frank G. *Catawba Texts*. Columbia Contributions to Anthropology Series, Vol. 24. 1934; rpt. New York: AMS Press, 1969. $7.50.

453. Spence, Lewis. *The Myths of the North American Indians*. With thirty plates in colour by James Jack and other illustrations. 1914; rpt. New York: Kraus Reprint Co., 1972. 393 pp. $17.50.

454. * Spencer, Katherine. *Mythology and Values: An Analysis of Navaho Chantway Myths*. Philadelphia: American Folklore Society, 1957. 240 pp. $3.50. Also: Austin: University of Texas Press.

455. Spinden, Herbert J., trans. *Songs of the Tewa*. Preceded by An Essay on American Indian Poetry with a selection of outstanding compositions from North and South America. New York: The Exposition of Indian Tribal Arts, Inc., 1933. 125 pp.

456. * Spott, Robert, and A. L. Kroeber. *Yurok Narratives*. See No. 4035.

457. Squire, Roger. *Wizards and Wampum: Legends of the Iroquois*. New York: Abelard-Schuman, Ltd., 1971. (Grades 4 up) $4.38.

458. Standing Bear, Luther. *The Land of the Spotted Eagle*. Boston: Houghton Mifflin, 1933. 259 pp.

459. * Steiner, Stan, and Shirley Hill Witt, eds. *The Way: An Anthology of American Indian Literature*. New York: Random House, 1972. 352 pp. $7.95. In paper: $1.95.

460. Storm, Hyemeyohsts. *Seven Arrows*. New York: Harper and Row, 1971. 388 pp. $9.95. Author is a Northern Cheyenne.

461. * Swanton, John R. *Haida Texts and Myths: Skidegate Dialect*. Landmarks in Anthropology. 1905; rpt. New York: Johnson Reprint Corp., 1970. $18.00.

462. ——. *Myths and Tales of the Southeastern Indians*. 1929; rpt. Nashville, Tennessee: The Blue and Gray Press, 1971. 275 pp. $10.00.

463. ——. *Tlingit Myths and Texts*. 39th Annual Report of the Bureau of American Ethnology. Washington, D.C., 1909; rpt. New York: Johnson Reprint Corp., 1970. $18.00.

464. * Tedlock, Dennis Trans. *Finding the Center: Narrative Poetry of the Zuni Indians*. New York: Dial Press, Inc., 1971. $8.50. In paper: $3.95.

465. * Thayer, Mrs. Carl T. *Indian Legends of Minnesota*. Small paperback. St. Paul: Minnesota Historical Society, [1969]. $ .35.

466. * Thibert, A. *Eskimo-English, English-Eskimo Dictionary*. Rev. ed. New York: William S. Heinma, Inc., 1969. $6.00.

467. * Thompson, Hildegard. *Navajo Life Series*. Navajo Series. Lawrence, Kansas: Haskell Press, 1970. English and Navajo Text. Preprimer .25; Primer .15.

468. * Thompson, Stith, ed. *Tales of the North American Indians*. 1929; rpt. Bloomington: Indiana University Press, 1966. 386 pp. $7.50. In paper: $2.95.

469. Thorne, J. Frederic. *In the Time that Was Being: Legends of the Tlingits.* 1909; rpt. Seattle: Shorey Publications, 1972. $2.50.

470. Thornton, M. Valley. *Indian Lives and Legends.* New York: William S. Heinman, 1966. $12.50.

471. Traveller Bird. *Tell Them They Lie: The Sequoyah Myth.* Great West and Indian Series, Vol. 40. Los Angeles: Westernlore Press, 1971. $7.95.

472. Tvedten, Benet, Compiler. *An American Indian Anthology.* Marvin, S.D.: Blue Cloud Quarterly Publication, 1971. Unpaged; approximately 100 pp.

473. Tyler, Hamilton A. *Pueblo. Gods and Myths.* Civilization of the American Indian Series, No. 71. Norman: University of Oklahoma Press, 1964; rpt. 1971. 310 pp. $7.95.

474. Vaudrin, Bill. *Tanaina Tales from Alaska.* Civilization of the American Indian Series, No. 96. Norman: University of Oklahoma Press, 1969. 127 pp. $4.95. Author is a Chippewa Indian.

475. Verlarde, Pablita. *Old Father, The Story Teller.* Globe, Arizona: Dale Stuart King, 1960. 66 pp. Author is Santa Clara Pueblo. Also Delux ed., $20.00.

476. Voight, Virginia F. *The Adventures of Hiawatha.* Reading Shelf in American Folk Tales Series. Champaign, Illinois: Garrard Publishing Company, 1969. (Grades 3-6) $2.39.

477. ———. *Close to the Rising Sun: Algonquian Indian Legends.* American Folk Tales Series. Champaign, Illinois: Garrard Publishing Company, 1972. (Grades 2-5) $2.95.

478. Walker, J. R. *The Sun Dance and Other Ceremonies of the Oglala Division of the Teton Dakota.* Anthropological Papers of the American Museum of Natural History. Vol. 46. Washington, D.C., 1936.

479. * Waters, Frank. *Book of the Hopi.* Walden Edition. New York: Ballantine Books, Inc., 1969. 423 pp. $1.25. Also: New York: Viking Press, 1963. $12.50.

480. ———. *Masked Gods: Navaho and Pueblo Ceremonialism.* Walden Editions. New York: Ballantine Books, Inc., 1970. 459 pp. $1.65. Also: Chicago: Swallow Press, 1971. $8.50.

480. Wetherill, Hilda F., see *Navaho Indian Poems*, No. 407.

482. Wheelwright, Mary C. *Navajo Creation Myth of the Emergence.* By Hasteen Klah. *Navajo Religion Series.* Vol. 1. Sante Fe: Museum of Navajo Ceremonial Art, 1942. 237 pp. Klah is the Indian speaker.

483. Wood, Charles E. *The Book of Indian Tales.* New York: Vanguard Press, Inc., 1971. $3.95. Also: Gordmik, 1972, $11.00.

484. Young, Egerton R., collector. *Algonquin Indian Tales*. New York: The Abingdon Press, 1903 (Rptd. 1909, 1915.) 258 pp.
485. ——, compiler. *Stories From Indian Wigwams and Northern Camp-Fires*. 1893; rpt. Detroit: Gale Research Company, 1970. $13.50. Also: Highland Park, N.J.: Gryphon Press, 1970. $13.50.
486. Zitkala-Sa (Gertrude Bonnin). *American Indian Stories*. Washington, D.C.: Hayworth Publishing House, 1921. 195 pp.
487. Zitkala-Sa (Gertrude Bonnin). *Old Indian Legends*. Boston: Ginn and Company, 1901. 157 pp.

ALL OTHER BOOKS

501. Abel, Annie H. *American Indian As a Participant in the Civil War*. American Studies Series. 1919; rpt. New York: Johnson Reprint, 1970. $10.50.

502. ——. *The American Indian As Slave-Holder and Secessionist*. 1915; rpt. St. Clair Shores, Michigan: Scholarly Press, 1970. $16.00.

503. ——. *The American Indian Under Reconstruction*. House American Studies Series. New York: Johnson Reprint Corp., 1970. $12.50.

504. ——. *A History of Events Resulting in Indian Consolidation West of the Mississippi River*. 1908; rpt. New York: AMS Press, 1970. $10.00.

505. ——. *Slaveholding Indians*. 1919; rpt. 3 vols. St. Clair Shores, Michigan: Scholarly Press, 1972. $14.50 each / $39.00 set.

506. * Aberle, David F. *Navajo and Ute Peyotism: A Chronological and Distributional Study*. 1957; rpt. New York: Kraus Reprint Co., 1970. $6.00.

507. ——. *The Peyote Religion Among the Navaho*. Chicago: Aldine Publishing Company, 1966. 454 pp. $12.50.

508. * Aberle, S.D. de. *The Pueblo Indians of New Mexico: Their Land, Economy and Civil Organization*. 1948; rpt. New York: Kraus Reprint Company, 1972. $5.00.

509. Adair, James. *The History of the American Indians.*, etc. London: Edward and Charles Dilly, 1775; rpt. New York: Johnson Reprint Corp., 1968. A photofacsimile reprint. 464 pp. $20.00. Also: New York: Arno Press, 1971. $22.50. Also: Ed. Samuel C. Wills. Nashville, Tennessee: The Blue and Gray Press, 1971. 508 pp. $15.00.

510. Adair, John. *The Navajo and Pueblo Silversmiths*. Civilization of the American Indian Series, No. 25. Norman: University of Oklahoma Press, 1966. 220 pp. $6.95.

511. Adair, John, and Kurt Deuschle. *The People's Health*. New York: Appleton-Century, Crofts, 1950. 186 pp. $6.95. Rpt. 1970. On the health of the Navajo Indian. See also Bunker, Robert.

512. Adams, Audrey. *Karankawa Boy*. San Antonio, Texas: Naylor Company, 1971. (Grades 4-8) $3.95.

513. Adams, Evelyn C. *American Indian Education: Government Schools and Economic Progress.* American Education Series, No. 2. 1946; rpt. New York: Arno Press, 1972. $7.00.

514. Adrian, Mary. *The Indian Horse Mystery.* New York: Hastings House Publishers, 1966. (Grades 4-6) $3.50.

515. * Aginsky, Burt W., and Ethel G. Aginsky. *Deep Valley: The Pomo Indians of California.* New York: Stein & Day, 1971. $2.45.

516. * Aginsky, Ethel G. *A Grammar of the Mende Language.* 1935; rpt. New York: Kraus Reprint Co., 1970. $4.00.

517. * *Alaska Natives and the Land.* Washington, D.C.: Government Printing Office, 1968. 565 pp. $16.00.

518. Alden, John R. *John Stuart and the Southern Colonial Frontier: A Study of Indian Relations, War, Trade, and Land Problems in the Southern Wilderness, 1754-1775.* 1944; rpt. Staten Island: Gordian Press, Inc., 1966. $9.50.

519. Alderman, Clifford L. *Joseph Brant: Chief of the Six Nations.* New York: Julian Messner, Inc., 1958. (Grades 8 up) $3.34.

520. Alford, Thomas Wildcat. *Civilization.* As Told to Florence Drake. Norman: University of Oklahoma Press, 1936. 203 pp. Author is Shawnee.

521. Allen, T. D., ed. *Red Eagle: A Collection of Poetry by Young American Indians.* New York: Doubleday & Co., 1971. See also Mitchell, Emerson Blackhorse.

522. * ——. *The Whispering Wind: A Collection of Poems by Young American Indians.* New York: Doubleday & Co., 1972. 144 pp. $1.95.

523. Allen, T. D. *Navajos Have Five Fingers.* Civilization of the American Indian Series, No. 68. Norman: University of Oklahoma Press, 1965. 249 pp. $6.95.

524. ——. *Tall As Great Standing Rock.* Philadelphia: Westminster Press, 1963. (Grades 7-10) $3.25.

525. Allman, C. B. *Lewis Wetzel, Indian Fighter.* Old Greenwich, Conn.: Devin-Adair Co., Inc., 1961. $5.95.

526. Alter, J. Cecil. *Jim Bridger.* Norman: University of Oklahoma Press, 1968. $7.50.

527. Alter, Robert E. *Time of the Tomahawk.* New York: G. P. Putman's Sons, 1964. (Grades 5 up) $3.95.

528. Altsheler, Joseph A. *Apache Gold.* New York: Hawthorn Books, Inc., 1952. (Grades 7-10) $4.50. Mr. Altsheler is the author of some thirty books of fiction about the pioneer and the Indian. We list only one here.

529. *American Friends Service Committee. *Uncommon Controversy: The Fishing Rights of the Muckleshoot, Puyallut, and Nisqually Indians.* Seattle: University of Washington Press, 1970. $5.59. In paper: $2.95.

530. *The American Indian,* See Carroll, John, No. 858.

531. * *The American Indian Today.* Ed. Stuart Levine and Nancy O. Lurie. Deland, Florida: Everett / Edwards, Inc., 1968. A book of essays by various scholars on current problems, conditions, etc. of the American Indians. 229 pp. $12.00. In paper: Baltimore: Penquin Books, Inc., 1971. $1.95.

532. *American Indians: Facts and Future.* Toward Economic Development for Native American Communities. 1969; rpt. New York: Arno Press, 1970. 566 pp.

533. Amon, Aline. *Talking Hands: Indian Sign Language.* Garden City, New York: Doubleday and Company, 1968. (Grades 5 up) $3.95.

534. *Amsden, Charles A. *Navaho Weaving. Its Technic and History.* Rpt. Glorietta, New Mexico: Rio Grande Press, Inc., 1964. $12.00. In paper: New York: Dover Publications, Inc., 1971. 263 pp. $3.50.

535. * *Analysis of Sources of Information on the Population of the Navaho.* Washington, D.C.: Government Printing Office, 1966. 220 pp. $2.00.

536. Anderson, Hobson D., and Walter C. Eells. *Alaska Natives: A Survey of their Educational Status.* Made Under the Auspices of the Stanford School of Education. 1935; rpt. New York: Kraus Reprint Company, 1971. 472 pp. $40.00.

537. Anderson, La Vere. *Black Hawk: Indian Patriot.* Champaign, Illinois: Garrard Publishing Company, 1972. (Grades 2-5) $2.95.

538. ——. *Quanah Parker, Indian Warrior for Peace.* Champaign, Illinois: Garrard Publishing Company, 1970. (Grades 7-12) 96 pp. $3.00.

539. ——. *Sitting Bull: Great Sioux Chief.* Ed. Elizabeth M. Graves. Champaign, Illinois: Garrard Publishing Company, 1970. (Grades 7-12) 80 pp. $2.59.

540. Andrews, Ralph W. *Curtis' Western Indians.* Seattle: Superior Publishing Company, 1962. 176 pp.

541. ——. *Indian Leaders Who Helped Shape America, 1620-1900.* Seattle: Superior Publishing Company, 1970. $12.95.

542. ——. *Indian Primitive.* New York: Bonanza Books, 1960. 175 pp.

543. ——. *Indians as the Westerners Saw Them.* Seattle: Superior Publishing Company, 1963. 176 pp. $12.95.

544. *Andrist, Ralph K. *The Long Death. The Last Days of the Plains Indians.* New York: Macmillan Company, 1964. 371 pp. $8.95. In paper: Collier Books Edition. New York: Macmillan Company, 1969. 371 pp. $2.45.

545. Andrist, Ralph K., and R. E. Bingham. *To the Pacific with Lewis and Clark.* New York: Harper and Row, 1967. (Grades 5 up) $5.95.

546. Ansen, Fridtjof N. *Eskimo Life.* 1883; rpt. Detroit: Gale Research Company, 1971.

547. Anson, Bert. *The Miami Indians.* Civilization of the American Indian Series, No. 103. Norman: University of Oklahoma Press, 1970. $8.95.

548. *Answers to Your Questions About American Indians.* Washington, D.C.: Government Printing Office, 1970. 42 pp. $ .35.

549. Anthropological Society of Washington, D.C. *New Interpretations of Aboriginal American Culture History.* 1955; rpt. New York: Cooper Square Publishers, Inc., 1970. $6.00.

550. *Anthropology in North America.* See Swanton, John R., et al.

551. *The Anthropology of the Numa.* John Wesley Powell's Manuscripts on the Numic Peoples of Western North America, 1868-1880. Smithsonian Institution Contributions to Anthropology, Vol. 14. Washington, D.C.: Government Printing Office, 1971. $3.25.

552. Anton, Ferdinand, and Frederick J. Dockstader. *Columbian Art and Later Indian Tribal Arts.* Panorama of World Art Series. New York: Harry N. Abrams, Inc., 1968. $7.95.

553. *The Appalachian Indian Frontier. The Second Atkin Report and Plan of 1755.* Ed. Wilbur R. Jacobs. 1954; rpt. Lincoln: University of Nebraska Press, 1967. 108 pp. $1.95. Also: Gloucester, Mass.: Peter Smith, 1971. $4.00.

554. Appel, Claude. *American Indians.* Ed. Matt Chisholm. Chicago: Follett Publishing Company, 1965. (Grades 5 up) $4.95.

555. *Appleton, Le Roy H. *American Indian Design and Decoration.* New York: Dover Publications, Inc., 1971. 246 pp. large paper. $4.00.

556. *An Archeaological Survey of Southwest Virginia.* Smithsonian Institution Contributions to Anthropology, Vol. 12. Washington, D.C.: Government Printing Office, 1970. 194 pp. $4.75.

557. Archer, Jules. *Indian Foe, Indian Friend.* New York: Macmillan, 1970. (Grades 7-12) 185 pp. $4.95.

558. Armer, Laura A. *In Navajo Land.* New York: David McKay Company, Inc., 1962. 107 pp. $3.95.

559. ——. *The Waterless Mountain.* New York: David McKay Company, Inc., 1931. (Grades 5-9) $5.75.

560. Armillas, Pedro. *Program of the History of American Indians.* Washington, D.C.: Pan American Union, 1962. (In English and Spanish.) $1.25.

561. * Armstrong, Virginia I., compiler, and Frederick W. Turner III. *I Have Spoken: American History Through the Voices of the Indians.* Chicago: Swallow Press, Inc., 1971. 206 pp. $2.95. Also: New York: Pocket Books, 1972. $1.50.

562. Arnold, Elliott. *Blood Brother.* Ed. Dale Nichols. New York: Hawthorn Books, Inc., 1947. $7.95.

563. ———. *Broken Arrow.* New York: Hawthorn Books Inc., 1954. (Grades 5-9) $4.95.

564. Arnold, R. Ross. *Indian Wars of Idaho.* Caldwell, Idaho: Caxton Printers, Ltd. 1932.

565. Artichoker, John. *Indians of South Dakota.* Pierre, South Dakota, 1956. 89 pp.

566. * Artichoker, John Jr., and Neil M. Palmer. *The Sioux Indian Goes to College.* An Analysis of Selected Problems of South Dakota Indian College Students. Vermillion, S.D.: Institute of Indian Studies, 1959. 47 pp.

567. *The Artist of 'Isleta Paintings' in Pueblo Society.* Washington, D.C.: Government Printing Office, 1967. 227 pp. $4.25.

568. * Atkin, Edmond. See *Appalachian Indian Frontier*, No. 553.

569. Austin, Mary, *American Rhythm: Studies and Reexpressions of Amer-Indian Songs.* 1930; ṛpt. New York: Cooper Square Publishers, Inc., 1966. 174 pp. $6.00.

570. ———. *Arrow-Maker.* Rev. ed. 1915; rpt. New York: AMS Press, 1969. $7.50.

571. Averill, Esther. *King Philip, the Indian Chief.* New York: Harper Row, 1950. (Grades 7 up) $3.95.

572. * *Aztec Ruins National Monument, New Mexico.* Washington, D.C.: Government Printing Office, 1963. $ .30.

573. Bachhofer, Ludwig. *Early Indian Sculpture.* 1929; rpt. New York: Hacker Art Books, 1971. $50.00.

574. Bad Heart Bull, Amos. *A Pictographic History of the Oglala Sioux.* Ed. Helen M. Blish. Lincoln, Nebraska: University of Nebraska Press, 1967. 530 pp.

575. Bahr, Donald M. et al. *Staying Sickness: A Study of Piman Knowledge and Speech About Sickness.* Tucson: University of Arizona Press, 1970. $9.50.

576. * Bahr, Howard M., et al., eds. *Native Americans Today: Sociological Perspectives.* New York: Harcourt Brace and Row, 1971. $4.95.

577. Bailey, Alfred G. *The Conflict of European and Eastern Algonkian Cultures, 1504-1700: A Study in Canadian Civilization.* Second Edition. Toronto: University of Toronto Press, 1969. $7.95.

578. * Bailey, Flora L. *Some Sex Beliefs and Practices in a Navaho Community.* Harvard University Peabody Museum of Archaeology and Ethnology Papers Series. 1950; rpt. New York: Kraus Reprint Co., 1971. 112 pp. $5.00.

579. * Bailey, L. R. *Indian Slave Trade in the Southwest.* New York: Tower Publications, Inc., 1966. $ .95. Also: Great West and Indian Series, Vol. 32. Los Angeles: Western Lore Press, 1971. $7.95.

580. Bailey, M. Thomas. *Reconstruction in Indian Territory.* Port Washington, New York: Kennikat Press, 1972. $11.50.

581. * Bailey, Paul. *Ghost Dance Messiah.* New York: Tower Publications, Inc., 1970. Fictionalized account of Wovoka's Life. 172 pp. $ .95.

582. Bailey, Ralph E. *Indian Fighter: The Story of Nelson A. Miles.* New York: William Morrow and Co., 1965. (Grades 7 up) $4.50.

583. Bailey, Robert G. *Nez Perce Indians.* Lewiston, Idaho: Bailey Publishing Co., 1943.

584. * Bailey, Tom. *The Comanche Wars.* The True Saga of a People Who Loved War and Knew No Fear of Death. Derby, Connecticut: Monarch Books, Inc., 1963. 142 pp.

585. Baird, W. David. *Peter Pitchlynn: Chief of the Choctaws.* Civilization of the American Indian Series, No. 116. Norman: University of Oklahoma Press, 1972. 244 pp. $7.95.

586. Baity, Elizabeth C. *Americans Before Columbus.* Rev. ed. New York: Viking Press, 1961. (Grades 7 up) 256 pp. $5.00.

587. Baker, Betty. *And One Was a Wooden Indian.* New York: Macmillan and Co., 1970. (Grades 5-9) $4.95.

588. ——. *Arizona.* States of the Nation Series. New York: Coward-McCann, Inc., 1969. (Grades 7-11) $4.29.

589. ——. *Blood of the Brave.* New York: Harper and Row, 1966. (Grades 9 up) $3.95.

590. ——. *Do Not Annoy the Indians.* New York: Macmillan and Co., 1968. (Grades 4-6) $4.50.

591. ——. *Dunderhead War.* New York: Harper and Row, 1967. (Grades 5 up) $3.95.

592. ——. *Killer-Of-Death.* New York: Harper and Row Publishers, Inc., 1963. (Grades 7 up) $3.95.

593. ——. *The Little Runner of the Longhouse.* I Can Read Books. New York: Harper and Row, 1962. (Grades K-3) $2.50.

594. ——. *Pig War.* I Can Read History Book Series. New York: Harper and Row, 1969. (Grades K-3) $2.50.

595. ——. *Shaman's Last Raid*. New York: Harper and Row, 1963. (Grades 3-6) $3.95.

596. ——. *Sun's Promise*. New York: Abelard-Schuman, Ltd., 1962. $2.75.

597. ——. *Treasure of the Padres*. New York: Harper and Row, 1964. (Grades 3-7) $3.95.

598. ——. *Walk the World's Rim*. New York: Harper and Row, 1965. (Grades 5 up) $3.95.

599. Baker, R. Ray. *Red Brother*. 1927; rpt. Ann Arbor, Mich.: George Wahr Publishing Co., 1971. $ .75.

600. * Balch, Glenn. *Indian Paint*. 1942; rpt. New York: Grosset and Dunlap, 1970. (Grades 4-6) $2.95. In paper: New York: Apollo Editions, 1970. $1.65.

601. * ——. *Indian Saddle-Up*. 1953; rpt. New York: Apollo Editions, 1970. $1.65.

602. Baldwin, Gordon C. *America's Buried Past: The Story of the North American Archaeology*. Science Survey Series. New York: G. P. Putnam's Sons, 1962. (Grades 5-8) $3.96.

603. ——. *Ancient Ones*. New York: Grosset and Dunlap, Inc., 1970. (Grades 5-8) 274 pp.

604. ——. *Games of the American Indians*. New York: Grosset and Dunlap, Inc., 1970. 150 pp. $4.25.

605. ——. *How the Indians Really Live*. Science Survey Series. New York: G. P. Putnam's Sons, 1967. (Grades 5-9) 223 pp. $4.29.

606. ——. *The Indians of the Southwest*. New York: G. P. Putnam's Sons, 1970. (Grades 6-8) $4.50.

607. Balikci, Asen. *The Netsilik Eskimo*. 1970; rpt. Garden City, New Jersey: Natural History, 1971. $3.95.

608. Ball, Eve. *The Warm Spring Apaches*. Tucson: University of Arizona Press, 1970. 222 pp. $6.50.

609. Bancroft, Hubert H. *Native Races*. 5 vols. New York: McGraw-Hill, 1967. $105.00.

610. ——. *The Works of Hubert H. Bancroft*. 39 vols. 1882-1890; rpt. St. Clair Shores, Michigan: Scholarly Press, 1970. $545.00.

611. Bandelier, Adolph F. *Scientist on the Trail*. Ed. George P. Hammond. Quivira Society Publications, Vol. 10. 1949; rpt. New York: Arno Press, 1967. $12.00.

612. ——. *The Southwestern Journals of Adolph F. Bandelier, 1880-1882*. Ed. Charles H. Lange and Carroll L. Riley. Albuquerque: University of New Mexico Press, 1966. 462 pp. $15.00. Vol. II, 1969. $17.50.

613. * *Bandelier National Monument, New Mexico*. Washington, D.C.: Government Printing Office, 1963. $ .35.

614. Bandi, Hans-Georg. *Eskimo Pre-history*. Seattle: University of Alaska Press, 1969. $6.50.

615. Bannon, Laura. *When the Moon is New*. Chicago: Albert Whitman and Co., 1971. (Grades 3-5) $3.50.

616. * Barbeau, Marius. *The Modern Growth of the Totem Pole on the Northwest Coast*. 1939; rpt. Facsimile Edition. Seattle: Shorey Publications, 1971. $1.00.

617. Barbe-Marbois, Francois. *Our Revolutionary Forefathers: The Letters of Francois, Marquis De Barbe-Marbois During His Residence in the United States as Secretary of the French Legation 1779-1785*. 1929; rpt. Select Bibliographies Reprint Series. Facsimile Edition. Freeport, New York: Books for Libraries, Inc., 1971. $11.50.

618. Barbour, Philip. *Pocahontas and Her World*. Boston, Mass.: Houghton Mifflin Co., 1971. $7.95.

619. *Bark Canoes and Skin Boats of North America*. Washington, D.C.: Government Printing Office, 1968. 242 pp. $3.75.

620. Barker, Arthur C. *The History of the Seneca Indians*. 1926; rpt. Kennikat, 1972. $7.50.

621. Barnett, Homer G. *The Coast Salish of British Columbia*. University of Oregon Monographs. Studies in Anthropology, IV. Eugene: University of Oregon Press, 1955. $5.00.

622. *———. *Indian Shakers: A Messianic Cult of the Pacific Northwest*. Carbondale: Southern Illinois University Press, 1957. $5.75. In paper: $2.95.

623. * Barnouw, Victor. *Acculturation and Personality Among the Wisconsin Chippewa*. 1950; rpt. New York: Kraus Reprint Co., 1971. $8.00.

624. Barnum, Francis. *Grammatical Fundamentals of the Innuit Language As Spoken by the Eskimo of the Western Coast of Alaska*. 1901; rpt. New York: Adler's Foreign Books, Inc., 1968. $19.20.

625. Barrett, Samuel A. *Pomo Indian Basketry*. Rpt. Glorieta, New Mexico: Rio Grande Press, Inc., 1971. $10.00. See also No. 4005, 4007, 4012, and 4014.

626. * Bartlet, Richard A. *The Wilderness and the Indians: Challenges in the New World*. Ed. Donald E. Worcester. Miscellany of History Series, No. 1. Austin, Texas: Stock-Vaughn Co., 1970. (Grades 7-9) $1.00.

627. Barton, Benjamin S. *New Views of the Origin of the Tribes and Nations of America*. 1798; rpt. New York: Kraus Reprint Co., 1971. $15.00.

628. Bass, Althea. *The Arapaho Way*. New York: Potter and Clarkson, 1966. A Life of Carl Sweezy, the Arapaho Indian.

629. ———. *Cherokee Messenger: A Life of Samuel Austin Worcester*. Civilization of the American Indian Series, No. 12. 1936; rpt. Norman: University of Oklahoma Press, 1968. 348 pp. $6.95.

630. * Basso, Keith H. *Cibecue Apache.* New York: Holt, Rinehart and Winston, 1970. $2.35.

631. ——. *Western Apache Witchcraft.* Anthropological Papers No. 15. Tucson: University of Arizona Press, 1969. 75 pp. $6.00.

632. Basso, Keith, H., and Morris E. Opler, eds. *Apachean Culture History and Ethnology.* Anthropological Paper, No. 21. Tucson: University of Arizona Press, 1970. 168 pp. $9.50.

633. Bateman, Walter L. *The Navajo of the Painted Desert.* Boston: Beacon Press, Inc., 1970. (Grades 4 up) 124 pp. $5.95.

634. Battey, Thomas C. *The Life and Adventures of a Quaker Among the Indians.* Western Frontier Library, No. 36. Norman: University of Oklahoma Press, 1968. 355 pp. $2.95.

635. Bauer, Helen. *California Indian Days.* Rev. ed. Garden City, New York: Doubleday and Co., 1971. (Grades 5-6) 192 pp. $4.50.

636. Baumhoff, Martin A. See No. 4049.

637. Baxter, James P. *The Pioneers of New France in New England.* 1894; rpt. Munsell's History Series. New York: Burt Franklin Pub., 1971. $20.00.

638. Baylor, Byrd. *When Clay Sings.* Illus. Tom Bahti. New York: Scribner's 1972. $495.

639. * Beaglehole, Ernest, and Pearl Beaglehole. *The Hopi of the Second Mesa.* 1935; rpt. New York: Kraus Reprint Co., 1970. $3.50.

640. * Beal, Merrill D. *"I Will Fight No More Forever"; Chief Joseph and the Nez Perce War.* Seattle: University of Washington Press, 1963. 366 pp. In paper: New York: Ballantine Books, 1971. 398 pp. $1.25.

641. Bealer, Alex. *Only the Names Remain: The Cherokees and the Trail of Tears.* Boston, Mass.: Little, Brown and Co., 1972. $5.75.

642. Beals, Alan R., and Bernard J. Siegel. *Divisiveness and Social Conflict: An Anthropological Approach.* Stanford: Stanford University Press, 1966. $6.00.

643. Beals, Ralph L. See Nos. 4031, 4042, and 4044.

644. Bean, Lowell J. *Mukat's People: The Cahuilla Indians of Southern California.* Berkeley: University of California Press, 1972. $6.75.

645. Bean, Lowell J., and William H. Mason, eds. *The Diaries and Accounts of the Romero Expeditions in Arizona and California, 1823-1826.* Los Angeles: Ward Ritchie Press, 1963. $10.00.

646. Beatty, Charles. *Journal of the Two-Months Tour, with a View to Promoting Religion.* 1768; rpt. St. Clair Shores, Michigan: Scholarly Press, 1970. $8.50.

647. ——. *Journals. Seventeen Sixty-Two to Seventeen Sixty-Nine.* Ed. Guy S. Klett. University Park: Pennsylvania State University Press, 1962. $7.50.

648. Beatty, Hetty B. *Little Owl Indian.* Eau Claire, Wisconsin: E. M. Hale and Co., 1951. (Grades 1-3) $3.06. Also: Boston: Houghton Mifflin Co., 1951. $3.40.

649. Beauchamp, William M. *The History of the New York Iroquois.* New York: Charles Scribners, 1913; rpt. Empire State Historical Publications Series, No. 3. Port Washington, New York: Ira J. Friedman, Inc., 1970. $8.50.

650. Beaver, R. Pierce. *Church, State, and the American Indians.* St. Louis, Missouri: Concordia Publishing House, 1966. $6.75.

651. ——. *Pioneers in Mission.* Grand Rapids, Michigan: William B. Eerdmans Pub. Co., 1966. $6.95.

652. * Beckham, Stephen D. *Requiem for a People: The Rogue Indians and the Frontiersmen.* Civilization of the American Indian Series, Vol. 108. Norman: University of Oklahoma Press, 1971. 214 pp. $7.95. In paper: 1972. $2.95.

653. Beckhard, Arthur J. *Black Hawk.* New York: Julian Messner Inc., 1957. (Grades 6 up) $3.34.

654. Beckwourth, James. *Black Frontiersman: Jim Beckwourth's Story.* Ed. Jeffrey Tarter. Black Autobiographies Series. New York: Richard W. Baron Pub., Co., 1970. $4.50. See also: Bonner, T. D., No. 726.

655. Beeler, Joe. *Cowboys and Indians.* Norman: University of Oklahoma Press, 1967. 80 pp. (last p. should be p. 81) Numbered on odd numbered pages only, which are always pictures; text on unnumbered left-hand pages. Beeler is Cherokee. $7.95.

656. Belous, Russell E., and Robert A. Weinstein. *Will Soule: Indian Photographer at Fort Sill, 1869-1874.* Los Angeles: War Ritchie Press, 1969. 120 pp. $12.50.

657. Belting, Natalia M. *Verity Mullens and the Indian.* New York: Holt, Rinehart and Winston, 1960. (Grades 5-8) $3.25.

658. Bemrose, John. *Reminiscences of the Second Seminole War.* Ed. John K. Mahon. Gainesville: University of Florida Press, 1966. $5.00.

659. Benchley, Nathaniel. *Only Earth and Sky Remain Forever.* New York: Harper and Row, 1972. $4.50.

660. * Benedict, Ruth F. *The Concept of the Guardian Spirit in North America.* 1923; rpt. New York: Kraus Reprint Co., 1970. $5.00.

661. Benedict, Rex. *Good Luck, Arizona Man.* New York: Pantheon Books, 1972. (Grades 5 up) $4.50.

662. * ——. *Patterns of Culture.* Boston: Houghton Mifflin, 1934. $6.95. In paper: New York: Houghton Mifflin, 1971. $2.25.

663. Bennett, Edna M. *Turquoise and the Indian*. Chicago: Swallow Press, 1966. $5.00.

664. Benson, Henry C. *Life Among the Choctaw Indians and Sketches of the South West*. 1860; rpt. American Studies. New York: Johnson Reprint Corp., 1970. $10.00.

665. Benton, Colbee C. *A Visitor to Chicago In Indian Days: Journal to the Far-Off West*. Ed. Paul M. Angle and James R. Getz. Rpt. New York: Burt Franklin, Pub., 1957, $14.50.

666. * Berger, Thomas. *Little Big Man*. 1954. Rptd. Greenwich, Connecticut: Fawcett Crest Book, (1969). 445 pp. $1.95. Hardbound: New York: Dial Press, 1964. $5.95.

677. Bergman, Tobi, ed. *The American Indian in the Continental Congress*. 2 Vols. New York: Bergman Publishers, 1971. $42.50.

668. Berke, Ernest. *The North American Indians: Life and Lore*. Garden City, New York: Doubleday and Co., 1964. (Grades 4-6) 64 pp. $5.95.

669. Berkhofer, Robert F., Jr. *Salvation and the Savage*. An Analysis of Protestant Missions and American Indian Response, 1787-1862. Lexington: University of Kentucky Press, 1965. 186 pp. $6.00.

670. Berlandier, Jean L. *The Indians of Texas in 1830*. Ed. by John C. Ewers. Trans. Patricia R. Leclerq. Washington, D.C.: Smithsonian Institution Press, 1969. 209 pp. $10.00.

671. * Berreman, J. V. *Tribal Distribution in Oregon*. American Anthropological Association Memoirs Series. 1937; rpt. New York: Kraus Reprint Co., 1970. $3.00.

672. * Berry, Brewton. *Almost White*. New York: Macmillan, 1963. $5.95. In paper: $1.25.

673. Berthrong, Donald J. *The Southern Cheyennes*. Civilization of the American Indian Series, No. 66. Norman: University of Oklahoma Press, 1963. 442 pp. $8.95.

674. * Beverley, Robert. *History and Present State of Virginia*. Ed. Louis B. Wright. Dominion Books. Charlottesville, Virginia: University Press of Virginia, 1968. $3.75. Also: 1947; rpt. Chapel Hill: University of North Carolina Press, 1960. $7.50. Also: In paper: Indianapolis: Bobbs Merrill, 1971. $2.95.

675. *Biesterfeldt, A Post-Contract Coalescent Site on the Northeastern Plains*. Smithsonian Institution Contributions to Anthropology, Vol. 15. Washington, D.C.: Goverment Printing Office, 1971. 108 pp. $1.50.

676. Bigelow, John. *On the Bloody Trail of Geronimo*. Ed. Arthur Woodward. Great West and Indian Series, Vol. 12. Los Angeles: Westernlore Press, 1968. 237 pp. $7.50.

677. Bilby, Julian W. *Among Unknown Eskimo: An Account of Twelve Years Intimate Relations with the Primitive Eskimo of Ice-Bound Baffin Land with a Description of Their Ways of Living, Hunting, Customs, and Beliefs.* 1923; rpt. Detroit: Gale Research Company, 1971. $12.50.

678. Bird Harrison. *War for the West, 1790-1813.* Fairlawn, New Jersey: Oxford University Press, 1972. 272 pp. $7.50.

679. Birket-Smith, Kaj. *Eskimos.* New York: Crown Publishers, Inc., 1971. $15.00.

680. Bissell, Benjamin H. *American Indian in English Literature of the Eighteenth Century.* Yale Studies in English, No. 68. 1925; rpt. Hamden, Connecticut: Shoe String Press, Inc., 1968. $6.25.

681. Bjorklund, Karna L. *The Indians of Northeastern America.* New York: Dodd, Mead, and Company, 1969. (Grades 9 up) 192 pp. $4.95.

682. Blackthunder, Elijah, et al. *Ehanna Woyakapi. History of the Sisseton Wahpeton Sioux Tribe.* Sisseton, S.D.: Tribal Publications, 1972. 130 pp. Text, appendices and photographs. $7.00. Blackthunder is Sioux.

683. Blaine, Thomas L. *Indian Tribes of North America.* Philadelphia: Rice and Company, 1870.

684. Blair, Emma H., ed. and Trans. *Indian Tribes of the Upper Mississippi Valley and Region of the Great Lakes as Described by Nicolas Perrot.* Cleveland, Ohio: Arthur Clark, 1911; rpt. 2 vols. in One. New York: Kraus Reprint Co., 1970. $25.00.

685. Blassingame, Wyatt. *Osceola: Seminole War Chief.* Indian Books Series. Champaign, Illinois: Garrard Publishing Company, 1967. (Grades 2-5) 80 pp. $2.59.

686. ——. *Sacagawea: Indian Guide.* Champaign, Illinois: Garrard Publishing Company, 1965. (Grades 2-5) $2.59.

687. * Bleed, Peter. *The Archaeology of Petaga Point.* St. Paul: Minnesota Historical Society, 1969. 51 pp. $2.00.

688. Bleeker, Sonia. *The Apache Indians: Raiders of the Southwest.* New York: William Morrow and Company, 1951. (Grades 4-6) 157 pp. $3.95.

689. ——. *The Cherokee, Indians of the Mountains.* New York: William Morrow and Company, 1952. (Grades 4-6) 159 pp. $3.95.

690. ——. *The Chippewa Indians: Rice Gatherers of the Great Lakes.* New York: William Morrow and Company, 1955. (Grades 4-6) 157 pp. $3.95.

691. ——. *The Crow Indians.* New York: William Morrow and Company, 1953. (Grades 4-6) 155 pp. $3.95.

692. ——. *The Delaware Indians.* New York: William Morrow and Company, 1953. (Grades 4-6) $3.78.

693. ——. *The Eskimo, Arctic Hunters and Trappers.* New York: William Morrow and Company, 1959. (Grades 4-6) 160 pp. $3.95.

694. ——. *Horsemen of the Western Plateaus: The Nez Perce Indians.* New York: William Morrow and Company, 1957. (Grades 4-6) 157 pp. $3.95.

695. ——. *Indians of the Longhouse.* New York: William Morrow and Company, 1959. (Grades 4-6) 160 pp. $3.78.

696. ——. *The Mission Indians of California.* New York: William Morrow and Company, 1956. (Grades 4-6) 142 pp. $3.95.

697. ——. *The Navajo, Herders, Weavers, and Silversmiths.* New York: William Morrow and Company, 1958. (Grades 4-6) 159 pp. $3.78.

698. ——. *The Pueblo Indians: Farmers of the Rio Grande.* New York: William Morrow and Company, 1955. (Grades 4-6) 155 pp. $3.95.

699. ——. *The Sea Hunters.* New York: William Morrow and Company, 1951. (Grades 4-6) 155 pp. $3.95.

700. ——. *The Seminole Indians.* New York: William Morrow and Company, 1954. (Grades 4-6) 156 pp. $3.36.

701. ——. *The Sioux Indians, The Hunters and Warriors of the Plains.* New York: William Morrow and Company, 1962. (Grades 4-6) 160 pp. $3.95.

702. Blish, Helen H. See Bad Heart Bull, Amos, No. 574.

703. * Bluecloud, Peter, ed. *Indians of all Tribes. Alcatraz is not an Island.* Wingbow Press, 1972. $3.95.

704. Blunt, Joseph. *A Historical Sketch of the Formation of the Confederacy, Particularly with Reference to the Provincial Limits and the Jurisdiction of the General Government over Indian Tribes and the Public Territory.* 1825; rpt. New York: Kraus Reprint Co., 1971. $10.00.

705. Boas, Franz. See also Rohner, Ronald P., and No. 4020.

706. * ——. *The Central Eskimo.* Rptd. Gloucester, Mass.: Peter Smith, 1970. $4.00. Also: Nashville, Tenn.: The Blue and Gray Press, 1972. In paper: Lincoln: University of Nebraska Press, 1964. $1.95.

707. ——. *The Chinook Indian Language.* 1911; rpt. Seattle: Shorey Publications, 1970. $5.00.

708. ——. *Contributions to the Ethnology of the Kwakiutl.* Columbia University Contributions to Anthropology Series, Vol. 3. Rpt. New York: AMS Press, 1969. $22.50.

709. ——. *The Theology of the Kwakiutl.* 35th Annual Report of the Bureau of American Ethnology. Washington, D.C., 1921. Part I, pp. 41-794; Part II, pp. 795-1481. Rpt. Helen Codere. Classics in Anthropology. Chicago: University of Chicago Press, 1966. $12.50.

710. ——. *The Geographical Names of the Kwakiutl Indians.* Columbia University Contributions to Anthropology Series, Vol. 20. 1934; rpt. New York: AMS Press, 1969. $25.00.

711. ——. *The Kwakiutl Indian Language.* 1911; rpt. Seattle: Shorey Publications, 1970. $7.50.

712. ——. *Materials for the Study of Inheritance in Man.* Columbia University Contributions to Anthropology Series, Vol. 6. Rpt. New York: AMS Press, 1969. $27.50.

713. ——. *The Mind of Primitive Man.* Rev. ed. Rpt. New York: Free Press, 1965. $1.95.

714. * ——. *Primitive Art.* 1927; rpt. New York: Dover Publications, 1970. $2.50.

715. * ——. *Race, Language, and Culture.* 1940; rpt. New York: Free Press, 1966. $3.95.

716. ——. *The Religion of the Kwakiutl Indians.* Columbia University Contributions to Anthropology. Vol. 10. New York: Columbia University Press, 1930; rpt. 2 vols. New York: AMS Press, 1969. $32.50; $17.50 ea.

717. ——. *The Social Organization and Secret Societies of the Kwakiutl Indians.* Based on Personal Observations and on Notes Made by Mr. George Hunt. 1895; rpt. Landmarks in Anthropology Series. New York: Johnson Reprint Corp., 1970. $30.00.

718. ——. *The Tsimshian Indian Language.* 1911; rpt. Seattle: Shorey Publications, 1970. $8.00.

719. Boas, Franz, and John R. Swanton. *Siouan—Teton and Santee Dialects—Dakota.* 1911; rpt. Seattle: Shorey Publications, 1970. $6.00.

720. Boatright, Moody C., and Donald Day, eds. *From Hell to Breakfast.* Dallas: Southern Methodist University Press, 1944. $5.95.

721. Bodge, George M. *Soldiers in King Philip's War.* 1906; rpt. Baltimore: Genealogical Publishing Co., Inc., 1967. $15.00.

722. Boelter, H. H. *The Hopi Kachina Portfolio.* Glendale, California: Arthur H. Clark, 1969. $65.00.

723. * Boller, Henry A. *Among the Indians: Four Years on the Upper Missouri, 1858-1862.* Ed. Milo M. Quaife. Lincoln: University of Nebraska Press, 1972. $2.25.

724. Bolton, Reginald P. *Indian Life of Long Ago in the City of New York.* New York: Crown Publishers, 1972. $4.95.

725. Bonner, Mary G. *Made in Canada.* New York: Alfred A. Knopf, Inc., 1943. (Grades 7-8) $4.97.

726. Bonner, T. D. *The Life and Adventures of James P. Beckwourth, Mountaineer, Scout and Pioneer and Chief of the Crow Nation of Indians.* 1856; rpt. American Negro: His History and Literature Series, No. 2. New York: Arno Press, 1969. $16.00. Also: Minneapolis: Ross and Haines, Inc., 1965. $10.00.

727. * Borland, Hal. *When the Legends Die.* New York: Bantam Pathfinder Edition. 1964. 216 pp. $ .60.

728. Bossu, Jena-Bernard. *Travels in the Interior of North America, 1751-1762.* Ed. Seymour Feiler. American Exploration and Travel Series, No. 35. Norman: University of Oklahoma Press, 1962. $8.95.

729. Bougainville, Louis Antoine de. *Adventure in the Wilderness: The American Journals . . . 1756-1760.* Tr. and ed. Edward P. Hamilton. American Expedition and Travel Series, No. 42. Norman: University of Oklahoma Press, 1970. $8.95.

730. Bounds, Thelma V. *The Children of Nanih Waiya.* San Antonio, Texas: Naylor Company, 1970. (Grades 6 up) $3.95.

731. * ——. *The Story of the Mississippi Choctaws.* Lawrence, Kansas: Haskell Press, 1970. (Grades 2-6) 25 pp. $ .35.

732. Bourke, John G. *Mackenzie's Last Fight with the Cheyenne's.* 1890; rpt. Ann Arbor, Michigan: University Microfilms, 1966. $7.50.

733. ——. *The Medicine Men of the Apaches.* Rpt. Glorieta, New Mexico: Rio Grande Press, Inc., 1970. $15.00.

734. ——. *On the Border with Crook.* 1891; rpt. Beautiful Rio Grande Classic Series, Vol. 12. Los Angeles: Westernlore Press, 1969. $10.00. Also: Westport, Connecticut: Greenwood Press, Inc., 1970. $16.00.

735. Bowers, Alfred W. *Mandan Social and Ceremonial Organization.* Chicago, Illinois: University of Chicago Press, 1950.

736. Boyd, Julian P., ed. *The Indian Treaties Printed by Benjamin Franklin, 1736-1762.* 1938; rpt. New York: AMS Press, 1970. $12.50.

737. Brackenridge, Henry M. *Views of Louisiana.* 1814; rpt. March of America Series. Ann Arbor, Michigan: University Microfilms, 1966. $4.55.

738. * Brackett, William S. *Indian Remains on the Upper Yellowstone River.* 1893; rpt. Seattle: Shorey Publications, 1972. $1.25.

739. Bradbury, John. *Travels in the Interior of America, in the Years 1809-1810 and 1811.* 1817; rpt. Landmarks in Anthropology Series. Ann Arbor, Michigan: University Microfilms, 1966. $7.75.

740. Bradfield, Wesley. *Cameron Creek Village, a Site in the Mimbres Area in Grant County, New Mexico.* 1931; rpt. New York: Kraus Reprint Co., 1971. $18.50.

741. * Brady, Byrus T. *Indian Fights and Fighters.* 1904; rpt. Lincoln: University of Nebraska Press, 1971. $2.25.

742. Brainerd, David, ed. *Memoirs of the Reverend David Brainerd: Missionary to the Indians on the Border of New York, New Jersey, and Pennsylvania.* 1822; rpt. American History Series. St. Clair Shores, Michigan: Scholarly Press, 1970. $11.00.

743. Brainerd, George W. See No. 4044.

744. Brandon, William. *Indians.* Deluxe Edition. New York: McGraw-Hill, 1961. $20.00.

745. * ——, ed. *American Heritage Book of the Indians.* New York: Dell, 1970. $ .75.

746. * ——, ed. *The Magic World: American Indian Songs and Poems.* New York: William Morrow and Co., Inc., 1970. 145 pp. $6.00. In paper: $2.50.

747. Brandon, William, and Anne T. White. *American Indians.* Landmark Giant, No. 3 New York: Random House, 1963. (Grades 5-9) $5.95.

748. Brant, Charles S. See Jim Whitewolf, No. 204.

749. Bray, Martha C., ed. *The Journals of Joseph N. Nicollet.* Trans. Andre Fertey. St. Paul: Minnesota Historical Society, 1970. 288 pp. $16.50.

750. Breetveld, Jim. *Getting to Know Alaska.* New York: Coward-McCann, Inc., 1958. (Grades 4-7) $3.29.

751. Brennan, Louis A. *American Dawn: A New Model of American Prehistory.* New York: Macmillan, 1970. 390 pp. $8.95.

752. ——. *Buried Treasure of Archaeology.* New York: Random House, 1964. (Grades 7-11) $4.95.

753. * Breternitz, David A. *The Excavations at Nantack Village, Point of Pines, Arizona.* Anthropological Papers, No. 1. Tucson: University of Arizona Press, 1959. $1.75.

754. * Brew, J. O. *The Archaeology of Alkali Ridge, Southeastern Utah.* 1946; rpt. New York: Kraus Reprint Co., 1970. $36.00.

755. Brewster, Benjamin. *The First Book of Indians.* New York: Franklin Watts, Inc., 1950. (Grades 4-6) 69 pp. $3.75.

756. Brickell, John. *The Natural History of North Carolina, with an Account of the Trade, Manners, and Customs of the Christian and Indian Inhabitants.* 1737; rpt. American Studies Series. New York: Johnson Reprint Corp., 1969. $20.00.

757. Briggs, Jean L. *Never in Anger: Portrait of an Eskimo Family.* Cambridge: Harvard University Press, 1970. 379 pp. $15.25.

758. Brigham, Besmilr. *Heaved from the Earth.* New York: Alfred A. Knopf, 1971. 76 pp. $4.95. Author is of Choctaw descent.

759. Bright, William. *Age of the Fathers.* 2 vols. 1913; rpt. New York: AMS Press, 1970. $35.00 / $18.00 each.

760. * ——. *The Karok Language.* University of California Publications in Linguistics Series, Vol. 13. Rpt. Berkeley: University of California Press, 1957. $6.50.

761. * ——, ed. *Studies in Californian Linguistics.* University of California Publications in Linguistics Series, Vol. 34. Berkeley: University of California Press, 1964. $5.00.

762. Brindze, Ruth. *The Story of the Totem Pole.* New York: Vanguard Press, Inc., 1951. (Grades 4-8) 64 pp. $4.50.

763. Brininstool, E. A. *Fighting Indian Warriors.* 1953; rpt. New York: Bonanza Books, 1972. 353 pp. $4.95.

764. Brinton, Daniel G. *American Race: A Linguistic Classification and Ethnographic Description of the Native Tribes of North and South America.* 1901; rpt. New York: Johnson Reprint Corp., 1970. $14.00.

765. ——. *Essays of an Americanist.* Series in American Studies. Rpt. New York: Johnson Reprint Corp., 1970. $14.00.

766. ——. *Notes on the Floridian Peninsala.* Rpt. New York: AMS Press, 1969. $12.50.

767. Britt, Albert. *The America That Was.* Barre, Mass.: Barre Publishers, 1964. $5.94.

768. ——. *Great Indian Chiefs.* New York: McGraw-Hill Book Co., 1938; rpt. Facsimile Edition. Freeport, New York: Books for Libraries, Inc., 1969. 280 pp. $9.75.

769. Brody, J. J. *Indian Painters and White Patrons.* Albuquerque: University of New Mexico Press, 1971. 238 pp. $15.00.

770. * Bronson, Edgar B. *Reminiscences of a Ranchman.* Rpt. Gloucester, Mass.: Peter Smith, 1971. $4.00. In paper: Lincoln: University of Nebraska Press, 1962. $1.95.

771. Bronson, Ruth Muskrat. *Indians are People Too.* New York: Friendship Press, 1944. 184 pp. Author is Cherokee.

772. Bronson, Wilfred S. *Pinto's Journey.* New York: Julian Messner, Inc., 1948. (Grades 5-8) $3.50.

773. The Brookings Institution. *The Problem of Indian Administration.* 1928; rpt. New York: Johnson Reprint Corp., 1971. $32.50.

774. Brophy, William A., Sophie D. Aberle, and others, compilers. *The Indian: America's Unfinished Business.* Civilization of the American Indian Series, No. 83. Norman: University of Oklahoma Press, 1966. 236 pp. This is the *Report of the Commission on the Rights, Liberties, and Responsibilities of the American Indian.*

775. Brower, Charles D. *Fifty Years Below Zero.* New York: Dodd, Mead and Company, 1942. 310 pp. $6.00.

776. * Brown, Dee. *Action at Beecher Island.* New York: Modern Literary Editions Publishing Co., 1967. 237 pp. Story of the 9-day siege of Forsyth's Scouts by Plains Indians at Beecher Island in September, 1868.

777. ———. *Bury My Heart at Wounded Knee.* An Indian History of the American West. New York: Holt, Rinehart, and Winston, 1970. 487 pp. $10.95. In paper: $1.95.

778. ———. *Galvanized Yankees.* Urbana: University of Illinois Press, 1963. $5.50.

779. * ———. *Showdown at Little Big Horn.* New York: Berkeley Publishing Corp., 1970. 190 pp. $ .95. Hardbound: New York: G. P. Putnam's Sons, 1964. (Grades 6-9) $4.50.

780. Brown, Douglas S. *The Catawba Indians: The People of River.* Columbia: University of South Carolina Press, 1966; rpt. 1968. 400 pp. $10.00.

781. Brown, John P. *Old Frontiers: The Story of the Cherokee Indians from the Earliest Times to the Date of Their Removal to the West.* 1838; rpt. First American Frontier Series. 1938; rpt. New York: Arno Press, 1970. $27.00.

782. * Brown, Joseph Epes. *The Spiritual Legacy of the American Indian.* Pendle Hill Pamphlet One Hundred and Thirty-Five. Lebanon, Pa.: Sowers Printing Co., 1970. 32 pp. $ .70.

783. Brown, Mark H. *The Flight of the Nez Perce.* New York: G. P. Putnam's, 1967. 480 pp.

784. * ———. *Plainsmen of the Yellowstone: A History of the Yellowstone Basin.* Lincoln: University of Nebraska Press, 1969. $2.50.

785. Brown, Mark H., and W. R. Felton. *Before Barbed Wire.* New York: Bramhall House, 1961. 214 pp. Mostly about cowboys, settlers. Many interesting photos; some of Indians and Indian camps.

786. ———. *The Frontier Years.* New York: Bramhall House, 1965. Over 250 pp.

787. Brown, Vinson. *Great Upon the Mountain: Crazy Horse of America.* Healdsburg, California: Naturegraph Publishers, 1971. 133 pp. $2.25.

788. * Brown, Vinson, and Douglas Andrews. *The Pomo Indians of California and Their Neighbors*. Ed. Albert B. Elsasser. Indian Map Books of America Series, Vol. 1. Healdsburg, California: Naturegraph Publishers, 1969. $4.50. In paper: $2.50.

789. Brown, William C. *Early Okanogan History, 1811-1911*. Enlarged Edition. Rpt. Fairfield, Washington: Ye Galleon Press, 1968. $3.50.

790. Browne, J. Ross. *Adventures in the Apache Country*. Rpt. Ed. Donald M. Powell. Tucson: University of Arizona Press, 1972.

791. ——. *A Peep at Washoe*. Includes *Washoe Revisited*. Lithographic Reprints. Ninety Browne Woodcuts. Balboa, California: Paisano Press, Inc., 1960. $7.50.

792. Bruemmer, Fred. *Seasons of the Eskimo*. Greenwich, Connecticut: New York Graphic Society, Ltd., 1971. $15.00.

793. * Bryan, Nonahbah G., and Stella Young. *Navajo Native Dyes*. Illust. Charles Keetsie Shirley. Washington, D.C.: Division of Education, Bureau of Indian Affairs, 1940. 75 pp. $ .60. Bryan and Shirley are Navajo.

794. Bryde, John. *Indian Psychology*. Vermillion, South Dakota: University of South Dakota Press, 1970. $5.00.

795. * ——. *Indian Students and Guidance*. Guidance Monograph Series. Boston: Houghton Mifflin, 1971. $1.60.

796. ——. *The Sioux Indian Student: A Study of Scholastic Failure and Personality Conflict*. 1966. 196 pp.

797. Buck, Daniel. *Indian Outbreaks*. 1904; rpt. Minneapolis: Ross and Haines, Inc., 1965. 284 pp. $8.75.

798. Buckmaster, Henrietta. *Seminole Wars*. New York: Macmillan and Company, 1966. (Grades 7 up) $2.95.

799. * *Buckskin and Blanket Days: Memoirs of a Friend of the Indians*. Written in 1905 by Thomas Henry Tibbles. Rptd. from the 1957 edition by Vivian K. Barris. Lincoln: University of Nebraska Press, 1969. A Bison Book. 336 pp. $2.25.

800. Budd, Lillian. *Full Moons*. New York: Rand McNally and Company, 1970. (Grades 4-6) $4.95.

801. Buechel, Eugene, S.J. *A Grammar of Lakota*. The Language of the Teton Sioux Indians. St. Louis: John S. Swift Co., 1939. 374 pp. $10.00.

802. Buff, Mary. *Dancing Cloud: The Navajo Boy*. With Lithographs by Conrad Buff. New York: The Viking Press, 1937. 80 pp. $3.95.

803. ——. *Hah-Nee*. With Lithographs by Conrad Buff. Boston: Houghton Mifflin Company, 1965. (Grades 4-6) $4.07.

804. ——. *Kemi: An Indian Boy Before the White Man Came*. With Lithographs by Conrad Buff. Los Angeles: Ward Ritchie Press, 1966. (Grades 3-7) $3.95.

805. ——. *Magic Maize*. With Lithographs by Conrad Buff. Boston: Houghton Mifflin, 1953. $4.00.
806. Bulla, Clyde R. *Eagle Feather*. New York: Thomas Y. Crowell, 1953. (Grades 2-5) $3.95.
807. ——. *Indian Hill*. New York: Thomas Y. Crowell, 1963. (Grades 2-5) $3.00.
808. ——. *John Billington, Friend of Squanto*. New York: Thomas Y. Crowell, 1970. (Grades 2-5) $3.50.
809. ——. *Squanto: Friend of the Pilgrims*. New York: Thomas Y. Crowell, 1954. (Grades 2-5) $3.50.
810. * Bullard, William R. *The Cerro Colorado Site and Pithouse Architecture in the Southwestern United States Prior to A.D. 900*. 1962; rpt. New York: Kraus Reprint Co., 1971. $20.00.
811. Bunker, Robert. *Other Men's Skies*. 1956; rpt. New York: Kraus Reprint Co., 1971. 256 pp. $13.00.
812. Bunker, Robert, and John Adair. *A First Look at Strangers*. New Brunswick: Rutgers University Press, 1959. $6.00.
813. Bunn, Iola F. *Growing Up in Alaska*. Jericho, New York: Exposition Press Inc., 1965. (Grades 2-5) $4.00.
814. * Bunn, Matthew. *The Journal of the Adventures of Matthew Bunn*. Rpt. Facsimile Edition. Chicago: Newberry Library, 1962. $1.75. Bunn was an Indian captive.
815. Bunnell, Lafayette H. *The Discovery of the Yosemite and the Indian War of 1851*. 1880; rpt. Facsimile Edition. Select Bibliographies Reprint Series. Freeport, New York: Books for Libraries, Inc., 1970.
816. * Bunzel, Ruth L. *Pueblo Potter: A Study of Creative Imagination in Primitive Art*. Columbia University Contributions to Anthropology, Vol. 8. 1929; rpt. New York: AMS Press, 1969. $55.00. In paper: New York: Dover Publications, 1972. $2.50.
817. ——. *Zuni Katcina: An Analytical Study*. 47th Annual Report of the Bureau of American Ethnology. Washington, 1932, pp. 837-1086.
818. * Burdick, Loraine. *Alaskan Homes*. Washington, D.C.: Hobby House Press, 1967. $2.00.
819. * ——. *Alaskan Indian Copper Money*. Washington, D.C.: Hobby House Press, 1967. $2.00.
820. * ——. *Alaskan Skin Clothing*. Washington, D.C.: Hobby House Press, 1970. $2.00.
821. * ——. *Alaskettes: Alaskan Lore and Crafts for Children*. Washington, D.C.: Hobby House Press, 1967. (Grades 3-6) $7.50. In paper: $3.50.
822. * ——. *Arctic Alaska Adventure*. Washington, D.C.: Hobby House Press, 1966. $3.95.

823. Burdick, Usher L. *The Last Battle of the Sioux Nation*. Stevens Point, Wisconsin: Worzalla Publishing Company, 1929. 164 pp.

824. ———. *The Marquis de Mores at War in the Bad Lands*. 1929; rpt. Seattle: Shorey Publications, 1970. $2.50.

825. Burland, Cottie. *The People of the Ancient Americas*. London: Paul Hamlyn, 1969. 159 pp.

826. Burnette, Robert. *The Tortured Americans*. Englewood Cliffs, New Jersey: Prentice-Hall, 1971. 155 pp. $7.95. Author is Sioux.

827. Burnford, Sheila. *Without Reserve*. With drawings by Susan Ross. Boston: Atlantic, Little Brown, 1969. 242 pp. $6.50. About her experiences with Indians in northern Ontario.

828. Burns, Robert I. *The Jesuits and the Indian Wars of the Northwest*. New Haven: Yale University Press, 1966. 512 pp. $15.00.

829. Burton, Frederick R. *American Primitive Music*. With Special Attention to the Music of the Ojibways. 1909; rpt. Port Washington, New York: Kennikat Press, Inc., 1969. $12.50.

830. Burton, Henrietta K. *The Re-Establishment of the Indians in Their Pueblo Life Through the Revival of Their Traditional Crafts: A Study of Home Extension Education*. 1936; rpt. New York: AMS Press, 1972. $10.00.

831. * Bushnell, David I. *The Cahokia and Surrounding Mound Groups*. 1904; rpt. New York: Kraus Reprint Co., 1971. $2.50.

832. ———. *Native Villages and Village Sites East of the Mississippi and Native Cemeteries and Forms of Burial East of the Mississippi*. 1919-1920; rpt. Nashville, Tennessee: The Blue and Gray Press, 1971. 271 pp. $12.50.

833. ———. *Villages of the Algonquian, Siouan, and Caddoan Tribes West of the Mississippi and Burials of the Algonquian, Siouan, and Caddoan Tribes West of the Mississippi*. Nashville, Tennessee: The Blue and Gray Press, 1972.

834. * Bushnell, Geoffrey H. *Ancient Arts of the Americas*. Prager World of Art Series Paperbacks. New York: Frederick A. Praeger, Publishers, 1965. (Grades 10 up) 287 pp. $7.50. In paper: $3.95.

835. * ———. *First Americans: The Pre-Columbian Civilizations*. Library of the Early Civilizations. New York: McGraw-Hill, 1968. $5.50. In paper: $2.95.

836. Butterfield, C. W. *The History of the Discovery of the Northwest by John Nicollet in 1634*. Port Washington, New York: Kennikat Press, Inc., 1969. $7.00.

837. ———. *The History of the Girtys*. Columbus, Ohio: Long's College Book Company, 1950. $7.50.

838. Cahill, Holger. *American Sources of Modern Art*. Museum of Modern Art Publications in Reprint Series. 1933; rpt. New York: Arno Press, 1970. $10.00.

839. * Cahn, Edgar S., ed. *Our Brother's Keeper: The Indian in White America.* New York: World Publishing Company, 1969. (New Community Press Book) 193 pp. $5.95. Seering indictment of white society. In paper: $2.95.

840. * Caldwell, Joseph R. *Trend and Tradition in the Prehistory of the Eastern United States.* 1958; rpt. New York: Kraus Reprint Co., 1971. $5.00.

841. Callan, Eileen T. *The Hardy Race of Men: America's Early Indians.* New York: Harcourt Brace Jovanovich, Inc., 1970. (Grades 7 up) $4.25.

842. Campbell, Walter S. See Vestal, Stanley. No. 2860-2864.

843. Cannon, Cornelia J. *Pueblo Boy: A Story of Coronado's Search for the Seven Cities of Cibola.* 1926; rpt. New York: Garrett Press, Inc., 970. $15.00.

844. Capps, Benjamin. *The Trail to Ogallala.* New York: Hawthorn Books, Inc., 1964. $4.95.

845. ——. *White Man's Road.* New York: Harper Row, 1969. $6.95.

846. * ——. *The Woman of the People.* New York: Hawthorn Books, Inc., 1966. $5.95. In paper: New York: Fawcett World Library, 1971. $ .95.

847. Capron, Louis. *The Red War Pole.* Indianapolis: Bobbs-Merrill Company, 1963. (Grades 5-9) $3.75.

848. Carcia, Andrew. *A Tough Trip Through Paradise, 1878-1879.* Rpt. Ed. Bennett H. Stein. Boston: Houghton Mifflin Company, 1967. $6.95.

849. * Cardinal, Harold. *The Unjust Society.* The Tragedy of Canada's Indians. Edmonton, Alberta: M. G. Hurtig, Ltd., 1969. 171 pp. Also: Trans. into French as *La Tragedie Des Indiens Du Canada.* By Raymond Gagne and Jacques Vallee. Intl. School Book Service. $3.50.

850. Carelton, Guy. *The Conditions of the Indian Trade in North America, 1767.* 1890; rpt. New York: Burt Franklin, Pub., 1971. $6.00.

851. * Carley, Kenneth. *The Sioux Uprising of 1862.* St. Paul: Minnesota Historical Society, 1961. 80 pp. $3.75. In paper: $2.50.

852. Carlson, Gerald F. *Two on the Rocks.* New York: David McKay Company, Inc., 1966. $4.95. On the Eskimo.

853. Carlson, Roy I. *White Mountain Redware.* Anthropological Papers Series, No. 19. Tucson: University of Arizona Press, 1970. $7.00.

854. Carpenter, Edmund. *The Story of Comock the Eskimo.* New York: Simon and Shuster, 1968. (Grades 5 up) 85 pp. $4.50.

855. * ——, et. al. *The Eskimo.* Canadian University Paperbooks. Toronto: University of Toronto Press, 1959. $4.95.

856. Carrighar, Sally. *Moonlight at Midday*. New York: Alfred A. Knopf, Inc., 1958. $7.95.

857. Carriker, Robert C. *Fort Supply, Indian Territory: Frontier Outpost on the Plains*. Norman: University of Oklahoma Press, 1971. $7.95.

858. Carroll, John, ed. *The American Indian*. New York: Liveright, 1970.

859. * Carter, George F. *Plant Geography and Culture History in the American Southwest*. 1945; rpt. New York: Johnson Reprint Corp., 1970. $10.00.

860. Cartier, Jacques. *A Shorte and Brief Narration of the Two Navigations and Discoveries to the Northwest Partes Called Newe Fraunce*. 1580; rpt. March of America Series. Ann Arbor, Michigan: University Microfilms, 1966. $4.55.

861. Caruso, John A. *The Mississippi Valley Frontier*. Indianapolis: Bobbs-Merrill, 1970. $8.50.

862. Carver, Jonathan. *Travels Through the Interior Parts of North America*. 1781; rpt. Facsimile Edition. Minneapolis: Ross and Haines, Inc. 1970. $10.00.

863. * Cash, Joseph H., and Herbert T. Hoover, eds. *To Be an Indian: An Oral History*. New York: Holt, Rinehart, Winston, 1971. 239 pp. $4.00.

864. Cassel, Jonathan F. *Tarahumara Indians*. San Antonio: Naylor Co., 1969. (Grades 7 up) 160 pp. $6.95.

865. * Castaneda, Carlos. *A Separate Reality*. New York: Pocket Books, 1972. 263 pp. $1.25.

866. * ———. *Teachings of Don Juan: A Yaqui Way of Knowledge*. Berkeley: University of California Press, 1968. $6.95. In paper: New York: Ballantine Books, 1971. 276 pp. $ .95.

867. Castetter, Edward F., and Willis H. Bell. *Pima and Papago Indian Agriculture*. Albuquerque: University of New Mexico Press, 1942. 215 pp.

868. ———. *Yuman Indian Agriculture*. Primitive Subsistence on the Lower Colorado and Gila Rivers. Albuquerque: University of New Mexico Press, 1951. 288 pp. $5.00.

869. Catlin, George. *Life Amongst the Indians: A Book for Youth*. London: Sampson, Low, Son, and Marston, 1867. 339 pp.

890. ———. *Letters and Notes on the Manners, Customs, and Condition of the North American Indians*. 2 vols. London: Published by the Author, 1841; rpt. Facsimile Edition. Minneapolis: Ross and Haines, 1970. $17.50. In paper: New York: Dover Publications, 1970. $2.50 each.

871. ———. *O-Kee-Pa. A Religious Ceremony and Other Customs of the Mandans*. Ed. John C. Ewers. Centennial Edition. New Haven, Connecticut: Yale University Press, 1967. 106 pp. $12.50.

872. ———. See also Ross, Marvin C., No. 2460.

873. Caughey, John W. *The American West: Frontier and Region*. Rpt. Ed. Norris Hundley and John A. Schultz. Los Angeles: Ward Ritchie Press, 1969. $10.00.

874. ———. *Hubert Howe Bancroft, Historian of the West*. Rpt. New York: Russell and Russell, 1970. $15.00.

875. ———. *McGillivray of the Creeks*. Norman: University of Oklahoma Press, 1938; rpt. 1959. 385 pp. $7.95.

876. Cawston, Vee. *Matuk, the Eskimo Boy*. New York: Lantern Press, Inc., 1965. (Grades 1-2) $3.81.

877. Ceram, C. W. *First American: A Story of North American Archaeology*. New York: Harcourt Brace Jovanovich, 1971. $9.95.

878. Chalmers, Harvey. *Joseph Brant: Mohawk*. See Monture, Ethel B., No. 2117.

879. ———. *The Last Stand of the Nez Perce: Destruction of a People*. New York: Twayne Publishers, 1962. 288 pp.

880. * Chamberlin, Ralph V. *The Ethno-Botany of the Gosiute Indians of Utah*. 1915; rpt. New York: Kraus Reprint Co., 1970. $5.00.

881. * Chance, Norman A. *The Eskimo of North Alaska*. Case Studies in Cultural Anthropology. New York: Holt, Rinehart, and Winston, 1966. $2.35.

882. * Chapman, Carl H., and Eleanor F. Chapman. *Indians and Archaeology of Missouri*. Columbia: University of Missouri Press, 1964. $1.00.

883. * Chapman, Kenneth M. *The Pottery of San Ildefonso Pueblo*. School of American Research Publication. Albuquerque: University of New Mexico Press, 1969. 408 pp. $25.00. / $15.00.

884. * ———. *The Pottery of Santo Domingo Pueblo: A Detailed Study of its Decoration*. School of American Research Publication. Albuquerque: University of New Mexico Press, 1953. 206 pp. $15.00.

885. Chapman, William. *Remember the Wind: A Prairie Memoir*. New York: J. B. Lippincott Co., 1965. 240 pp. $5.95.

886. * Cheshire, Cliff. *Thunder on the Mountain*. New York: Modern Literary Editions Publishing Co., 1960. 239 pp. $1.25.

887. Chief Eagle, Dallas. *Winter Count*. Boulder, Colorado: Johnson Publishing Co., 1967. 211 pp. $5.95. Author is Sioux.

888. Chittenden, Hiram M., and Alfred T. Richardson. *The Life, Letters and Travels of Father Pierre Jean De Smet, S.J., 1801-1873: Missionary Labors and Adventures Among the Wild Tribes of the North American Indians.* 4 vols. 1905; rpt. Religion in America Series. New York: Arno Press, 1969. $55.00.

889. * Christensen, Gardell D. *The Buffalo Kill.* Rpt. New York: Washington Square Press, Inc., 1968. (Grades 4-6) $ .50.

890. * *Chronicles of American Indian Protest.* Compiled and edited by the Council on Interracial Books for Children. Greenwich, Connecticut: Fawcett Publications, 1970. 374 pp. $1.25.

891. * Claflin, W. H. *The Stalling's Island Mound*, Columbia County, Georgia. 1931; rpt. New York: Kraus Reprint Co., 1971. $6.50.

892. * Clark, Ann N. *Brave Against the Enemy.* Sioux Text by Emil Afraid-of-Hawk. Ed. Willard W. Beatty. Photographic Illustrations by Helen Post. Sioux Series. Washington, D.C.: Division of Education, Bureau of Indian Affairs, [c. 1940]. For junior and senior high. 95 pp. $ .75.

893. * ——. *Bringer of the Mystery Dog.* Sioux Text by Emil Afraid-of-Hawk. Illustrated by Oscar Howe. Sioux Series. Washington, D.C.: Division of Education, Bureau of Indian Affairs, 1950. (For junior high) $ .40.

894. ——. *The Desert People.* New York: Viking Press, Inc., 1962. (Grades 1-5) $3.00.

895. ——. *Father Kino, Priest to the Pimas.* Vision Book. New York: Farrar, Straus and Giroux, Inc., 1963. (Grades 3-7) $2.95.

896. * ——. *The Grass Mountain Mouse.* Sioux Text by Emil Afraid-of-Hawk. Just for Fun Series. Illustrated by Andrew Standing Soldier. Washington, D.C.: Division of Education, Bureau of Indian Affairs, [c. 1950]. (Grades K-5) In English and Sioux. 108 pp. $ .60.

897. * ——. *The Hen of Wahpeton.* Sioux Text by Emil Afraid-of-Hawk. Just for Fun Series. Illustrated by Andrew Standing Soldier. Washington, D.C.: Division of Education, Bureau of Indian Affairs, [c. 1950]. (Grades K-5) In English and Sioux. 97 pp. $ .50.

898. ——. *In My Mother's House.* New York: Viking Press, Inc., 1941. (Grades K-5) $3.50.

899. * ——. *Little Boy with Three Names.* Spanish Text by Christina Jenkins. Illustrated by Tonita Lujan. Pueblo Series. Washington, D.C.: Division of Education, Bureau of Indian Affairs, [c. 1950]. (Grades K-5) $ .60.

900. *——. *Little Herder in Autumn*. Navajo Text by Robert W. Young and John P. Harrington. Illustrated by Hoke Denetsosie. Washington, D.C.: Division of Education, Bureau of Indian Affairs, [c. 1950] (Grades K-5) $ .60.

901. *——. *Little Herder in Spring*. Navajo Text by Robert W. Young and John P. Harrington. Illustrated by Hoke Denetsosie. Washington, D.C.: Division of Education, Bureau of Indian Affairs, [c. 1950]. (Grades K-5) $ .60.

902. *——. *Little Herder in Summer*. Navajo Text by Robert W. Young and John P. Harrington. Illustrated by Hoke Denetsosie. Washington, D.C.: Division of Education, Bureau of Indian Affairs, [c. 1950]. (Grades K-5) $ .60.

903. *——. *Little Herder in Winter*. Navajo Text by Robert W. Young and John P. Harrington. Illustrated by Hoke Denetsosie. Washington, D.C.: Division of Education, Bureau of Indian Affairs, [c. 1950]. (Grades K-5) $ .60.

904. *——. *The Little Indian Basket Maker*. Chicago: Melmont Publishers, 1957. (Grades 1-5) $2.75.

905. ——. *The Little Indian Pottery Maker*. Chicago: Melmont Publishers, Inc., 1955. (Grades 1-5) $3.25.

906. ——. *The Little Navajo Bluebird*. New York: Viking Press, Inc., 1943. (Grades 2-5) $3.50.

907. ——. *The Medicine Man's Daughter*. New York: Farrar, Straus and Giroux, Inc., 1963. (Grades 4-8) $3.50.

908. *——. *The Pine Ridge Porcupine*. Sioux Text by Emil Afraid-of-Hawk. Just for Fun Series. Ed. William W. Beatty. Illustrated by Andrew Standing Soldier. Washington, D.C.: Division of Education, Bureau of Indian Affairs, 1940. (Grades K-5) 42 pp. $ .40.

909. *——. *Singing Sioux Cowboy*. Sioux Text by Emil Afraid-of-Hawk. Just for Fun Series. Ed. Willard W. Beatty. Illustrated by Andrew Standing Soldier. Washington, D.C.: Division of Education, Bureau of Indian Affairs, [c. 1940] . (Grades K-5) $ .50.

910. *——. *Sioux Cowboy*. Sioux Text by Emil Afraid-of-Hawk. Just for Fun Series. Ed. Willard W. Beatty. Illustrated by Andrew Standing Soldier. Washington, D.C.: Division of Education, Bureau of Indian Affairs, [c. 1940]. (Grades K-5) $ .50.

911. *——. *Slim Butte Raccoon*. Sioux Text by Emil Afraid-of-Hawk. Just for Fun Series. Ed. Willard W. Beatty. Illustrated by Andrew Standing Soldier. Washington, D.C.: Division of Education, Bureau of Indian Affairs, 1942. 48 pp. $ .40.

912. *——. *Sun Journey*. Pueblo Series. Illustrated by Percy Sandy. Washington, D.C.: Division of Education, Bureau of Indian Affairs, [c. 1950]. (Grades 5-8) $ .65.

913. *——. *There Still Are Buffalo.* Ed. Willard W. Beatty. Illustrated by Andrew Standing Soldier. Washington, D.C.: Division of Education, Bureau of Indian Affairs, 1942. (Grades 5-7) 44 pp. $ .40.

914. *——. *Young Hunter of Picuris.* Spanish Text by Christina Jenkins. Illustrated by Velino Herrera. Pueblo Series. Washington, D.C.: Division of Education, Bureau of Indian Affairs, [c. 1950]. (Grades 3-7) $ .35.

915. Clark, Electa. *Cherokee Chief; The Life of John Ross.* New York: Macmillan Company, 1970. (Grades 5-8) 118 pp. $3.95.

916. ——. *Osceola: Young Seminole Indian.* Indianapolis: Bobbs-Merrill Company, 1970. (Grades 3-7) $2.75.

917. Clark, Joshua V. H. *Onondaga: Or, Reminiscences of Earlier and Later Times.* 1849; rpt. 2 vols in 1. New York: Kraus Reprint Company, 1971. $30.00.

918. Clark, Laverne H. *They Sang For Horses: The Impact of the Horse on Navajo Apache Folklore.* Tucson: University of Arizona Press, 1966. $12.00.

919. Clark, William P. *The Indian Sign Language With Brief Explanatory Notes of the Gestures Taught Deaf-Mutes . . . And a Description of the Peculiar Laws, Customs, Myths, Superstitions, Ways of Living, Code of Peace and War Signals of our Aborigines.* 1885; rpt. San Jose, California: The Rosicrucian Press, Ltd. 1959. 443 pp.

920. Clarke, George F. *Someone Before Us: Our Maritime Indians.* Brunswick Press, 1968. 240 pp.

921. Clarke, Mary W. *Chief Bowles and the Texas Cherokees.* Civilization of the American Indian series, No. 113. Norman: University of Oklahoma Press, 1971. 154 pp. $6.95.

922. Clarke, T. Wood. *The Bloody Mohawk.* New York: The Macmillan Company, 1940; rpt. Empire State Historical Publications Series, No. 53. Port Washington, New York: Ira J. Friedman, Inc., 1968. $11.00.

923. Cleven, Catherine S. *Black Hawk: A Young Sauk Warrior.* Indianapolis: Bobbs-Merrill Company, 1966. (Grades 3-7) $2.75.

924. Coatsworth, Elizabeth. *Indian Encounters.* New York: Macmillan and Company, 1960. (Grades 6-8) 264 pp. $4.50.

925. ——. *Indian Mound Farm.* New York: Macmillan and Company, 1969. (Grades 2-5) $4.50.

926. ——. *Ronnie and the Chief's Son.* New York: Macmillan and Company, 1967. (Grades 4-6) $3.95.

927. * Coatsworth, Emerson, and Robert C. Dailey. *Indians of Quetico.* Toronto: University of Toronto Press, 1957. $2.50.

928. * Cobe, Albert. *Great Spirit*. Open Door Books. Chicago: Children's Press, Inc., 1970. (Grades 5 up) 64 pp. $3.00. In paper: $ .75.

929. Codere, Helen. *Fighting with Property: A Study of Kwakiutl Potlatching and Warfare, 1792-1930*. American Ethnological Society Monographs. Seattle: University of Washington Press, 1966. $5.95.

930. * Cody, Iron Eyes. Assisted by Ye-Was. *How Indian Sign Talk in Pictures*. Hollywood, California: Homer H. Boelter Lithography, 1952. Unpaged; approximately 30 pp. Also: Healdsburg, California: Naturegraph Pub., 1970. $3.50. Paper: $1.50.

931. Coen, Rena N. *The Red Man in Art*. Fine Arts Books for Young People Series. Minneapolis: Lerner Publications, 1972. (Grades 5-12) $4.50.

932. *The Coeur D'Alene Indian Reservation*. A Senate Document. Rpt. Fairfield, Washington: Ye Galleon Press, 1970. $5.00.

933. Cohen, Felix S. *Legal Conscience*. Selected Papers. Ed. Lucy K. Cohen. 1960; rpt. Hamden, Connecticut: Shoe String Press, 1970. $15.00.

934. Cohen, Myer M. *Notices of Florida and the Campaigns*. Ed. O. Z. Tyler. Rpt. Floridiana Facsimile and Reprint Series. Gainesville: University of Florida Press, 1964. $8.50.

935. Cohoe, William. *A Cheyenne Sketchbook*. Commentary by E. H. Hoebel and K. D. Peterson. Civilization of the American Indian Series, No. 75. Norman: University of Oklahoma Press, 1964. 96 pp. $5.95.

936. Colbv, Carroll B. *Cliff Dwellings: Ancient Ruins from America's Past*. New York: Coward McCann, 1971. $3.49.

937. * Colden, Cadwallader. *The History of the Five Nations of Canada*. Ithaca: Cornell University Press, 1958. $1.95. Also: Gloucester, Mass.: Peter Smith, 1972. $4.00.

938. * Collier, Donald, et al. *Archaeology of the Upper Columbia Region*. Publications in Anthropology. Seattle: University of Washington Press, 1942. $5.00.

939. Collier, John. *American Indian Ceremonial Dances*. Navajo-Pueblo, Apache-Zuni. New Ed. New York: Crown Publishers, 1972. 192 pp. $3.95.

940. ——. *The Indians of the Americas*. New York: W. W. Norton, Inc., 1947. 326 pp.

941. *——. *On the Gleaming Way: Navajos, Eastern Pueblos, Zunis, Hopis, Apaches, and Their Land; and Their Meanings to the World.* Chicago: Swallow Press, Inc., 1962. 163 pp. $5.00. Revision and Updating of his original book entitled *Patterns and Ceremonials of the Indians of the Southwest,* 1949. In paper: Sage Book. $2.25.

942. Collins, Dennis. *The Indians Last Fight or the Dull Knife Raid.* 1914; rpt. New York: AMS Press, 1970. $22.50.

943. *Collins, H. B. *Archaeology of the Bering Sea Region.* 1933; rpt. Facsimile Edition. Seattle: Shorey Publications, 1971. $1.50.

944. Colson, Elizabeth. *The Makah Indians.* Minneapolis: University of Minnesota Press, 1953. 308 pp. Also: New York: Humanities Press, Inc., 1971. $7.50.

945. Colton, C. *A Tour of the American Lakes, and Among the Indians of the North-West Territory, 1830.* 2 vols. 1833; rpt. Port Washington, New York: Kennikat Press, Inc., 1971. $35.00.

946. *Colton, Harold S. *Hopi Kachina Dolls With a Key to their Identification.* Color Photographs by Jack Breed. Rev. ed. Albuquerque: University of New Mexico Press, 1959. 160 pp. $7.50. In paper: University New Mexico Paperback. 150 pp. $3.45. Definitive work on the subject.

947. Colyer, Vincent. *Peace with the Apaches of New Mexico and Arizona.* 1872; rpt. Select Bibliographies Reprint Series. Freeport, N.Y.: Books for Libraries, 1972. $6.50.

948. *Comparison of the Formative Cultures in the Americas, Diffusion or the Psychic Unity of Men.* Smithsonian Institution Contributions to Anthropology, Vol. 11. Washington, D.C.: Government Printing Office, 1969. 211 pp. $7.75.

949. Cone, Molly, *Number Four.* Boston: Houghton-Mifflin Co., 1972. $3.95.

950. *Contemporary Sioux Painting.* An Exhibition organized by the Indian Arts and Crafts Board of the United States Department of the Interior. Rapid City, S.D.: Tipi Shop, Inc., 1970. Approximately 80 pp. of text and representative art by Indian painters. $2.50.

951. Cook, Sherburne F. See Nos. 4040 and 4043.

952. Cooke, David C. *Apache Warrior.* New York: Grosset and Dunlap, Inc., 1970. 212 pp. $3.95.

953. ——. *Fighting Indians of America.* New York: Dodd, Mead, and Company, 1966 (Grades 6 up) 36 pp. $6.00.

954. ——. *Tecumseh: Destiny's Warrior.* New York: Julian Messner, Inc., 1970. (Grades 6 up) $3.34.

955. Cooke, David C., and William Moyers. *Famous Indian Tribes.* New York: Random House, Inc., 1954. (Grades 1-4) $1.95.

956. Coolidge, Dane, and Mary R. Coolidge. *The Navajo Indians.* Boston: Houghton Mifflin, 1930.

957. Cooper, John M. *The Gros Ventres of Montana*: Part II— *Religion and Ritual.* Ed. Regina Flannery. Washington, D.C.: Catholic University of America Press, 1956. Catholic University of America Anthropological Series No. 16. 491 pp.

958. Copeland, Donalda M. *True Book of Little Eskimos.* Chicago: Children's Press, Inc., 1953. (Grades K-4) $3.00.

959. Corcos, Lucille. *From Ungskah One to Oyaylee Ten: A Counting Book for All Little Indians.* New York: Pantheon Books, 1965. (Grades K-3) $3.50.

960. * Corkran, David H. *The Carolina Indian Frontier.* Tricentennial Booklet, No. 6. Columbia: University of South Carolina Press, 1970. $1.95.

961. ——. *The Cherokee Frontier: Conflict and Survival, 1740-1762.* Norman: University of Oklahoma Press, 1962; rpt. 1966. 302 pp. $6.95.

962. ——. *The Creek Frontier, 1540-1783.* Civilization of the American Indian Series, No. 86. Norman: University of Oklahoma Press, 1968. 343 pp. $6.95.

963. * Corle, Edwin. *Fig Tree John.* 1935; rpt. New York: Liveright, 1970. 310 pp. $2.45.

964. Cortlett, William T. *The Medicine Man of the American Indian and His Cultural Background.* 1935; rpt. Medicine Classics Series. Clifton, New Jersey: Thomas Kelley, 1972. $15.00.

965. * Cosgrove, C. B. *Caves of the Upper Gila and Hueco Areas in New Mexico and Texas.* 1947; rpt. New York: Kraus Reprint Co., 1970. $18.00.

966. * Cosgrove, Harriet S., and C. B. Cosgrove. *Swarts Ruin: A Typical Mimbres Site in Southwestern New Mexico.* 1932; rpt. New York: Kraus Reprint Co., 1970. $27.00.

967. * Costo, Rupert. *Contributions and Achievements of the American Indian.* San Francisco: The Indian Historian Press, 1971. $10.00. In paper: $4.00. Author is Cahuilla.

968. ——. *Redman of the Golden West.* San Francisco: The Indian Historian Press, 1970. 184 pp.

969. * ——, ed. *Textbooks and the American Indian.* San Francisco, California: American Indian Historical Society, 1970. $4.25.

970. Cotterill, Robert S. *The Southern Indians: The Story of the Civilized Tribes Before Removal.* Civilization of the American Indian Series, No. 37. Norman: University of Oklahoma Press, 1954; rpt. 1966. 254 pp. $6.50.

971. * The Council on International Books for Children, ed. *The Chronicles of American Indian Protest.* New York: Fawcett World Library, 1970. $1.25.

972. Country Beautiful Editors. *The Story of the Sioux.* New York: G. P. Putnam's Sons, 1972. $4.69.

973. Courchene, Richard. *Hell, Love, and Fun.* Billings, Montana: Available from the Author, 1969. 138 pp. Author is Assiniboine-Sioux.

974. Coutant, Charles G. *A History of Wyoming and the Far West.* 1899; rpt. Ann Arbor, Michigan: University Microfilms, 1966. $35.00.

975. Cox, Ross. *Adventures on the Columbia River.* Ed. Alfred Powers. 1957; rpt. Portland, Oregon: Binfords and Mort, Publishers, 1970. $3.00. Also: Norman: University of Oklahoma Press, 1957; rpt. American Exploration and Travel Series. 1972. $9.95.

976. Cozzens, Samuel W. *The Marvelous Country.* Rpt. Minneapolis: Ross and Haines, Inc., 1967. $10.00.

977. Crane, Leo. *Desert Drums: The Pueblo Indians of New Mexico, 1540-1928.* 1928; rpt. Detroit: Gale Research Co., 1970. $12.50.

978. ——. *Indians of the Enchanted Desert, Arizona.* 1925; rpt. Detroit: Gale Reprint Company, 1970. $12.50. Also: Glorietta, New Mexico: Rio Grande Press, Inc., 1972. $10.00.

979. * Crane, Verner W. *The Southern Frontier, Sixteen Seventy-Seventeen Thirty-Two.* Ann Arbor: University of Michigan Press, 1956. $2.25.

980. Crapanzano, Vincent. *The Fifth World of Forster Bennett: Portrait of a Navaho.* New York: Viking Press, 1972. 245 pp. $7.95.

981. Creekmore, Raymond. *Lokoshi Learns to Hunt Seals.* New York: Macmillan Company, 1967. (Grades K-3) $4.25.

982. Creighton, Luella B. *Tecumseh: The Story of the Shawnee Chief.* 1965; rpt. New York: St. Martin's Press, Inc., 1971. (Grades 3-5).

983. Cremony, John C. *Life Among the Apaches.* 1868; rpt. Beautiful Rio Grande Classic Series. New Mexico: Rio Grande Press, Inc., 1969. 327 pp. $10.00.

984. * Cresson, H. T. *Report Upon Pile-Structures in Naaman's Creek, near Claymont, Delaware.* 1892; rpt. New York: Kraus Reprint Co., 1971. $ .50.

985. Creswell, Rev. R. J. *Among the Sioux: A Story of the Twin Cities and the Two Dakotas.* Minneapolis: The University Press, 1906.

986. Cuoq, Jean A. *Etudes Philologiques Sur Quelques Langues Sauvages De L'Amerique.* 1866; rpt. New York: Johnson Reprint Corp., 1970. $9.00.

987. Curtis, Edward S. *Indian Days of the Long Ago.* Ed. F. N. Wilson. 1914; rpt. Detroit, Michigan: Gale Research Corp., 1970. $7.50.

988. ——. *Portraits from North American Indian Life.* Ed. A. D. Coleman and T. C. McLahan. New York: Outerbridge and Lazard, 1972. $25.00. Also: Barre, Mass.: Barre Publishers, 1972. $15.00.

989. ——. *The North American Indian.* Being a Series of Volumes Picturing and Describing the Indians of the United States and Alaska, Written, Illustrated, and Published by Edward S. Curtis. Ed. Frederick W. Hodge. 20 vols. Supplement, 4 vols. Cambridge: Cambridge University Press, 1907-30; rpt. New York: Johnson Reprint Corp., 1970. $500.00 ($30.00. each).

990. * Cushing, Frank. *My Adventures in Zuni.* Rpt. Wild and Wooly West Series, No. 5. Palmer Lake, Colorado: Filter Press, 1967. $4.00. In paper: $2.00.

991. ——. *Nation of the Willows.* Flagstaff, Arizona: Northland Press, 1965. $4.00.

992. ——. *Zuni Breadstuff.* Museum of the American Indian, Heye Foundation. Vol. 8. New York, 1920.

993. Cushman, Dan. *Stay Away, Joe.* New York: The Viking Press, 1953.

994. Cushman, Horatio B. *History of the Choctaw, Chickasaw, and Natchez Indians.* Ed. Angie Debo. 1962; rpt. New York: Russell and Russell, 1972. $20.00.

995. Dale, Edward E. *Frontier Ways: Sketches of Life in the Old West.* Rpt. Austin: University of Texas Press, 1959. $4.50.

996. ——. *The Indians of the Southwest: A Century of Development Under the United States.* Civilization of the American Indian Series, No. 28. 1949; rpt. Norman: University of Oklahoma Press, 1971. 283 pp. $8.95.

997. ——. *Range Cattle Industry: Ranching on the Great Plains from 1865 to 1925.* 1930; rpt. Norman: University of Oklahoma Press, 1969. $6.50.

998. ——, and Gaston Litton, eds. *Cherokee Cavaliers: Forty Years of Cherokee History as Told in the Correspondence of the Ridge-Watie-Boudinot Family.* Civilization of the American Indian Series, No. 19. Norman: University of Oklahoma Press, 1939; rpt. 1969. 319 pp. $7.95.

999. Dall, William H., et al. *Languages of the Tribes of the Extreme Northwest, Alaska, the Aleutians and Adjacent Territories.* 1877; rpt. Seattle: Shorey Publications, 1970. $6.00.

1000. ——. *Masks, Labrets, and Certain Aboriginal Customs.* 1844; rpt. Facsimile ed. Seattle: Shorey Publications, 1972, $8.50.

1001. ——, et al. *Tribes of the Extreme Northwest, Alaska, the Aleutians and Adjacent Territories.* 1877; rpt. Seattle: Shorey Publications, 1970. $15.00.

1002. D'Amato, Alex, and Janet O'Amato. *American Indian Craft Inspirations.* Philadelphia: M. Evans and Co., 1972. $7.95.

1003. * Daniels, John S. *Ute Country.* New York: New American Library, 1971. $ .60.

1004. Daniels, Walter M., ed. *American Indians.* New York: H. W. Wilson, 1957. 219 pp. $4.50.

1005. Darbois, Dominique. *Achound, Boy of the Arctic.* Chicago: Jollett Publishing Company, 1962. (Grades 3-5) $3.48.

1006. D'Aulaire, Ingri, and Edgar P. D'Aulaire. *Pocahontas.* New York: Doubleday and Company, 1971. $3.95.

1007. * David, Jay, ed. *The American Indian: The First Victim.* New York: William Morrow and Company, 1972. $6.95. In paper: $2.95.

1008. Davis, Britton. *The Truth About Geronimo.* New Haven: Yale University Press, 1929. 253 pp.

1009. Davis, Christopher. *North American Indian.* With Introduction by Marlon Brando. London: Hamlyn, 1969. In 2 parts: "The Trail of the Indian," pp. 10-80; "The Indian Today," pp. 82-139. $7.50.

1010. Davis, Francis M. *Cherokee Woman.* Boston: Branden Press, Inc., 1972. $8.95.

1011. Davis G. T. *Metlakahtla: Mission to the Tsimshean Indians.* 1904; rpt. Facsimile edition. Seattle: Shorey Publications, 1970. $3.50.

1012. Davis, Robert T., ed. *Native Arts of the Pacific Northwest.* From the Rasmussen Collection of the Portland Art Museum. 1949; rpt. New York: Kraus Reprint Company, 1971. $30.00.

1013. Dawson, E. J. See No. 4025.

1014. * Dawson, George M. *The Haidas.* 1882; rpt. Facsimile edition. Seattle, Washington: Shorey Publications, 1970. $1.00.

1015. * Day, A. Grove. *Coronado's Quest: The History-Making Adventures of the First White Men to Invade the Southwest.* Rpt. Berkeley: University of California Press, 1964. $2.25.

1016. * De Aberle, S. B. *The Pueblo Indians of New Mexico: Their Land, Economy, and Civil Organizations.* 1948; rpt. American Anthropological Association Memoirs Series. New York: Kraus Reprint Co., 1970. $5.00.

1017. DeBarthe, Joe. *The Life and Adventures of Frank Grouard.* Ed. Edgar I. Stewart. Norman: University of Oklahoma Press, 1958. $7.95.

1018. Debo, Angie. *And Still the Waters Run.* 1940; rpt. Staten Island: Gordian Press, Inc., 1966. $9.00.

1019. ——. *A History of the Indians of the United States*. Civilization of the American Indian Series, No. 106. Norman: University of Oklahoma Press, 1970. 386 pp. $8.95.

1020. ——. *The Rise and Fall of the Choctaw Republic*. Civilization of the American Indian Series, No. 6. 2nd ed. Norman: University of Oklahoma Press, 1967. 314 pp. $7.95.

1021. ——. *The Road to Disappearance*. 1941; rpt. Civilization of the American Indian Series, No. 22. Norman: University of Oklahoma Press, 1967. 399 pp. $8.95.

1022. DeChamplain, Samuel. *The Voyages of Samuel DeChamplain*. Rpt. E. F. Slafter, ed. 3 vols. New York: Burt Franklin, Publisher, 1970. $20.00 each. See also: March of America Series. Ann Arbor, Michigan: University Microfilms, 1966. $8.95.

1023. DeCharlevoin, Pierre F. *Journal of a Voyage to North America, 1682-1761*. 2 vols. 1923; rpt. Ed. L. P. Kellogg. New York: Burt Franklin, Publisher, 1969. $25.00. Originally published in 1761, and this edition is reprinted: Ann Arbor: University Microfilms, 1971. $15.95.

1024. De Coccola, Raymond, and Paul King. *Ayorama*. Fair Lawn, New Jersey: Oxford University Press, 1956. $6.75.

1025. De Crevecoeur, Michel-Guillaume J. *Journey Into Northern Pennsylvania and the State of New York*. Rpt. Clarissa S. Bostelmann, trans. Ann Arbor: University of Michigan Press, 1964. $15.00. Also: Trans. Percy G. Adams. Lexington: University Press of Kentucky, 1961. $5.00.

1026. Deer, Ada. *Speaking Out*. Chicago: Children's Press, 1970.

1027. * Deetz, James. *The Dynamics of Stylistic Change in Arikara Ceramics*. Urbana: University of Illinois Press, 1965. $2.50.

1028. DeForest, John W. *The History of the Indians of Connecticut from the Earliest Known Period to 1850*. 1851; rpt. Hamden, Connecticut: Shoe String Press, Inc., 1964. $10.00. Also: St. Clair Shores, Michigan: Scholarly Press, 1971. $10.00. Also: Ed. Donald Pizer. American Authors Series. New York: Garrett Press, Inc., 1970. $26.95.

1029. De Grazia, Ted. *De Grazia Paints the Yaqui Easter*. Ltd. ed. with original painting. Tucson: University of Arizona Press, 1968. $18.00.

1030. De Grazia, Ted, and William N. Smith. *The Seri Indians*. Flagstaff, Arizona: Northland Press, 1970.

1031. DeHass, Wills. *The History of the Early Settlement and Indian Wars of Western Virginia*. 1851; rpt. Parsons, West Virginia: McClaim Printing Company, 1970. $9.00.

1032. Delaguna, Frederica. *Church Prehistory: The Archaeology of Prince William Sound, Alaska*. Seattle: University of Washington Press. 1967. $7.50.

1033. De Lahontan. *Dialogues Curieux Entre L'auteur Et Un Sauvage De Bon Sens Qui a Voyage, Et Memoires De L'Amerique Septentrionale.* Ed. Gilbert Chinard. Baltimore: John Hopkins University Press, 1931. $12.00.

1034. DeLand, Charles Edmund. *Tragedy of the White Medicine. A Story of Indian Mystery, Revenge, and Love.* New York: The Neale Publishing Company, 1913.

1035. Delano, Alonzo. *Life on the Plains and Among the Diggings.* 1854; rpt. Ann Arbor, Michigan: University Microfilms, 1966. $8.95.

1036. De Las Casas, Bartolome. *Tears of the Indians* and *The Life of Las Casas by Sir Arthur Helps.* Ed. Louis Hanke. 2 vols. in 1. Williamstown, Mass.: John Lilburne Company, 1970. 393 pp. $12.50.

1037. De L'Incarnation, Marie. *Word from New France: Selected Letters of Marie De. L'Incarnation.* Rpt. Trans. Joyce Marshall. New York: Oxford University Press, 1968. $6.50.

1038. Deloria, Ella C. *Speaking of Indians.* New York: Friendship Press, 1944. 163 pp. Author was Sioux.

1039. * Deloria, Vine, Jr. *Custer Died For Your Sins: An Indian Manifesto.* New York: Macmillan, 1969. 279 pp. Author is Sioux. In paper: New York: Avon Books, 1970.

1040. ———. *Of Utmost Good Faith.* San Francisco: Straight Arrow Books, 1971. 262 pp.

1041. ———. *We Talk, You Listen. New Tribes, New Turf.* New York: The Macmillan Company, 1970. 227 pp.

1042. Deloria, Vine, Jr., and Jennings C. Wise. *Red Man in the New World Drama.* New York: Macmillan, 1971. 418 pp. $10.95. A revision by Deloria of the book by Wise.

1043. Dempsey, Hugh A. *Crowfoot, Chief of the Blackfeet.* Civilization of the American Indian Series, No. 122. Norman: University of Oklahoma Press, 1972. 230 pp. $7.95.

1044. Denig, Edwin Thompson. *Five Indian Tribes of the Upper Missouri: Sioux, Arickaras, Assiniboines, Crees, Crows.* Ed. by John C. Ewers. Civilization of the American Indian Series, No. 59. Norman: University of Oklahoma Press, 1961. 217 pp. $6.95. Also: Facsimile edition. Extracts. Seattle: Shorey Publications, 1970. $7.50.

1045. Dennis, Henry C. *The American Indian, 1492-1970, A Chronology and Fact Book.* Dobbs Ferry, New York: Oceana Publications, Inc., 1970. (Grades 7-12) $5.00.

1046. Dennis, Wayne. *The Hopi Child.* 1940; rpt. Family in America Series. New York: Arno Press, 1972. $11.00.

1047. Densmore, Frances. *American Indians and Their Music.* American Studies Series. 1926; rpt. New York: Johnson Reprint Corp., 1970. $7.00.

1048. ——. *Chippewa Customs.* 1929; rpt. Landmarks in Anthropology Series. New York: Johnson Reprint Corp., 1970. $12.50. Also: Minneapolis: Ross and Haines, 1970. $10.00.

1049. ——. *Chippewa Music.* Bureau of American Ethnology, No. 45, 1910; No. 53, 1913; rpt. 2 vols. New York: Plenum Publishing Co., 1971. $29.50.

1050. ——. *Choctaw Music.* Bureau of American Ethnology, Bulletin 136. Washington, D.C., 1943, pp. 101-188. Rpt. Da Capo Music Reprint Series. New York: Plenum Publishing Co., 1972. $7.95.

1051. ——. *Mandan and Hidatsa Music.* Bureau of American Ethnology, Bulletin 80. Washington, D.C., 1923. 192 pp. Rpt. Da Capo Music Reprint Series. New York: Plenum Publishing Co., 1972. $12.50.

1052. ——. *Menominee Music.* Bureau of American Ethnology, Bulletin 102. Washington, D.C., 1932. 230 pp. Rpt. Da Capo Music Reprint Series. New York: Plenum Publishing Co., 1972. $12.95.

1053. ——. *Music of Acoma, Isleta, Cochiti, and Zuni Pueblos.* 1957; rpt. Da Capo Music Reprint Series. New York: Plenum Publishing Co., 1972. $8.95.

1054. ——. *Music of the Indians of British Columbia.* Bureau of American Ethnology, Bulletin 136. Washington, D.C., 1943. 99 pp. Rpt. Da Capo Music Reprint Series. New York: Plenum Publishing Co., 1972. $8.50.

1055. ——. *Nootka and Quileute Music.* Bureau of American Ethnology, Bulletin 124. Washington, D.C., 1939. 358 pp. Rpt. Da Capo Music Reprint Series. New York: Plenum Publishing Co., 1972. $16.50.

1056. ——. *Northern Ute Music.* Bureau of American Ethnology, Bulletin 75. Washington, D.C, 1922. 213 pp. Rpt. Da Capo Music Reprint Series. New York: Plenum Publishing Co., 1972. $12.50.

1057. ——. *Papago Music.* Bureau of American Ethnology, Bulletin 90. Washington, D.C., 1929. 229 pp. Rpt. Da Capo Music Reprint Series. New York: Plenum Publishing Co., 1972. $12.50.

1058. ——. *Pawnee Music.* Bureau of American Ethnology, Bulletin 93. Washington, D.C., 1929. 129 pp. Rpt. Da Capo Music Reprint Series. New York: Plenum Publishing Co., 1972. $8.95.

1059. ——. *Seminole Music.* 1956; rpt. Da Capo Music Reprint Series. New York: Plenum Publishing Co., 1972. $12.50.

1060. *——. *A Study of Indian Music.* 1941; rpt. Facsimile ed. Seattle, Washington: Shorey Publications, 1970. $1.50.

1061. ——. *Teton Sioux Music*. Bureau of American Ethnology, Bulletin 61. Washington, D.C., 1918. 516 pp. Rpt. Da Capo Music Reprint Series. New York: Plenum Publishing Co., 1972. $24.50.

1062. ——. *Yuman and Yaqui Music*. Bureau of American Ethnology. Bulletin 110. Washington, D.C., 1932; rpt. Da Capo Music Reprint Series. New York: Plenum Publishing Co., 1972. 216 pp. $12.50.

1063. Denton, Daniel. *A Brief Description of New-York: Formerly Called New-Netherlands*. 1670; rpt. Ann Arbor: University Microfilms, 1966. $3.55.

1064. Denys, Nicolas. *A Description and Natural History of the Coasts of North America*. Ed. William F. Ganong. 1908; rpt. Westport, Connecticut: Greenwood Press, Inc., 1968. $36.50.

1065. DePoncins, Gontran, and Lewis Galantiere. *Kabloona*. 1941; rpt. New York: Reynal and Company, 1966.

1066. DePourtales, Albert-Alexandre. *On the Western Tour with Washington Irving: The Journal and Letters of Count DePourtales*. Ed. George F. Spaudling. Trans. Seymour Feiler. American Exploration and Travel Series, Vol. 54. Norman: University of Oklahoma Press, 1968. $5.95.

1067. DeRosier, Arthur H., Jr. *The Removal of the Choctaw Indians*. Knoxville: The University of Tennessee Press, 1970. 208 pp. $7.50.

1068. DeSchweinitz, Edmund. *The Life and Times of David Zeisberger, the Western Pioneer and Apostle of the Indians*. First American Frontier Series. 1870; rpt. New York: Arno Press, 1970. $30.00. Also: 1871; rpt. New York: Kraus Reprint Co., 1971. $21.00.

1069. De Smet, P. J. *Life, Letters, and Travels, Eighteen Hundred One to Eighteen Seventy-Three*. 4 vols. in 2. 1905; rpt. New York: Kraus Reprint Co., 1971. $49.50. See also: Chittenden, Hiram M., No. 888.

1070. ——. *New Indian Sketches*. 1904; rpt. Seattle: Shorey Publications, 1970. $8.50.

1071. ——. *Western Missions and Missionaries*. 1863; rpt. White Plains, New York: Irish University Press, Inc., 1970. $25.00.

1072. Deuel, Leo. *Conquistadors Without Swords: Archaeologists in the Americas*. New York: St. Martin's Press, 1967. $12.50.

1073. Deur, Lynne. *Indian Chiefs*. Minneapolis: Lerner Publications Company, 1971. (Grades 6-11) $3.95.

1074. Devereux, George. *Mohave Ethnopsychiatry: The Psychic Disturbances of an Indian Tribe*. Bureau of American Ethnology Bulletin, No. 175. 1961; rpt. Washington: Smithsonian Institution Press, 1969. 586 pp. $16.50.

1075. * ——. *Reality and Dream: Psychotherapy of a Plains Indian.* Rev. ed. 1951; rpt. New York: New York University Press, 1969. $12.00. In paper: Anchor Books. New York: Doubleday, Doran Company, 1969. $3.95.

1076. De Vorsey, Louis, Jr. *The Indian Boundary in the Southern Colonies, 1763-1775.* Chapel Hill: University of North Carolina Press, 1966. $7.50.

1077. * DeVoto, Bernard. *The Course of Empire.* Boston, Mass.: Houghton Mifflin Company, 1952. $8.50. In paper: Houghton Mifflin, 1962. $2.65.

1078. Dewdney, Selwyn, and Kenneth E. Kidd. *Indian Rock Paintings, the Great Lakes.* 2nd ed. Toronto: University of Toronto Press, 1967. 191 pp. $6.75.

1079. * Dick, Herbert W. *Bat Cave.* School of American Research Monograph, No. 27. Albuquerque: University of New Mexico Press, 1965. $4.75.

1080. *Digest of Decisions of the Department of Interior in Cases Relating to the Public Lands.* Vols. 52-61, January 1927-December 1954. Part I, 1962. Washington, D.C.: Government Printing Office, 1963. Indian Matters Included. 505 pp. $2.50.

1081. Dines, Charles. *Crazy Horse.* See and Read Biographies Series. New York: G. P. Putnam's Sons, 1966. (Grades 1-3) $2.68.

1082. Dines, Glen. *Long Knife.* New York: Macmillan and Company, 1962. (Grades 4-6) $3.44.

1083. * Dittert, Alfred E., et al. *Archaeological Survey of the Navajo Reservoir District, Northwestern New Mexico.* School of American Research Monographs, No. 23. Albuquerque: University of New Mexico Press, 1961. $5.00.

1084. * Dixon, Joseph K. *The Vanishing Race.* New York: Popular Library, Inc., 1972. $1.25.

1085. Dixon, Roland B. *The Chimariko Indians and Language.* See Nos. 4005 and 4016.

1086. Dobie, J. Frank. *Apache Gold and Yaqui Silver.* New York: Barmhall House, 1939. 366 pp.

1087. * ——. *Tales of Old-Time Texas.* New York: Little, Brown and Company, 1955. $6.95. In paper: $1.95.

1088. Dobrin, Norma. *The Delawares.* Chicago: Melmont Publishers, Inc., 1963. (Grades 2-5) 32 pp. $3.25.

1089. Dockstader, Frederick J. *Indian Art in America: The Arts and Crafts of the North American Indian.* Greenwich, Connecticut: New York Graphic Society, 1961. 3rd ed. 1968. 224 pp. Author is Oneida.

1090. ——. *Indian Art in Middle America.* Greenwich, Connecticut: New York Graphic Society, 1964. 221 pp.

1091. ——. *Indian Art in South America: Pre-Columbian and Contemporary Arts and Crafts.* Greenwich, Connecticut: New York Graphic Society, 1967. 222 pp.

1092. ——. *The Kachina and the White Man: The Influences of the White Culture on the Hopi Kachina Culture.* Bulletin No. 35. Bloomfield Hills, Michigan: Cranbrook Institute of Science, 1954. 204 pp.

1093. Doddridge, Joseph. *Notes on the Settlement and Indian Wars.* 1824; rpt. Parsons, West Virginia: McClain Printing Company, 1970. $8.00. Also: 1876 ed.; rpt. New York: Burt Franklin, Pub., 1967. $18.50.

1094. Dodge, Richard I. *Our Wild Indians: Thirty-Three Years' Personal Experience Among the Red Men of the Great West.* 1882; rpt. Select Bibliographies Reprint Series. Freeport, New York: Books for Libraries, Inc., 1970. $39.50.

1095. * Dolores, Juan. See Nos. 4010 and 4020.

1096. Donaldson, Thomas. *Moqui Pueblo Indians of Arizona and Pueblo Indians of New Mexico.* Extra Census Bulletin. Eleveneth Census of the United States. Washington, D.C.: Government Printing Office, 1893. 136 pp.

1097. ——. *A Report on Indians Taxed and Indians Not Taxed in the United States at the Eleventh Census, 1890.* 1894; rpt. New York: AMS Press, 1970. $49.50.

1098. ——. *The Idaho of Yesterday.* 1941; rpt. Westport, Connecticut: Greenwood Press, Inc., 1970. $19.00.

1099. * Dorchester, Guy C. *Condition of the Indian Trade in North America, 1767: As Described in a Letter to Sir William Johnson.* 1890; rpt. New York: Burt Franklin, 1972. $6.00.

1100. Dorian, Edith M. *Hokahey: American Indians Then and Now.* New York: McGraw-Hill, 1957. (Grades 5 up) $4.33.

1101. Dorn, Edward. *The Shoshoneans.* The People of the Basin-Plateau. New York: William Morrow and Company, 1966. 96 pp.

1102. * Dorsey, George A. *The Arapaho Sun Dance: The Ceremony of the Offerings Lodge.* Chicago Field Museum of Natural History Fieldiana Anthropology Series. 1903; rpt. New York: Kraus Reprint Co., 1970. $6.25.

1103. * ——. *The Cheyenne.* Chicago Field Museum of Natural History Fieldiana Anthropology Series. 1905; rpt. New York: Kraus Reprint Co., 1970. $15.00.

1104. ——. *The Traditions of the Caddo.* Washington, D.C.: Carnegie Institution of Washington, 1905.

1105. * ——. *Traditions of the Skidi Pawnee.* Publications of the American Folklore Society. Boston: Houghton, Mifflin, 1940; rpt. New York: Kraus Reprint Co., 1970. $15.00.

1106. * Dorsey, George A., and A. L. Kroeber. *The Traditions of the Arapaho*. Chicago Field Museum of Natural History Fieldiana Anthropology Series. 1903; rpt. New York: Kraus Reprint Co., 1970. $6.25.

1107. * Dorsey, George A., and H. R. Voth. *The Oraibi Soyal Ceremony, and Oraibi Powamu Ceremony, and Mishongnovi Ceremonies of the Snake and Antelope Fraternities, and Oraibi Summer Snake Ceremony*. 4 bks. in 1 vol. 1901-03; rpt. New York: Kraus Reprint Co., 1970. $35.00.

1108. Dorsey, James O. *Omaha Sociology*. Rpt. New York: Johnson Reprint Co., 1971. $9.50.

1109. ———. *The Study of Siouan Cults*. 1894; rpt. Seattle: Shorey Publications, 1972. $10.00.

1110. Douglas, Frederic, and Rene D'Harnoncourt. *Indian Art of the United States*. New York: The Museum of Modern Art, 1941; rpt. Museum of Modern Art Publications in Reprint Series. New York: Arne Press, 1970. 219 pp. $16.00.

1111. Douglas, Loretto. *People We Call Indians*. Deer Park, New York: Brown Book Company, 1971. $2.00.

1112. * Downes, Randolph C. *Council Fires on the Upper Ohio*. 1940; rpt. Pittsburgh: University of Pittsburgh Press, 1969. $2.50.

1113. Downey, Fairfax. *The Buffalo Soldiers in the Indian Wars*. New York: McGraw-Hill Company, 1969. (Grades 5 up) $4.95.

1114. ———. *The Indian Wars of the United States Army, 1776-1885*. New York: Doubleday Doran Company, 1965. $6.95.

1115. * Downs, James F. *Animal Husbandry in Navajo Society and Culture*. University of California Publications in Anthropology Series, Vol. 1. Berkeley: University of California Press, 1964. $2.00.

1116. * ———. *The Two Worlds of the Washo: An Indian Tribe of California and Nevada*. Case Studies in Cultural Anthropology. New York: Holt, Rinehart and Winston, 1966. 113 pp. $2.35.

1117. * Downs, James F., and G. S. Downs. *Nez Ch'ii: A Pastoral Community of Navajo Indians*. New York: Holt, Rinehart and Winston, Inc., 1971. 144 pp. $1.75.

1118. * Dozier, Edward P. *Hano, A Tewa Community in Arizona*. New York: Holt, Rinehart, and Winston, 1966. 104 pp. $2.35. Author is Santa Clara Pueblo.

1119. * ———. *The Kalinga of Northern Luzon, Philippines*. Case Studies in Cultural Anthropology. New York: Holt, Rinehart, and Winston, 1967. $1.95.

1120. ———. *Mountain Arbiters: The Changing Life of the Philippine Hill People*. Tucson: University of Arizona Press, 1966. $10.00.

1121. *———. *The Pueblo Indians of North America.* New York: Holt, Rinehart, and Winston, 1970. $4.50.

1122. *———. *Pueblo Indians of the Southwest.* New York: Holt, Rinehart, and Winston, 1970. 192 pp.

1123. Drake, Benjamin. *The Life and Adventures of Black Hawk.* Rpt. American Biography Series. New York: Garrett Press, Inc., 1970. $15.95.

1124. ———. *Life of Tecumseh, and of His Brother the Prophet; with a Historical Sketch of the Shawanoe Indians.* 1852; rpt. New York: Kraus Reprint Co., 1969. 235 pp. $10.00. Also: 1841; rpt. Mass Violence in America Series. New York: Arno Press, 1971. $8.50.

1125. Drake, Samuel G. *Biography and History of the Indians of North America from its First Discovery.* 1851; rpt. Detroit: Gale Research Co., 1970. $24.00.

1126. * Driver, Harold E. *Indians of North America.* 2nd ed. Rev. Chicago, Illinois: University of Chicago Press, 1969. 632 pp. See also Nos. 4031, 4035, and 4036.

1127. *———, ed. *The Americans on the Eve of Discovery.* Spectrum Books. New York: Prentice-Hall, Inc., 1964. $1.95.

1128. *———, and William C. Massey. *Comparative Studies of North American Indians.* Transactions of the American Philosophical Society, New Series, 47, Part 2 (1957), 165-456; rpt. Philadelphia: American Philosophical Society, 1971. $5.00.

1129. Drucker, Philip. *Archaeological Surveys on the Northern Northwest Coast.* 1943; rpt. Seattle: Shorey Publications, 1970. $7.00. See also Nos. 4035 and 4036.

1130. *———. *Cultures of the North Pacific Coast.* Scranton, Pa. Chandler Publishing Co., 1965. $4.75.

1131. *———. *Indians of the Northwest Coast.* Anthropological Handbook Number Ten for the American Museum of Natural History. New York: McGraw-Hill Company, 1955. 208 pp. In paper: Garden City, New York: The Natural History Press, 1963. An American Museum Science Books Edition. 224 pp.

1132. Drucker, Philip, and Robert F. Heizer. *To Make My Name Good: A Re-Examination of the Southern Kwakiutl Potlatch.* Berkeley: University of California Press, 1967. 167 pp. $6.00.

1133. Drury, Clifford M. *Nez Perce Indian Missions.* Caldwell, Idaho: The Caxton Printers, 1936.

1134. DuBois, Constance M. See Nos. 4008, 4028, and 4036.

1135. Ducheneaux, Frank. "The Peace Treaty of Fort Laramie, April 29, 1868." 1968. Mimeographed. Written and compiled by F. D. 42 pp. Author is Sioux.

1136. DuCreux, Francois. *The History of Canada, or New France.* Ed James B. Conacher. Trans. Percy J. Robinson. 2 vols. 1951; rpt. Westport, Connecticut: Greenwood Press, Inc., 1969. $46.00.

1137. * Dumarest, Noel. *Notes on Cochiti, New Mexico.* 1919; rpt. New York: Kraus Reprint Company, 1970. $5.00.

1138. Dunn, Dorothy. *American Indian Painting of the Southwest and Plains Areas.* Albuquerque: University of New Mexico Press, 1968. 429 pp. $25.00.

1139. * Dunn, J. P. *Massacres of the Mountains: A History of the Indian Wars of the Far West, 1815-1875.* [1880?] Rpt. New York: Archer House, Inc., 1965. 669 pp. Also: Gloucester, Mass.: Peter Smith, 1971. $5.50. Also: in paper: New York: G. P. Putnam's Sons, 1969. $3.25.

1140. * Dunning, R. W. *Social and Economic Change Among the Northern Ojibwa.* Toronto: University of Toronto Press, 1972. 217 pp. $8.50. In paper: $3.50.

1141. Dutton, Bertha P. *Sun Father's Way. The Kiva Murals of Kuaua.* Albuquerque: University of New Mexico Press, 1963. 237 pp. $15.00.

1142. Duval, John C. *Early* Times in Texas. Rpt. Facsimile ed. Austin, Texas: Steck-Vaughn Company, 1970. $5.95.

1143. Dyck, Paul. *Brulé: The Sioux People of the Rosebud.* Flagstaff, Arizona: Northland Press, 1970. 365 pp. $20.00.

1144. Dyk, Walter. See Left Handed and Old Mexican, Nos. 177 and 186.

1145. Easby, Elizabeth K., and John F. Easby. *Before Cortes: Sculpture of Middle America.* New York: Metropolitan Museum of Art, 1970. $16.95.

1146. * Eastman, Charles A. (Ohiyesa). *The Soul of An Indian: An Interpretation.* Boston: Houghton Mifflin. 1911; rpt. New York: Johnson Reprint Corp., 1971. $7.50. Author was Sioux. In paper: Rapid City, South Dakota: Fenwyn Press Books, 1970. $2.95.

1147. Eastman, Mary. *Romance of Indian Life.* 1852; rpt. Upper Saddle River, New Jersey: Literature House / The Gregg Press, 1971. $11.50.

1148. Eckert, Allan W. *Blue Jacket: War Chief of the Shawnees.* New York: Little, Brown, and Company, 1969. (Grades 9 up) $4.50.

1149. ——. *The Frontiersmen.* Boston: Little, Brown and Company, 1967. $10.00.

1150. ——. *Wilderness Empire.* Boston: Little, Brown and Company, 1969. 653 pp. $10.00.

1151. Editors of the National Geographic Society. *Discovering Man's Past in America.* Washington, D.C.: National Geographic, 1971. $4.25.

1152. * Edmonds, Walter D. *Drums Along the Mohawk.* New York: Little, Brown and Company, 1936. (Grades 7 up) $5.95. In paper: New York: Bantam Press, 1970. $ .75.

1153. ——. *In the Hands of the Senecas.* New York: Little, Brown and Company, 1947. (Grades 7-9) $4.95.
1154. ——. *The Matchlock Gun.* New York: Dodd, Mead and Company, 1941. (Grades 7-9) 50 pp. $3.95.
1155. ——. *The Musket and the Cross.* New York: Little, Brown and Company, 1968. 514 pp. $10.00.
1156. ——. *They Had a Horse.* New York: Dodd, Mead and Company, 1962. (Grades 7-9) 60 pp. $3.50.
1157. ——. *Two Logs Crossing.* New York: Dodd, Mead and Company, 1943. (Grades 7-9) 82 pp. $3.50.
1158. Edmonson, Munro S. *The Status Terminology and the Social Structure of the North American Indians.* American Ethnological Society Monographs. Seattle: University of Washington Press, 1958. 84 pp. $5.00.
1159. Edwards, Cecile P. *King Philip.* Boston: Houghton Mifflin Co., 1970. (Grades 3-8) $2.20.
1160. Edwards, Everett E. *Agriculture of the American Indians.* A Classified List of Annotated Historical References. 2nd ed. 1933; rpt. New York: Burt Franklin Pub., 1970. $18.50.
1161. * Edwards, Jonathan, ed. *David Brainerd: His Life and Diary.* Tyndale Series of Great Biographies. Chicago: Moody Press, 1968. In paper: $ .95.
1162. Edwards, Jonathan, and Sereno E. Dwight, eds. *Memoirs of the Reverend David Brainerd: Missionary to the Indians on the Border of New York, New Jersey and Pennsylvania.* American Indian History Series. St. Clair Shores, Michigan: Scholarly Press, 1970. $15.00.
1163. Eells, Myron. *A History of Indian Missions on the Pacific Coast.* 1882; rpt. Seattle: Shorey Publications, 1970. $12.50.
1164. ——. *Ten Years of Missionary Work Among the Indians at Skokomish.* 1881; rpt. Seattle: Shorey Pub., 1970. $12.50.
1165. ——. *The Twana, Chemakum and Klallam Indians of Washington Territory.* 1887; rpt. Seattle: Shorey Publications, 1971. $3.00.
1166. Egan, Ferol. *Sand in a Whirlwind: The Paiute Indian War of 1860.* New York: Doubleday and Company, 1972. $8.95.
1167. Eggan, Fred. *The American Indian.* Perspectives for the Study of Social Change. Chicago: Aldine Publishing Company, 1966. The Lewis Henry Morgan Lectures for 1964 at the University of Rochester. 193 pp. $6.00.
1168. ——. *The Social Organization of the Western Pueblos.* Chicago: University of Chicago Press, 1950. 373 pp. $6.00.
1169. ——, ed. *The Social Anthropology of the North American Tribes.* Rev. ed. Chicago: University of Chicago Press, 1955. $8.00.

1170. *Ellis, Florence H. *A Reconstruction of the Basic Jemez Pattern of Social Organization.* Anthropological Series No. 11. Albuquerque: University of New Mexico Press, 1964. $2.00.

1171. Ellis, George E. *Red Man and the White Man in North America From Its Discovery to the Present Time.* 1882; rpt. East Orange, New Jersey: Thomas Kelley, 1970. $15.00.

1172. Ellis, Richard N. *General Pope and U.S. Indian Policy.* Albuquerque: University of New Mexico Press, 1970. 287 pp. $10.00.

1173. *——, ed. *The Western American Indian.* Case Studies in Tribal History. Lincoln: University of Nebraska Press, 1972. $6.95. In paper: $2.95.

1174. Elting, Mary. *The Hopi Way.* Two World Book Series, No. 1. Philadelphia: J. B. Lippincott Company, 1969. (Grades 3 up) 63 pp. $3.95.

1175. Elting, Mary, and Franklin Folsom. *If You Lived in the Days of the Wild Mammoth Hunters.* New York: Four Winds Press, 1969. $3.95.

1176. Elting, Mary and Michael Folsom. *The Secret Story of Pueblo Bonito.* Science Parade Series. Irvington-on-Hudson, New York: Harvey House, 1963. (Grades 2-5) $3.50.

1177. ——. *Story of Archaeology in the Americas.* Story of Science Series. Irvington-on-Hudson, New York: Harvey House, 1960. (Grades 4-7) $4.50.

1178. *Embree, Edwin R. *Indians of the Americas.* Boston: Houghton Mifflin, 1939. 260 pp. $5.95. In paper: Collier Paperback. New York: Macmillan, 1970.

1179. *Emmerich, Andre. *Art Before Columbus.* New York: Simon and Shuster, 1963. $10.00.

1180. ——. *Sweat of the Sun and Tears of the Moon: Gold and Silver in Pre-Columbian Art.* Seattle: University of Washington Press, 1965. $15.00.

1181. *Emmitt, Robert. *The Last War Trail. The Utes and the Settlement of Colorado.* Rpt. Norman: University of Oklahoma Press, 1972. 352 pp. $8.95. In paper: $4.50.

1182. Emmons, Della Gould. *Sacajawea of the Shoshones.* Portland, Oregon: Metropolitan Press, 1943; rpt. Portland, Oregon: Binfords and Mort, Pubs., 1955. 312 pp. $5.50. Fictionalized, but based on reading of records of the time.

1183. Emmons, G. T. *The Tahltan Indians.* 1911; rpt. New York: Humanities Press, 1972. $7.25.

1184. Engel, Lorenz. *Among the Plains Indians.* Nature and Man Series. Minneapolis: Lerner Publications Company, 1970. (Grades 5-12) $6.95.

1185. *An English-Dakota Dictionary.* Compiled by Working Indians Civil Association, Inc. Ft. Pierre, South Dakota: Working Indians Civil Association, Inc., 1969. 264 pp. $5.00.

1186. *English-Eskimo, Eskimo-English Dictionary.* Brooklyn, New York: P. Shalom Publications, Inc., 1971. $8.50.

1187. Enochs, J. B. *Little Man's Family.* Navajo Series. Lawrence, Kansas: Haskell Press, 1970. English and Navajo Text. Preprimer .25; Primer .30; Reader .50.

1188. Epple, Jess C. *Custer's Battle of the Washita and the History of the Plains Indians.* Jericho, New York: Exposition Press, Inc., 1970. $7.00.

1189. Erdoes, Richard. *The Pueblo Indians.* New York: Funk and Wagnalls, Inc., 1968. (Grades 5 up) 128 pp. $5.95.

1190. ——. *The Sun Dance People: The Plains Indians, Their Past and Present.* New York: Alfred Knopf, Inc., 1972. (Grades 5-8) $4.95.

1191. Erickson, Erik H. See No. 4035.

1192. Espinosa, J. Manuel, ed. *First Expedition of De Vargas into New Mexico, 1692.* Albuquerque: University of New Mexico Press, 1940.

1193. *Essays in Anthropology Presented to A. L. Kroeber in Celebration of His Sixtieth Birthday, June 11, 1936.* 1936; rpt. Facsimile ed. New York: Books for Libraries, 1972. $17.50.

1194. Estep, Irene. *The Iroquois.* Chicago: Melmont Publishers, Inc., 1961. (Grades 2-6) $2.75.

1195. ——. *The Seminoles.* Chicago: Melmont Publishers, Inc., 1963. (Grades 3-6) 31 pp. $2.75.

1196. * *The European and the Indian.* 1956; rpt. New York: Johnson Reprint Corp., 1971. $4.50.

1197. Evans, W. McKee. *To Die Game: The Story of the Lowry Band.* Indian Guerrillas of Reconstruction. Baton Rouge: Louisiana State University Press, 1970. $8.95.

1198. Evarts, Jeremiah, ed. *Speeches on the Passage of the Bill for the Removal of the Indians.* See United States Twenty-First Congress, No. 2834.

1199. Ewers, John C. *Artists of the Old West.* Garden City, New York: Doubleday and Company, 1965. $12.95.

1200. * ——. *Blackfeet Crafts.* Lawrence, Kansas: Haskell Press, 1960. $ .55.

1201. ——. *The Blackfeet: Raiders on the Northwestern Plains.* Civilization of the American Indian Series, No. 49. Norman: University of Oklahoma Press, 1958; rpt. 1967. 345 pp. $7.95.

1202. ——. *Early White Influence Upon Plains Indians Painting: George Catlin and Carl Bodmer Among the Mandan.* Seattle: Shorey Publications, 1957. $2.00.

1203. ——. *The Horse in the Blackfoot Indian Culture*. Bureau of American Ethnology Bulletin, No. 159. Rpt. Washington, D.C.: Smithsonian Institution Press, 1969. $12.50.

1204. ——. *Indian Life on the Upper Missouri*. Civilization of the American Indian Series, No. 89. Norman: University of Oklahoma Press, 1968. 222 pp. $7.95. See also: Rachlis, Eugene, No. 2378.

1205. *——. *The Story of the Blackfeet*. Lawrence, Kansas: Haskell Institute, 1958. $ .55.

1206. *Excavations at Tse-Ta's, Canyon de Chelly National Monument, Arizona*. Washington, D.C.: Government Printing Office, 1966. 160 pp. $2.25.

1207. *Excavations in a 17th-Century Jumano Pueblo Gran Quivira*. Washington, D.C.: Government Printing Office, 1964. 168 pp. $1.75.

1208. *The Expedition Against the Sauk and Fox Indians in 1932*. Rpt. Fairfield, Washington: Ye Galleon Press, 1971. $2.00.

1209. *Ezell, Paul H. *The Hispanic Acculturation of the Gila River Pimas*. 1961; rpt. New York: Kraus Reprint Co., 1971. $10.00.

1210. Fairchild, Hoxie N. *Noble Savage: A Study in Romantic Naturalism*. 1928; rpt. New York: Russell and Russell, 1961. $12.00.

1211. Falk, Elsa. *The Borrowed Canoe; a Story of the Hupa Indians of Northern California*. Los Angeles: Ward Ritchie Press, 1969. (Grades 4-6) 47 pp. $3.95.

1212. ——. *Fence Across the Trail*. Chicago: Follett Publishing Co., 1957. (Grades 4-6) $2.97.

1213. ——. *Fog Island*. Chicago: Follett Publishing Company, 1953. (Grades 7 up) $3.63.

1214. ——. *Tohi Chumash Indian Boy*. Chicago: Melmont Publishers, Inc., 1959. $2.75.

1215. *Famous Indians, A Collection of Short Biographies*, Washington, D.C.: Government Printing Office, 1966. 47 pp. $ .35.

1216. Fanshel, David. *Far From the Reservation: The Transracial Adoption of American Indian Children*. Metuchen, New Jersey: Scarecrow Press, Inc., 1972. $10.00.

1217. Faraud, Henri J. *Dix-Huit Ans Chez Les Sauvages: Voyages et Missions de Monseigneur Henry Faraud*. 1866; rpt. New York: Johnson Reprint Corp., 1970. $15.00.

1218. Farb, Peter. *Man's Rise to Civilization as Shown by the Indians of North America from Primeval Times to the Coming of the Industrial State*. New York: E. P. Dutton and Company, 1968. 332 pp.

1219. Farnham, Thomas. *Travels in the Great Western Prairies*. 2nd ed. American Scene Series. Rpt. New York: Plenum Pub. Company, 1968. $32.50.

1220. Farquhar, Margaret C. *Colonial Life in America: A Book to Begin On*. Book to Begin On Series. New York: Holt, Rinehart and Winston, 1962. (Grades K-4) $3.27.

1221. * ——. *The Indian Children of America: A Book to Begin On*. New York: Holt, Rinehart and Winston, 1964. (Grades K-3) $3.27. In paper: $1.25.

1222. Farrand, Livingston. *Basis of American History, 1500-1900*. Rpt. New York: Frederick Ungar Publishing Company, 1971. $6.50.

1223. ——. *The Traditions of the Quinault Indians*. 1902; rpt. Facsimile ed. Extracts. Seattle: Shorey Publications, 1970. $4.00.

1224. Faulk, Odie B. *The Geronimo Campaign*. Fairlawn, New Jersey: Oxford University Press, 1969. 245 pp.

1225. ——. *The Land of Many Frontiers: A History of the American Southwest*. Fairlawn, New Jersey: Oxford University Press, 1970. $7.50.

1226. Faye, Paul-Louis. See No. 4020.

1227. Featherstonhaugh, George W. *A Canoe Voyage Up the Minnay Sotor*. 2 vols. St. Paul, Minnesota; Minnesota Historical Society, 1970. 372 pp. $20.00.

1228. Feder, Norman. *Art of the American Indian*. New York: Harry N. Abrams, Inc., 1971. $35.00.

1229. * ——. *North American Indian Painting*. Greenwich, Connecticut: New York Graphic Soceity, 1967. Approximately 24 pp. $2.50.

1230. ——. *Two Hundred Years of North American Indian Art*. New York: Praeger Publishers, 1972. $12.50.

1231. * *Federal and State Indian Reservations*. Washington, D.C.: Government Printing Office, 1971. 416 pp. $3.75.

1232. Fee, Chester A. *Chief Joseph: The Biography of a Great Indian*. New York: Wilson-Erickson, Inc., 1936.

1233. Fehrenbach, T. R. *The Comanches*. New York: World Publishing Company, 1972. $12.50.

1234. Fejes, Claire. *Enuk, My Son*. New York: Pantheon Books, 1969. (Grades K-3) $3.95.

1235. ——. *People of the Noatak*. New York: Alfred Knopf, 1966. 368 pp. $6.95.

1236. Fenton, Carroll L., and Alice Epstein. *The Cliff Dwellers of Walnut Canyon*. New York: John Day Company, 1960. (Grades 1-3) $3.69.

1237. Fenton, William. *American Indian and White Relations to 1830.* Chapel Hill: University of North Carolina Press, 1957; rpt. New York: Russell and Russell, 1970. $10.00.

1238. ———. *Contrasts Between Indian Herbalism and Colonial Medicine.* 1941; rpt. Seattle: Shorey Publications, 1970. $2.00.

1239. ———, ed. *Parker on the Iroquois.* Syracuse, New York: Syracuse University Press, 1968. Editions of "Iroquois Uses of Maize and Other Food Plants," "The Code of Handsome Lake," and "The Constitution of the Five Nations" bound in One Volume. 119 pp.; 148 pp.; 158 pp.

1240. * Ferdon, Edwin N. *Excavation of Hermit's Cave, New Mexico.* School of American Research Monograph, No. 10. Albuquerque: University of New Mexico Press, 1946. $2.50.

1241. * Fergusson, Erna. *Dancing Gods. Indian Ceremonials of New Mexico and Arizona.* 1931; rpt. Albuquerque: University of New Mexico Press, 1957. 312 pp. In paper: 286 pp. $2.45.

1242. ———. *New Mexico.* Rev. ed. Rpt. New York: Alfred A. Knopf, Inc., 1964. $7.95.

1243. * Fergusson, Harvey. *The Rio Grande.* New York: Apollo Editions, 1971. (Grades 9-12) $1.95.

1244. Fernow, Berthold. *The Ohio Valley in Colonial Days.* 1890; rpt. New York: Burt Franklin, Pub., 1971. $19.50.

1245. Fewkes, Jesse W. *Antiquities of the Mesa Verde National Park: Spruce Tree House* and *Antiquities of the Mesa Verde National Park: Cliff Palace.* 1909 / 1911; rpt. Nashville, Tennessee: The Blue and Gray Press, 1971. 139 pp. $10.00.

1246. ———. *Hopi Katchinas Drawn by Native Artists.* Glorieta, New Mexico: Rio Grande Press, Inc., 1967. $15.00.

1247. * Fey, Harold E., and D'Arcy McNickle. *Indians and Other Americans: Two Ways of Life Meet.* New York: Harper and Bros., 1959. 220 pp. McNickle is a Flathead Indian. In paper: Rev. ed. New York: Harper and Row, 1970. A Perennial Library Book. 274 pp. $1.25.

1248. * Filler, Louis, and Allen Guttmann, eds. *The Removal of the Cherokee Nation: Manifest Destiny or National Dishonor.* Problems in American Civilization Series. Indianapolis: D.C. Heath and Company, 1962. (Grades 11-12) $2.25.

1249. Filson, John. *Filsons Kentucky.* 1830; rpt. New York: Burt Franklin, Pub., 1969. $12.50.

1250. ———. *The Discovery, Settlement and Present State of Kentucky.* Rpt. Gloucester, Mass: Peter Smith, 1971. $4.00.

1251. Finley, James B. *Life Among the Indians; Or Personal Reminiscences and Historical Incidents Illustrative of Indian Life and Character.* 1857; rpt. Ed. D. W. Clark. Select Bibliographies Reprint Series. New York: Books for Libraries, 1972. $18.50.

1252. * Finnerty, John F. *War-Path and Bivouac: or The Conquest of the Sioux*. Chicago: M. A. Donohue and Company, 1890. 460 pp. In paper: Ed. Milo M. Quaife. Lincoln: University of Nebraska Press, 1966. 375 pp. $2.40. Also: Ed. Oliver Knight. Western Frontier Library, No. 18. Norman: University of Oklahoma Press, 1960. $2.95.

1253. Fishler, S. A. *Navajo Picture Writing*. See Newcomb, Franc J. *A Study of Navajo Symbolism*, No. 2201.

1254. Flaherty, Robert. *Nanook of the North*. New York: Windmill Books, 1971. (Grades 5 up) $4.95.

1255. Flannery, Regina. *The Gros Ventres of Montana: Part I— Social Life*. Washington, D.C.: Catholic University of America Press, 1953. Catholic University of America Anthropological Series No. 15. 221 pp.

1256. Fleishchmann, Glen H. *The Cherokee Removal, 1838: An Entire Indian Nation is Forced Out of Its Homeland*. Focus Books. New York: Franklin Watts, Inc., 1971. (Grades 7 up) 88 pp. $3.95.

1257. Fletcher, Alice C. *Indian Education and Civilization*. 1888; rpt. New York: Kraus Reprint Co., 1971. $25.00.

1258. ——. *Indian Games and Dances with Native Songs*. 1915; rpt. New York: AMS Press, 1971. $7.50. See also La Flesche, Francis.

1259. Fletcher, Alice C., and Francis La Flesche. *The Omaha Tribe*. 27th Report of the Bureau of American Ethnology. Washington, D.C., 1911; rpt. New York: Johnson Reprint Corp., 1970. $27.50. Also: 2 vols. Lincoln: University of Nebraska Press, 1972. 312 pp. $3.50 / 348 pp. / $3.50.

1260. * Fletcher, Alice C., and Francis La Flesche. *A Study of Omaha Indian Music with a Report of the Structural Peculiarities of the Music by J. C. Fillmore*. 1893; rpt. New York: Kraus Reprint Co., 1970. $6.00.

1261. Fletcher, J. G. *John Smith—Also Pocahontas*. 1928; rpt. New York: Kraus Reprint Co., 1970. $15.00.

1262. Fletcher, Sydney E. *The American Indians*. Silver Dollar Library. New York: Grosset and Dunlap, 1954. (Grades 4-6) 152 pp. $1.00.

1263. Flint, Timothy. *Indian Wars of the West, Containing Biographical Sketches of Those Pioneers Who Headed the Western Settlers in Repelling the Attacks of the Savages*. 1833; rpt. First American Frontier Series. New York: Arno Press, 1971. $11.00.

1264. Floethe, Louise L., and Richard Floethe. *The Indian and His Pueblo*. New York: Charles Scribner's Sons, 1960. (Grades 1-5) $5.95.

1265. Floethe, Louise L., and Richard Floethe. *Sea of Grass.* New York: Charles Scribner's Sons, 1963. (Grades 1-5) $3.65.

1266. * Florida Anthropological Society. *The Florida Anthropological Society Publications, Nos. 1-5.* 1949-58; rpt. New York: Johnson Reprint Corp., 1970. $17.50.

1267. * Flying Cloud, Chief (Francis B. Zahn). *The Crimson Carnage of Wounded Knee.* Bottineau, North Dakota: Edward A. Milligan, 1967. 12 pp. Author is Sioux.

1269. Folsom-Dickerson, William E. *The Cliff Dwellers.* San Antonio, Texas: Naylor Company, 1968. (Grades 5-8) $4.95. Author is Choctaw.

1269. ——. *White Path.* San Antonio, Texas: Naylor Company, 1971. (Grades 7 up) $4.95.

1270. Fontana, Bernard I., et al. *Papago Indian Pottery.* American Ethnological Society Monograph. Seattle: University of Washington Press, 1962. $6.50.

1271. Forbes, Jack D. *The Apache, Navaho, and Spaniard.* Civilization of the American Indian Series, No. 115. 1960; rpt. Norman: University of Oklahoma Press, 1963. 304 pp. $7.95.

1272. * ——. *The Indian in America's Past.* Englewood Cliffs, New Jersey: Prentice Hall, 1964. 181 pp. In paper: Prentice-Hall, 164 and film strip. $1.95 / $6.00.

1273. * ——. *Native Americans of California and Nevada.* Healdsburg, California: Naturegraphs Book, 1969. 208 pp. $5.95. In paper: $3.95.

1274. ——. *Nevada Indians Speak.* Tucson: University of Nevada Press, 1967. 293 pp. $5.75.

1275. ——. *Warriors of the Colorado: The Yumas of the Quechan Nation and Their Neighbors.* Civilization of the American Indian Series, No. 76. Norman: University of Oklahoma Press, 1965. 378 pp. $8.95.

1276. Ford, Clellan S. *Smoke From Their Fires: The Life of a Kwakiutl Chief.* New Haven: Yale University Press, 1941; rpt. Hamden, Connecticut: Shoe String Press, 1968. $6.50.

1277. * Ford James A., and George I. Quimby. *The Tchefuncte Culture, an Early Occupation of the Lower Mississippi Valley.* 1945; rpt. New York: Kraus Reprint Co., 1971. $10.00.

1278. Forde, C. Daryll. *Ethnography of the Yuma Indians.* University of California Publications in American Archaeology and Ethnology. Vol. 38. Berkeley, California: University of California Press, 1931; rpt. 1972. See No. 4028.

1279. * Foreman, Grant. *Advancing the Frontier, 1830-1860.* 1933; rpt. Civilization of the American Indian Series, No. 4. Norman: University of Oklahoma Press, 1968. 363 pp. $8.95. In paper: 1964. $1.95.

1280. * ——. *The Five Civilized Tribes.* Civilization of the American Indian Series, No. 8. 1934; rpt. Norman: University of Oklahoma Press, 1966. 455 pp. In paper: 455 pp. $3.95.

1281. ——. *Indian Removal: The Emigration of the Five Civilized Tribes of Indians.* Civilization of the American Indian Series, No. 2. Norman: University of Oklahoma Press, 1969. 415 pp. $6.00.

1282. ——. *Indian and Pioneers: The Story of the American Southwest Before 1830.* 1936; rpt. Civilization of the American Indian Series, No. 14. Norman: University of Oklahoma Press, 1967. 300 pp. $7.95.

1283. ——. *Last Trek of the Indians.* 1946; rpt. New York: Russell and Russell, 1972. $16.00.

1284. ——, ed. *A Pathfinder in the Southwest.* The Itinerary of Lieutenant A. W. Whipple during his exploration for a Railway Route from Fort Smith to Los Angeles in the years 1853 to 1854. Norman: University of Oklahoma Press, 1968. 298 pp. $5.95.

1285. ——. *Sequoyah.* Civilization of the American Indian Series, No. 16. Norman: University of Oklahoma Press, 1959. 94 pp. $5.95.

1286. Forrest, Earle R. *The Missions and Pueblos of the Old Southwest.* Glorieta, New Mexico: Rio Grande Press, 1962. $7.50.

1287. * ——. *The Snake Dance of the Hopi Indians.* Great West and Indian Series, Vol. 21. Los Angeles: Westernlore Press, 1970. 172 pp. $6.95. In paper: New York: Tower Publications, Inc., 1970. $ .95.

1288. ——. *With A Camera In Old Navaholand.* Norman: University of Oklahoma Press, 1970. 274 pp. $5.95.

1289. Fortune, R. F. *Omaha Secret Societies.* Columbia University Contributions in Anthropology. Vol. XIV. New York: Columbia University Press, 1932; rpt. New York: AMS Press, 1969. 193 pp. $12.50.

1290. Foster, George M. See No. 4042.

1291. Fox, Robin. *Keresan Bridge: A Problem in Pueblo Ethnology.* Social Anthropology, No. 35. New York: Humanities Press, Inc., 1968. $6.75.

1292. Frazer, Robert W. *Forts of the West: Military Forts and Presidios and Posts Commonly Called Forts West of the Mississippi River to 1898.* Norman: Oklahoma University Press, 1971. $6.95.

1293. Frazier, Neta L. *Sacajawea: The Girl Nobody Knows.* New York: David McKay Co., 1970. (Grades 9 up) $3.95.

1294. Freeland, L. S. See No. 4020.

1295. Freeland M. D. *The Records of Oxford, Massachusetts, Including Chapters of English History, 1630.* 1894; rpt. New York: Burt Franklin, Pub., 1969. $22.50.

1296. French, David H. *Factionalism in the Isleta Pueblo*. Seattle: University of Washington Press, 1966. $5.00.

1297. *The French-Iroquois Diplomatic and Military Relations 1609-1701*. Studies in American History, Vol. 9. New York: Humanities Press, Inc., 1970. $10.50.

1298. Freuchen, Dagmar, ed. *Peter Freuchen's Adventures in the Arctic*. New York: Simon and Shuster, 1960. $4.95.

1299. * Freuchen, Peter. *Book of the Eskimos*. Ed. Dagmar Freuchen. Cleveland, Ohio: World Publishing Company, 1951. 441 pp. In paper: Crest Books. New York: Fawcett World Library, 1970. $ .95.

1300. Freuchen, Peter, and Finn Salomonsen. *Whaling Boy*. New York: G. P. Putnam's Sons, 1958. (Grades 4-6) $4.50.

1301. Freuchen, Pipaluk. *Eskimo Boy*. New York: Lothrop, Lee and Shepard Company, 1970. (Grades 4-6) $3.75.

1302. * Frink, Maurice. *Fort Defiance and the Navajos*. Boulder, Colorado: Pruett Publishing Company, 1969. 124 pp. $3.50.

1303. Frink, Maurice, and Casey E. Barthelmess. *Photographer on an Army Mule*. Norman: University of Oklahoma Press, 1970. $8.95.

1304. Frisbie, Charlotte J. *Kinaalda: A Study of the Navajo Girl's Puberty Ceremony*. Middletown, Connecticut: Wesleyan University Press, 1967. 437 pp. $15.00.

1305. Fritz, Henry E. *The Movement for Indian Assimilation: 1860-1890*. Philadelphia: University of Pennsylvania Press, 1963. 244 pp. $9.00.

1306. Frost, Lawrence A. *The Court-Martial of General George Armstrong Custer*. Norman: University of Oklahoma Press, 1970. $7.95.

1307. Fry, Alan. *How a People Die*. New York: Doubleday and Company, 1970. $4.95.

1308. Fuchs, Estelle, and Robert J. Havighurst. *To Live on This Earth: American Indian Education*. Garden City, New York: Doubleday and Company, 1972. 390 pp. $8.95.

1309. Fuller, Emaline. *Left By the Indians*. Fairfield, Washington: Ye Galleon Press, 1970.

1310. Fuller, Henry B. *Cliff Dwellers*. Upper Saddle River, N. J.: Gregg Press, Inc., 1971. $9.00.

1311. * Fuller, Iola. *The Shining Trail*. New York: Hawthorn Books, Inc., 1951. $6.50. In paper: New York: Popular Library, Inc., 1970. $1.25.

1312. Fundaburk, Emma L., ed. *Southeastern Indians: Life Portraits*. A Catalogue of Pictures 1564-1860. 1958. Rptd. Metuchen, New Jersey: Scarecrow Reprint Corporation, 1969. 136 pp. $7.50.

1313. Fundaburk, Emma L., and Mary D. Foreman, eds. *Sun Cities and Human Hands: The Southeastern Indians Art and Industries.* Luverne, Alaska: Emma Lila Fundaburk, Publisher, 1971. $7.50.

1314. Furman, Abraham L., ed. *Indian Stories.* New York: Lantern Press, Inc., 1970. $3.81.

1315. Fynn, A. J. *The American Indian as a Product of Environment.* 1907; rpt. New York: Augustus M. Kelly, 1969. $10.00.

1316. * Gagliano, Sherwood M. *The Occupation Sequence at Avery Island.* Baton Rouge: Louisiana State University Press, 1967. $3.50.

1317. Galvin, John, ed. *Through The Country of the Commanche Indians in the Fall of the Year 1845: The Journal of a U.S. Army Expedition Led by Lieutenant James W. Albert of the Topographical Engineers.* San Francisco: John Howell Books, 1970. $7.50.

1318. Garbarino, Merwin S. *Big Cypress: A Changing Seminole Community.* New York: Holt, Rinehart and Winston, Inc., 1972. 144 pp.

1319. Garcia, Andrew. *Tough Trip Through Paradise, 1878-1879.* Ed. Bennett H. Stein. Boston: Houghton Mifflin, 1967. $6.95.

1320. Gardner, Jeanne L. *Mary Jemison: Seneca Captive.* New York: Harcourt Brace Jovanovich, 1966. (Grades 5-7) $3.50.

1321. * Gardner, Richard. *Grito: Reies Tijerina and the New Mexico Land Grant War of 1967.* New York: Harper and Row, 1971. $2.25.

1322. * Garfield, Viola E., and Linn A. Forrest. *The Wolf and the Raven: Totem Poles of Southeastern Alaska.* 2nd ed. Seattle: University of Washington Press, 1961. 151 pp. $3.95.

1323. * Garfield, Voila, and W. L. Chafe, eds. *Symposium on Language and Culture.* American Ethnological Society Proceedings. Seattle: University of Washington Press, 1962. $3.50.

1324. * Garfield, Viola E., and Ernestine Friedl, eds. *Symposium on Community Studies in Anthropology.* American Ethnological Society Proceedings. Seattle: University of Washington Press, 1963. $3.50.

1325. * Garfield, Viola E., and Paul S. Wingert. *The Tsimshian Indians and their Arts.* Washington Paperbacks. Seattle: University of Washington Press, 1966. $6.50.

1326. Garland, Hamlin. *The Book of the American Indian.* Pictured by Frederic Remington. New York: Harper and Brothers, 1923; rpt. New York: Garrett Press, Inc., 1970. 274 pp. $12.75.

1327. * Garrard, Lewis H. *Wah-to-Yah and the Taos Trail.* 1955; rpt. Norman: University of Oklahoma Press, 1966. 298 pp. $2.95. In paper: 1972. 298 pp. $2.95.

1328. Garst, Shannon. *Chief Joseph of the Nez Perces.* New York: Julian Messner, 1953. (Grades 6 up).

1329. ——. *Crazy Horse.* Eau Claire, Wisconsin: E. M. Hale and Company, 1950. (Grades 6-12) $2.67.Also: Boston: Houghton Mifflin Company, 1950. $3.75.

1330. ——. *Custer: Fighter of the Plains.* New York: Julian Messner, 1944. (Grades 6 up) $3.50.

1331. ——. *Red Eagle.* New York: Hastings House Publishers, Inc., 1959. (Grades 4-6) $3.50.

1332. ——. *Sitting Bull Champion of His People.* New York: Julian Messner, Inc., 1946. 189 pp.

1333. * Gatschet, Albert S. *Karankawa Indians: Coast People of Texas.* 1891; rpt. New York: Kraus Reprint Co., 1971. $5.50.

1334. ——. *An Ethnographic Sketch of the Klamatch Indians of Southwestern Oregon.* 1890; rpt. Facsimile ed. Seattle: Shorey Publications, 1970. $4.50.

1335. * ——. *Zwolf Sprachen Aus Dem Sudwestern Nord Amerikas.* Rpt. New York: Humanities Press, Inc., 1970. $7.75.

1336. * Gearing, Frederick O. *The Face of the Fox.* Chicago: Aldine Publishing Company, 1970. 158 pp. $6.00. In paper: $2.75.

1337. * ——. *Priests and Warriors. Social Structures for Cherokee Politics in the 18th Century.* 1962; rpt. New York: Kraus Reprint Co., 1971. $8.00.

1338. * Geary, Edward. *The Depredations and Massacre by the Snake River Indians.* Rpt. Fairfield, Washington: Ye Galleon Press, 1966. $2.00.

1339. Gessner, Robert. *Massacre: A Survey of Today's American Indian.* Civil Liberties in American History Series. 1931; rpt. New York: Da Capo Press, 1972. $15.00.

1340. * Ghobashy, Omar Z. *The Caughnawaga Indians.* Old Greenwich, Connecticut: Devin-Adair Company, 1970. $2.75.

1341. Gibbs, George. *The Alphabetical Vocabularies of the Clallam and Lumni.* 1863; rpt. New York: AMS Press, 1970. $10.00.

1342. ——. *The Alphabetical Vocabulary of the Chinook Language.* 1863; rpt. New York: AMS Press, 1970. $10.00.

1343. ——, et al. *Comparative Vocabularies of the Tribes of Western Washington and Northwestern Oregon.* 1877; rpt. Seattle: Shorey Publications, 1971. $5.00.

1344. ——. *A Dictionary of the Chinook Jargon, or Trade Languages of Oregon.* 1863; rpt. New York: AMS Press, 1970. $10.00.

1345. ——. *A Dictionary of the Nisqually Indian Language.* 1877; rpt. Seattle: Shorey Publications, Inc., 1970. $10.00.

1346. * ——. *Indian Tribes of Washington Territory.* Rpt. Fairfield, Washington: Ye Galleon Press, 1967. 56 pp.

1347. ——, et al. *Tribes of Western Washington and Northwestern Oregon*. 1877; rpt. Seattle: Shorey Publications, 1971. $20.00.

1348. * Gibson, Arrell M. *The Chickasaws*. Civilization of the American Indian Series, No. 109. Norman: University of Oklahoma Press, 1971. 307 pp. $7.50. In paper: 1972. 339 pp. $3.95.

1349. ——. *The Kickapoos: Lords of the Middle Border*. Civilization of the American Indian Series, No. 70. Norman: University of Oklahoma Press, 1963. 389 pp. $8.95.

1350. Giddings, James L. *The Ancient Men of the Arctic*. New York: Alfred A. Knopf, Inc., 1967. $12.50.

1351. ——. *The Archaeology of Cape Denbigh*. Providence: Brown University Press, 1964. $12.50.

1352. * ——. *Kobuk River People*. Studies of Northern Peoples, No. 1. Seattle: University of Alaska Press, 1970. $2.50.

1353. Giddings, Joshua R. *Exiles of Florida*. Ed. Arthur W. Thompson. Rpt. Floridiana Facsimile and Reprint Series. Gainesville: University of Florida Press, 1964. $8.50. Also: 1858; rpt. New York: Arno Press, 1969. $12.00.

1354. Gifford, Edward W. See Nos. 4011, 4012, 4014, 4018, 4020, 4022, 4023, 4029, 4031, 4034, 4037, and 4043.

1355. * Giles, Janice H. *Johnny Osage*. Boston, Mass.: Houghton Mifflin, 1960. $6.95. In paper: New York: Paperback Library, 1967. $ .75.

1356. Gillham, Charles E. *Beyond the Clapping Mountains*. New York: Macmillan Company, 1964. (Grades 4-6) $3.95.

1357. ——. *The Medicine Men of Hooper Bay*. New York: Macmillan Company, 1966. (Grades 4-6) $3.95.

1358. * Gillin, John. *Archaeological Investigations in Central Utah*. 1941; rpt. New York: Kraus Reprint Co., 1971. $3.00.

1359. * Gillmor, Frances, and Louisa Wade Wetherill. *Traders to the Navajos*. The Story of the Wetherills of Kayenta. 1953; rpt. Albuquerque: University of New Mexico Press, 1967. 271 pp. $2.45.

1360. Gilpin, Laura. *The Enduring Navaho*. Austin: University of Texas Press, 1968. 263 pp. $17.50.

1361. Gladwin, Harold, et al. *Excavations at Snaketown: Material Culture*. Tucson: University of Arizona Press, 1965. $10.00.

1362. Glassley, R. Howard. *Pacific Northwest Indian Wars*. Portland, Oregon: Binfords and Mort, 1953. $5.50.

1363. Glubok, Shirley. *The Art of the Eskimo*. New York: Harper and Row, Inc., 1964. (Grades 2-6) $4.50.

1364. ——. *The Art of the North American Indian*. New York: Harper and Row, Inc., 1964. (Grades 2-6) $4.50.

1365. ——. *The Art of the Southwest Indians*. New York: Macmillian, 1971. (Grades 4 up) 48 pp. $5.95.

1366. Goble, Paul, and Dorothy Goble. *Brave Eagle's Account of the Fetterman Fight*. New York: Pantheon Books, 1972. (Grades 5 up) $4.50.

1367. Goddard, Pliny E. *Hupa Texts*. 1904; rpt. New York: Kraus Reprint Co., 1970. $25.00. Bound with Goddard, *Life and Culture of the Hupa*, Part II.

1368. ——. *The Indians of the Northwest Coast*. 2nd ed. 1934; rpt. Handbook Series, No. 10. New York: Cooper Squares Publishers, 1972.

1369. ——. *Morphology of the Hupa Language*. 1905; rpt. New York: Kraus Reprint Co., 1971. $25.00. See also Nos. 4001, 4003, 4005, 4010, 4011, 4017, 4020, 4023, and 4024.

1370. * ——. *Life and Culture of the Hupa*. University of California Publications in American Archaeology and Ethnology. Berkeley, California: University of California Press, 1903; rpt. New York: Kraus Reprint Co., 1970. $25.00.

1371. Goggin, John. *Indian and Spanish Selected Writings*. Miami: University of Miami Press, 1964. $5.50.

1372. Golden, Gertrude. *Red Moon Called Me: Memoirs of a Schoolteacher in the Government Indian Service*. San Antonio, Texas: The Naylor Company, 1954. 211 pp.

1373. Goldfrank, Esther S. *Changing Configurations in the Social Organization of a Blackfoot Tribe During the Reserve Period. Observations on Northern Blackfoot Kinship*. American Ethnological Society Monographs Series. Seattle: University of Washington Press, 1966. 104 pp. $5.00.

1374. * ——. *The Social and Ceremonial Organization of Cochiti*. 1927; rpt. New York: Kraus Reprint Co., 1971. $6.50.

1375. * Goldschmidt, Walter, ed. *The Anthropology of Franz Boas*. Essays on the Centennial of His Birth. 1959; rpt. New York: Kraus Reprint Co., 1971. $8.00. See also Nos. 4035 and 4042.

1376. Goldstein, Robert A. *French-Iroquois Diplomatic and Military Relations, 1609-1701*. The Hague, Netherlands: Mouton, 1969. 212 pp. $9.00. Also: Studies in American History, Vol. 9. New York: Humanities Press, Inc., 1970. $9.00.

1377. Goodnough, David. *Pontiac's War, 1763-1766*. New York: Franklin Watts, Inc., 1971. $3.95.

1378. Goodpaster, Ed. *Ladonna Harris*. Story of an American Indian Series. Minneapolis: Dillon Press, 1972. $3.95.

1379. Goodrich, Samuel G. *Manners, Customs and Antiquities of the Indians of North and South America*. 1856; rpt. Ann Arbor, Mich.: Finch Press, 1972. $15.00.

1380. Goodwin, Grenville. *The Social Organization of the Western Apache*. Tucson: University of Arizona Press, 701 pp. $10.00.

1381. ——. *Western Apache Raiding and Warfare*. Ed. Keith H. Basso. Tucson: University of Arizona Press, 1971. 330 pp. $10.00.; $5.95.

1382. Gookin, Daniel. *An Historical Account of the Doings and Sufferings of the Christian Indians in New England in the Years 1675, 1676, 1677*. 1836; rpt. Research Library of Colonial Americana Series: Personal Narratives and Promotional Literature. New York: Arno Press, 1970. $10.00.

1383. ——. *Historical Collections of the Indians in New England*. 1792; rpt. Research Library of Colonial Americana Series: Personal Narratives and Promotional Literature. New York: Arno Press, 1970. $10.00.

1384. Goossen, Ivry W. *Navajo Made Easier*. 2nd ed. Flagstaff, Arizona: Northland Press, 1971. 271 pp. $6.95.

1385. Gordon, Cyrus H. *Before Columbus: Links Between the Old World and Ancient America*. New York: Crown Publishers, 1971. $6.50.

1386. * Gossain, Robert, et al. *Eskimo Art*. Boston: Boston Book and Art Shop, Inc., 1970. $9.95.

1387. * Gould, Richard A. *Archaeology of the Point St. George Site and Tolowa Prehistory*. University of California Publications in Anthropology Series, Vol. 4. Berkeley: University of California Press, 1966. $3.00.

1388. * Graburn, Nelson, H. H. *Eskimos Without Igloos: Social and Economic Development in Sugluk*. Boston: Little, Brown, and Company, 1969. 244 pp. $3.50.

1389. Graff, Stewart, and Polly A. Graff. *Squanto: Indian Adventurer*. Champaign, Illinois: Garrard Publishing Co., 1971. $2.59.

1390. Graham, W. A. *The Custer Myth*. New York: Bonanza, 1953. 413 pp.

1391. Grant, Bruce. *The American Indians: Yesterday and Today*. New ed. Rev. New York: E. P. Dutton and Company, 1958. (Grades 7 up) 351 pp. $5.95.

1392. * Grant, Campbell. *Rock Art of the American Indian*. New York: T. Y. Crowell Co., 1967. $12.95. In paper: $2.95.

1393. ——. *The Rock Paintings of the Chumash: The Study of a California Indian Culture*. Berkeley: University of California Press, 1965. 163 pp. $10.00.

1394. * Grant, Paul Warcloud. *Sioux Dictionary: Over 4,000 Words*. Pronunciation-at-a-glance. Pierre, South Dakota: State Publishing Co., [1971]. 172 pp. Author is Sioux.

1395. Grant, W. L., ed. *Voyages of Samuel De Champlain, Sixteen Four to Sixteen Eighteen.* Original Narratives. New York: Barnes and Noble, 1959. $5.75.

1396. * *Graphic Arts of the Alaskan Eskimo.* Washington, D.C.: Government Printing Office, 1969. 88 pp. $1.00.

1397. Grassmann, Thomas. *The Mohawk Indians and Their Valley.* Albany, New York: Magi Books, Inc., 1969. $20.00.

1398. Graymont, Barbara. *The Iroquois in the American Revolution.* New York State Study. Syracuse: University of Syracuse Press, 1972. 359 pp. $11.50.

1399. * *Great Western Indian Fights.* By Members of the Potomac Corral of the Westerners. Washington, D.C. Lincoln: University of Nebraska Press, 1966. Bison Book (Rptd. from 1960). $1.95. 336 pp.

1400. Gregg, Alexander. *The History of the Old Cheraws.* 1867; rpt. Spartanburg, North Carolina: Reprint Co., 1970. $15.00.

1401. Gregg, Alexander, and J. J. Dargan. *The History of the Old Cheraws.* Rev. ed. 1925; rpt. Baltimore: Genealogical Publishing Co., Inc. $15.00.

1402. Gregg, Elinor D. *The Indians and the Nurse.* Western Frontier Library Book, No. 28. Norman: University of Oklahoma Press, 1965. 170 pp. $2.95.

1403. Gregg, Josiah. *Commerce of the Prairies.* Ed. Max L. Moorhead. American Exploration and Travel Series, No. 17. Norman: University of Oklahoma Press, 1958. 469 pp. $8.50. Also: Ed. Milo M. Quaife. Gloucester, Mass.: Peter Smith, 1971. $4.58. Also: 2 vols. 1844; rpt. March of American Series. Ann Arbor, Michigan: University Microfilms, 1966. $14.95.

1404. * Gridley, Marion E. *American Indian Landmarks.* Chicago: Swallow Press, 1971. $10.00. In paper: $4.95.

1405. ——. *Contemporary American Indian Leaders.* New York: Dodd, Mead and Company, 1972. (Grades 7 up) $4.95.

1406. ——. *America's Indian Statues.* Chicago: The Amerindian Press, 1972. $2.50.

1407. ——. *Indians of Yesterday.* Chicago: M. A. Donohue and Company, 1970. $3.95.

1408. ——. *Pontiac.* See and Read Biography Series. New York: G. P. Putnam's Sons, 1970. $2.68.

1409. ——. *The Story of the Haida.* New ed. Indian Nations Series. New York: G. P. Putnam's Sons, 1972. (Grades 4-7) $4.69.

1410. ——. *The Story of the Iroquois.* Ed. Country Beautiful Editors. New York: G. P. Putnam's Songs, 1969. (Grades 5-7) 63 pp. $4.69.

1411. ——. *The Story of the Navajo.* Ed. Country Beautiful Editors. Indian Nations Series. New York: G. P. Putnam's Sons, 1971. (Grades 3-6) $4.69.

1412. ——. *The Story of the Sioux.* Ed. Country Beautiful Editors. Indian Nations Series. New York: G. P. Putnam's Sons, 1972. (Grades 5-7) $4.97.

1413. Griffin, James B., et al. *Archaeology of Eastern United States.* Chicago: University of Chicago Press, 1952. $13.50.

1414. * Griffin, John W., and Ripley P. Bullen. *Safety Harbor Site.* Pinellas County, Florida. 1950; rpt. New York: Johnson Reprint Corp., 1950. $3.50.

1415. Grinnell, George B. *The Cheyenne Indians, Their History and Ways of Life.* 2 vols. 1923; rpt. New York: Cooper Square Publs., 1970. $20.00.

1416. ——. *The Fighting Cheyennes.* Civilization of the American Indian Series, No. 44. Norman: University of Oklahoma Press, 1966. 450 pp. $5.95.

1417. ——. *The Indians of Today.* Chicago: Herbert S. Stone and Company, 1900.

1418. ——. *Story of the Indian.* 1895; rpt. Detroit, Michigan: Gale Research Company, 1971.

1419. ——. *When Buffalo Run.* Western Frontier Library, No. 31. Norman: University of Oklahoma Press, 1966. $2.95.

1420. Grisham, Noel. *A Serpent for a Dove: The Suppression of the American Indian.* Austin, Texas: Jenkins Publishing Company, 1972. $5.95.

1421. * Grower, Charlotte D. *Northern and Southern Affiliations of Antillean Culture.* 1927; rpt. New York: Kraus Reprint Co., 1971. $3.50.

1422. * Guernsey, Samuel J. *Explorations in Northeastern Arizona.* 1931; rpt. New York: Kraus Reprint Co., 1971. $11.00.

1423. * Guernsey, Samuel J., and A. V. Kidder. *The Basket-Maker Caves of Northeastern Arizona.* 1921; rpt. New York: Kraus Reprint Co., 1970. $8.50.

1424. Gunnerson, Dolores A. *The Jicarilla Apaches; A Study in Survival.* De Kalb, Illinois: Northern Illinois University Press, 1972. $10.00.

1425. Gunther, Erna. *Indian Life on the Northwest Coast of North America as Seen by Early Explorers and Fur Traders During the Last Decade of the 18th Century.* Chicago: University of Chicago Press, 1972. $15.00.

1426. Haberland, Wolfgang. *The Art of North America.* Art of the World Library. New York: Crown Publishers, Inc., 1968. $6.95.

1427. * Hack, John T. *The Changing Physical Environment of the Hopi Indians of Arizona*. Harvard University Peabody Museum of Archaeology and Ethnology Papers Series. 1942; rpt. New York: Kraus Reprint Co., 1970. $2.00.

1428. * ——. *Prehistoric Coal Mining in the Jeddito Valley, Arizona*. 1942; rpt. New York: Kraus Reprint Co., $1.00.

1429. Hackett, Charles W. *Revolt of the Pueblo Indians of New Mexico and Otermin's Attempted Reconquest, 1680-1682*. Coronado Historical Series, Vols. VIII and IX. 2 vols. 1942; rpt. Albuquerque: University of New Mexico Press, 1970. 472 and 430 pp. $30.00.

1430. Hader, Berta, and Elmer Hader. *Reindeer Trail*. New York: Macmillan Company, 1959. $4.95.

1431. * Haeberlin, Herman K. *The Idea of Fertilization in the Culture of the Pueblo Indians*. The American Anthropological Association, Memoirs. Vol. 3., Part I. Lancaster, Pennsylvania, 1916; rpt. New York: Kraus Reprint Co., 1970. $3.50.

1432. * Haeberlin, Hermann K., and Erna Gunther. *The Indians of Puget Sound*. Publications in Anthropology. Seattle: University of Washington Press, 1930. 83 pp. $1.50.

1433. Hafen, LeRoy, and Ann W. Hafen. *The Powder River Campaigns and Sawyer's Expedition, 1865*. Glendale, California: Arthur H. Clark, 1961. $12.00.

1434. Hafen, LeRoy R. and Ann W. Hafen, eds. *Relations with the Indians of the Plains, 1857-1861*. Documentary of P. G. Lowe, R. M. Pick, and others. Glendale, California: Arthur H. Clark, Company, 1959. 310 pp.

1435. Hafer, Flora V. *Captive Indian Boy*. New York: David McKay Company, 1963. (Grades 4-6) $3.50.

1436. * Hagan, William T. *American Indians*. Chicago: The University of Chicago Press, 1961. 190 pp. $5.95. In paper: $1.95.

1437. * ——. *The Indian in American History*. Publication No. 50 of the American Historical Association's Service Center for Teachers of History. New York: Macmillan Company, 1963. 26 pp.

1438. ——. *Indian Police and Judges: Experiments in Acculturation and Control*. New Haven: Yale University Press, 1966. 194 pp. $6.50.

1439. ——. *The Sac and Fox Indians*. Civilization of the American Indian Series, No. 48. Norman: University of Oklahoma Press, 1958. 284 pp. $6.95.

1440. Haines, Francis. *The Buffalo*. New York: Thomas Y. Crowell Company, 1970. 242 pp. $7.95.

1441. ——. *The Indians of the Great Basin and Plateau*. New York: G. P. Putnam's Sons, 1969. (Grades 6-9) $4.50.

1442. ——. *The Nez Perces: Tribesmen of the Columbia Plateau.* Civilization of the American Indian Series, No. 42. 1955; rpt. Norman: University of Oklahoma Press, 1972. 329 pp. $7.95.

1443. Hale, Horatio. *Ethnography and Philogy, United States Exploring Expedition During the Years 1838-1842.* Rpt. Upper Saddle River, New Jersey: Gregg Press, Inc., 1968. $44.00.

1444. ——, ed. *The Iroquois Book of Rites.* 1883; rpt. Toronto: University of Toronto Press, 1963. $7.50. Also: New York: AMS Press, 1971. 222 pp. $8.00.

1445. Hall, Charles F. *Life with the Esquimaux: A Narrative of Arctic Experience in Search of Survivors of Sir John Franklin's Expedition.* Rpt. Rutland, Utah: Charles E. Tuttle Company, 1970. $7.50.

1446. Hall, Gordon L. *Osceola.* New York: Holt, Rinehart and Winston, 1964. (Grades 4-7) $3.25.

1447. ——. *Peter Jumping Horse at the Stampede.* New York: Holt, Rinehart and Winston, 1970. (Grades 4-6) $2.95.

1448. Hall, Robert L. *The Archaeology of Carcajou Point: With an Interpretation of the Development of Oneonta Culture in Wisconsin.* 2 vols. Madison, Wisconsin: University of Wisconsin Press, 1962. $12.00.

1449. * Hallowell, A. Irving. *Culture and Experience.* Philadelphia: University of Pennsylvania Press, 1957. $12.50. In paper: New York: Schocken Books, Inc., 1967. $2.95.

1450. Hamilton, Charles, ed. *Cry of the Thunderbird: The American Indian's Own Story.* New York: Macmillan, 1951. 283 pp. Also: Civilization of the American Indian Series, No. 119. Norman: University of Oklahoma Press, 1972. $7.95.

1451. Hamilton, Henry W., and Jean T. Hamilton. *The Sioux of the Rosebud: A History in Pictures.* Civilization of the American Indian Series, Vol. III. Norman: University of Oklahoma Press, 1971. $12.50.

1452. Hamilton, William T. *My Sixty Years on the Plains Trapping, Trading, and Indian Fighting.* 1960; rpt. Western Frontier Library, No. 15. Norman: University of Oklahoma Press, 1965. $2.95. Also: Columbus, Ohio: Long's College Book Co., 1951. $6.00.

1453. Hammerer, John D. *An Account of a Plan for Civilizing the North American Indians.* Ed. P. L. Ford. 1890; rpt. New York: Burt Franklin, Publisher, 1969. $7.50.

1454. Hanauer, Elsie V. *The Dolls of the Indians.* Cranbury, New Jersey: A. S. Barnes and Company, 1970. $5.95.

1455. Hancock, Mary A. *The Sioux Ghost Dance Uprising.* Philadelphia: Macrea Smith Company, 1972. (Grades 7 up) $4.95.

1456. *Handbook of American Indians.* See Hodge, Frederick W., Nos. 138 and 1525.

1457. * Hanke, Lewis. *Aristotle and the American Indians: A Study in Race Prejudice.* Bloomington: Indiana University Press, 1970. $1.95.

1458. ——. *The First Social Experiments in America.* Gloucester, Mass.: Peter Smith, 1964. $4.00.

1459. * ——. *The Spanish Struggle for Justice in the Conquest of America.* New York: Little Brown, and Company, 1966. $3.25.

1460. Hanks, L. M., and Jane Richardson. *Observations on Northern Blackfoot Kinship.* Seattle: University of Washington Press, 1966. $5.00.

1461. Hanks, L. M., and Jane Richardson. *Tribe Under Trust: A Study of the Blackfoot Reserve of Alberta.* Toronto: University of Toronto Press, 1950. $15.00.

1462. Hanna, Charles A. *Wilderness Trail.* 2 vols. 1911; rpt. New York: AMS Press, 1971. $42.50.

1463. Hannum, Alberta. *Paint the Wind.* New York: Viking Press, 1958. $5.00. This and the following book tell the story of the life of Beatien Yazz, modern Navajo artist.

1464. ——. *Spin a Silver Dollar.* New York: Viking Press, 1945. $6.50.

1465. Hans, Fred M. *The Great Sioux Nation. A Complete History of Indian Life and Warfare in America.* c. 1900; rpt. Minneapolis, Minnesota: Ross and Haines, Inc., 1964. 586 pp. $10.00.

1466. Hansen, L. Taylor. *He Walked the Americas.* Amherst, Wisconsin: Amherst Press, 1963. $6.95.

1467. Hanson, Lee H. *Hardin Village Site.* Lexington: University Press of Kentucky, 1966. $5.00.

1468. Hanzeli, Victor E. *Missionary Linguistics in New France: A Study of the 17th and 18th Century Descriptions of American Indian Languages.* Janua Lingarum Series Maior, No. 29. New York: Humanities Press, Inc., 1970. $13.00.

1469. Hare, Lloyd C. *Thomas Mayhew: Patriarch to the Indians.* 1932; rpt. New York: AMS Press, 1970. $10.00. Also: New York: Reprint House International, 1970. $13.50.

1470. Harkins, Lee F. ed. *The American Indian.* 2 vols. Rpt. New York: Liveright, 1970. $100.00.

1471. Harmon, Daniel. *A Journey of Voyages and Travels in the Interior of North America.* 2nd ed. Rpt. American Scene Series. New York: Plenum Pub. Company, 1968. $17.50.

1472. Harmon, G. D. *Sixty Years of Indian Affairs Political, Economic, and Diplomatic.* 1941; rpt. New York: Kraus Reprint Co., 1970. $15.50.

1473. * Harrington, J. P. See No. 2048.

1474. Harrington, Lyn. *Ootook, Young Eskimo Girl.* Eau Claire, Wisconsin: E. M. Hale and Company, Inc., 1956. (Grades 4-7) $2.76.

1475. * Harrington, M. R. *The Indians of New Jersey: Dickon Among the Lenapes.* New Brunswick: Rutgers University Press, 1963. $6.00. In paper: $2.75. See also No. 4025.

1476. * ——. *Iroquois Trail: Dickon Among the Onondagas and Senecas.* New Brunswick: Rutgers University Press, 1965. (Grades 4-8) $6.00. In paper: $2.75.

1477. Harris, Christie. *Once Upon a Totem.* New York: Atheneum Publishers, 1963. (Grades 4 up) $3.81.

1478. ——. *West With the White Chiefs.* New York: Atheneum Publishers, 1965. (Grades 5 up) $3.95.

1479. Harrod, Howard L. *Mission Among the Blackfeet.* Civilization of the American Indian Series, No. 112. Norman: University of Oklahoma Press, 1971. 213 pp. $7.95.

1480. Harston J. Emmon. *Comanche Land.* San Antonio, Texas: Naylor Company, 1964. (Grades 7 up) $5.95.

1481. * Harvey, Byron. *Ritual in Pueblo Art.* New York: Museum of the American Indian, Heyl Foundation, 1970. $8.00.

1482. Harvey, H. *The History of the Shawnee Indians, from the Year 1681 to 1854.* 1855; rpt. New York: Kraus Reprint Co., 1970. $13.50.

1483. Hassrick, Royal B., et al. *The Sioux: Life and Customs of a Warrior Society.* Civilization of the American Indian Series, No. 72. Norman: University of Oklahoma Press, 1967. $6.95.

1484. * Haury, E. W. *The Excavation of Los Muertos and Neighboring Ruins in the Salt River Valley, Southern Arizona.* 1945; rpt. New York: Kraus Reprint Co., 1970. $18.00.

1485. Havighurst, Robert J., and Bernice L. Neugarten. *American Indian and White Children: A Sociopsychological Investigation.* Chicago: University of Chicago Press, 1955; rpt. 1969. 335 pp. $5.00. Also: Deer Park, New York: Brown Book Company, 1970. $5.00.

1486. Hawkes, Ernest W. *The Labrador Eskimo. 1916; rpt. New York: Johnson Reprint Company, 1971. $10.00.*

1487. Hawkins, B. *A Sketch of the Creek Country, in 1798 and 99.* 1848; rpt. New York: Kraus Reprint Co., 1971. $9.50.

1488. Hawthorn, Audrey. *The Art of the Kwakiutl Indians and Other Northwest Coast Tribes.* Seattle: University of Washington Press, 1967. 410 pp. $25.00.

1489. Hawthorn, H. B., C. S. Belshaw, and S. M. Jamieson. *The Indians of British Columbia.* Toronto: University of Toronto Press, 1958.

1490. * Hayden, Julian D. *Excavations, 1940, at University Indian Ruin*. Globe, Arizona: Southwest Parks and Monuments Association, 1958. $4.00.

1491. Hays, Wilma, and R. Vernon Hays. *Food the Indians Gave Us*. New York: Washburn, Ives Co., 1972. (Grades 7 up) $4.95.

1492. Hearne, Samuel. *A Journey from Prince of Wale's Fort in Hudson's Bay to the Northern Ocean in the Years 1769-1772*. 1911; rpt. Westport, Conn.: Greenwood Press, Inc., 1968. $32.75. Also: 1795; rpt. New York: Plenum Publishing Company, 1968. $20.00.

1493. * Heath, Virginia S. *The Dramatic elements in American Indian Ceremonials*. Americana Series, No. 37. Rpt. New York: Haskell House Publishers, 1970. $2.95.

1494. Hebard, George R. *Sacajawea*. A guide and interpreter of the Lewis and Clark expedition, with an account of the travels of Toussaint Charbonneau, and of Jean Baptiste, expedition papoose. Glendale, California: The Arthur H. Clark Company, 1957. 340 pp. $12.50.

1495. Heckewelder, John. *The History, Manners, and Customs of the Indian Nations Who Once Inhabited Pennsylvania and the Neighboring States*. 1819; rpt. First American Frontier Series. New York: Arno Press, 1971. $19.00.

1496. ———. *Narrative of the Mission of the United Brethren Among the Delaware and Mohegan Indians*. 1820; rpt. First American Frontier Series. New York: Arno Press, 1971. $17.00.

1497. Hegemann, Elizabeth C. *Navaho Trading Days*. Albuquerque: University of New Mexico Press, 1963. 400 pp. $7.50.

1498. Heiderstadt, Dorothy. *Indian Friends and Foes*. New York: David McKay Company, 1958. (Grades 3-7) $3.75.

1499. ———. *More Indian Friends and Foes*. New York: David McKay Company, Inc., 1963. (Grades 3-7) 146 pp. $3.24.

1500. ———. *Stolen By the Indians*. New York: David McKay Company, 1968. (Grades 4-6) $3.50.

1501. * Heizer, Robert F., and Adam E. Treganza. *Mines and Quarries of the Indians of California*. Phoenix: Balleen Press, 1972. $2.95.

1502. Heline, Theodore. *American Indian: Our Relations and Responsibilities*. Studies in This Changing World Series. Oceanside, California: New Age Press, Inc., 1971.$1.00.

1503. Helms, Mary W. *Asang: Adaptations to Culture Contact in a Miskito Community*. Gainesville: University of Florida Press, 1971. $10.00.

1504. Helps, Arthur. *Spanish Conquest in America and its Relation to the History of Slavery and to the Government of Colonies*. Ed. M. Oppenheim. 4 vols. New York: AMS Press, 1972. $57.00. Also: 4 vols. St. Clair Shores, Michigan: Scholarly Press, 1972. $21.50 ea / $79.00 set.

1505. Hennepin, Louis. *A Description of Louisiana*. 1880; rpt. March of America Series. Ann Arbor, Michigan: University Microfilms, 1966. $8.95.

1506. * Henry, Alexander. *Massacre at Mackinac, Seventeen Sixty-Three*. Ed. David Armour. Mackinac Island, Michigan: Mackinac Island State Park Commission, 1966. $1.00.

1507. ——. *Travels and Adventures in Canada and the Indian Territories*. 1809; rpt. March of America Series. Ann Arbor, Michigan: University Microfilms, 1966. $3.55. Also: Rutland, Vermont: Charles E. Tuttle Company, 1969. $6.00.

1508. ——. *Travels and Adventures in Canada and the Indian Territories Between 1760 and 1776*. 1901; rpt. Ed. James Bain. American Classics in History and Social Science Series No. 74. New York: Burt Franklin, Inc., 1969. $18.50. Also: St. Clair Shores, Michigan: Scholarly Press, 1970. $16.50.

1509. * Henry, Will. *Custer's Last Stand: The Story of the Little Big Horn*. Philadelphia: Chilton Book Company, 1966. (Grades 9 up) $3.95. In paper: Tempo Books, New York: Grosset and Dunlap, 1970. $ .75.

1510. ——. *The Day Fort Larking Fell: The Legend of the Last Great Indian Fight*. Philadelphia: Chilton Book Company, 1969. (Grades 8 up) $4.95.

1511. * ——. *Feleen Brand*. New York: Bantam Books, 1968. $ .50.

1512. ——. *The Last Warpath*. New York: Random House, 1966. $6.95.

1513. Hermann, Ralph. *Children of the North Pole*. New York: Harcourt, Brace and World, Inc., 1964. (Grades 2-5) $2.95.

1514. Hertzberg, Hazel W. *The Search for an American Indian Identity: Modern Pan-Indian Movements*. Syracuse: Syracuse University Press, 1971. 362 pp. $12.00.

1515. Heuman, William. *Famous American Indians*. New York: Dodd Mead and Company, 1972. (Grades 7-11) $3.50.

1516. Hewett, Edgar I. *Ancient Life in the American Southwest*. 1930; rpt. New York: Biblo and Tannen Booksellers and Publishers, Inc., 1968. $12.50.

1517. * Hibben, Frank C. *The Lost Americans*. New York: Thomas Y. Crowell Company, 1946. Apollo Editions. 200 pp.

1518. * Hickerson, Harold. *The Chippewa and Their Neighbors: A Study in Ethnohistory*. New York: Holt, Rinehart and Winston, 1970. $3.00.

1519. * ——. *The Southwestern Chippewa*. An Ethnohistorical Study. 1962; rpt. New York: Kraus Reprint Co., 1971. $8.00.

1520. Hill, Alex S. *From Home to Home: Autumn Wanderings of the North-West in the Years 1881, 1882, 1883, 1884*. 1885; rpt. New York: Arno Press, 1966. $22.50.

1521. Hill, James N. *Broken K Pueblo*. Anthropological Paper Series. Tucson: University of Arizona Press, 1970. $7.00.

1522. Hill, W. W. *The Agricultural and Hunting Methods of the Navaho Indians*. Yale University Publications in Anthropology, No. 18. New Haven: Yale University Press, 1938.

1523. Hinsdale, Wilbert B. *The Indians of Washtenaw County, Michigan*. 1927; rpt. Ann Arbor, Michigan: George Wahr Publishing Company, 1970. $ .60.

1524. * Hobson, Richard. *Navaho Acquisitive Values*. 1954; rpt. New York: Kraus Reprint Co., 1971. $4.00.

1525. Hodge, Frederick W. *The Indian Tribes of North America with Biographical Sketches of the Principal Chiefs*. 1933; rpt. St. Clair Shores, Michigan: Scholarly Press, 1972. $49.50.

1526. Hodge, Frederick W., and Theodore H. Lewis, eds. *Spanish Explorers in the Southern United States, 1528-1543*. New York: Barnes and Noble, 1959. $5.75.

1527. Hodge, Gene M. *Kachinas Are Coming*. Rpt. Facsimile Edition. Flagstaff, Arizona: Northland Press, 1967. $14.50.

1528. * Hodge, William H. *The Albuquerque Navajos*. Anthropological Papers of the University of Arizona, No. 11. Tucson: The University of Arizona Press, 1969. 76 pp. $4.00.

1529. Hodgson, Adam. *Remarks During a Journey Through North America in the Years 1819, 1820, 1821*. 1823; rpt. Westport, Connecticut: Negro Universities Press, 1970. $12.25.

1530. * Hoebel, E. Adamson. *The Cheyennes: Indians of the Great Plains*. Case Studies in Cultural Anthropology. Ed. George and Louise Spindler. New York: Holt, Rinehart, and Winston, 1960. 103 pp. In paper: $2.35.

1531. ——. *The Political Organizations and Law-Ways of the Comanche Indians*. 1940; rpt. New York: Kraus Reprint Co., 1970. $6.00.

1532. Hoffman, Charles. *American Indians Sing*. New York: John Day Co., 1967. (Grades 3-6) 96 pp. $3.27.

1533. Hoffman, Charles Fenno. *Greyslaer, A Romance of the Mohawk*. 1841; rpt. 2 vols. in one. Ed. J. V. Ridgely. American Fiction Series. New York: Garrett Press, 1970. $23.50. Also: St. Clair Shores, Michigan: Scholarly Press, 1968. $21.00.

1534. ——. *Wild Scenes in the Forest and Prairie*. 2 vols. 1842; rpt. Upper Saddle River, New Jersey: Gregg Press, Inc., 1970. $15.50.

KALAMAZOO VALLEY
COMMUNITY COLLEGE
LIBRARY

1535. ——. *Winter in the West by a New Yorker.* 2 vols. 1835; rpt. New York: Burt Franklin Publisher, 1968. $28.50. Also: March of America Series. Ann Arbor, Michigan: University Microfilms, 1966. $14.95. Also: St. Clair Shores, Michigan: Scholarly Press, 1970. $24.00.

1536. Hoffman, J. Jacob. *Comments on the Use and Distribution of Tipi Rings in Montana, North Dakota, South Dakota, and Wyoming.* Anthropology and Sociology Papers, No. 14. Missoula: Montana State University Press, 1953.

1537. Hoffman, Walter J. *The Menomini Indians.* 1896; rpt. New York: Johnson Reprint Co., 1970. $25.00.

1538. ——. *The Midewiwin or Grand Medicine Society of the Ojibwa.* 7th Annual Report. Bureau of American Ethnology. Washington, D.C., 1891, pp. 143-300.

1539. Hofsinde, Robert. *Indian Arts.* New York: William Morrow and Company, Inc., 1970. (Grades 4-6) $3.56.

1540. ——. *Indian Beadwork.* New York: William Morrow and Company, Inc., 1958. (Grades 4-6) $3.56.

1541. ——. *The Indian and the Buffalo.* New York: William Morrow and Company, Inc., 1961. (Grades 4-6) 96 pp. $3.56.

1542. ——. *Indian Costumes.* New York: William Morrow and Company, 1968. (Grades 3-6) 94 pp. $3.56.

1543. ——. *Indian Fishing and Camping.* New York: William Morrow and Company, Inc., 1963. (Grades 4-6) $3.56.

1544. ——. *Indian Games and Crafts.* New York: William Morrow and Company, Inc., 1957. (Grades 4-6) 127 pp. $3.75.

1545. ——. *The Indian and His Horse.* New York: William Morrow and Company, Inc., 1960. (Grades 4-6) 96 pp. $3.56.

1546. ——. *Indian Hunting.* New York: William Morrow and Company, 1962. (Grades 4-6) 96 pp. $3.56.

1547. ——. *Indian Medicine Man.* New York: William Morrow and Company, Inc., 1966. (Grades 4-6) 94 pp. $3.56.

1548. ——. *Indian Music Makers.* New York: William Morrow and Company, 1967. (Grades 4-6) 94 pp. $3.75.

1549. ——. *Indian Picture Writing.* New York: William Morrow and Company, 1959. (Grades 4-6) 96 pp. $3.36.

1550. ——. *The Indian Sign Language.* New York: William Morrow and Company, 1956. (Grades 4-6) 96 pp. $3.56.

1551. ——. *Indian Warriors and Their Weapons.* New York: William Morrow and Company, 1965. (Grades 4-6) 96 pp. $3.36.

1552. ——. *Indians at Home.* New York: William Morrow and Company, Inc., 1964. (Grades 4-6) 96 pp. $3.56.

1553. ——. *Indians on the Move.* New York: William Morrow and Company, Inc., 1970. (Grades 4-6) $3.36.

1554. ———. *The Indian's Secret World.* New York: William Morrow and Company, Inc., 1955. (Grades 7-9) 96 pp. $4.65.

1555. Hoig, Stan. *The Sand Creek Massacre.* Norman: University of Oklahoma Press, 1961. $5.25.

1556. * Hoijer, Harry, et al. *The Linguistic Stuctures of Native America.* Ed. Cornelius Osgood. 1946; rpt. New York: Johnson Reprint Corp., 1963. $12.50.

1557. * Hoijer, Harry, et al. *Studies in the Athapaskan Languages.* University of California Publications in Linguistics Series, Vol. 29. Rpt. Berkeley: University of California Press, 1963. $3.00.

1558. Holder, Preston. *The Hoe and the Horse on the Plains: A Study of Cultural Development Among North American Indians.* Lincoln: University of Nebraska Press, 1970. $6.95.

1559. * Holland, James W. *Andrew Jackson and the Creek War Victory at the Horseshoe.* Birmingham: University of Alabama Press, 1969. $ .95.

1560. Holling, Holling, C. *The Book of Indians.* Illustrated by H. C. and Lucille Holling. New York: The Platt and Munk Company, Inc., 1935. (Grades 7 up) 127 pp. $3.50.

1561. Hollmann, Clide. *Pontiac, King of the Great Lakes.* New York: Hastings House Publishers, Inc., 1971. $5.25.

1562. * Holm, Bill. *Northwest Coast Indian Art: An Analysis of Form.* Seattle: University of Washington Press, 1970. $4.95.

1563. Holmes, Louis A. *Fort McPherson, Nebraksa Territory.* Lincoln, Nebraska: Johsen Publishing Company, 1963. $7.50.

1564. Holmes, William H. *The Pottery of the Ancient Pueblos.* 1886; rpt. Seattle: Shorey Publications, 1971. $6.00.

1565. Holmes, William F. *The White Chief: James Kimble Vardaman.* Southern Biography Series. Baton Rouge: Louisiana State University Press, 1970. $10.95.

1566. Holt, Ray D. *Heap Many Texas Chiefs.* San Antonio, Texas: Naylor Company, 1966. (Grades 7 up) 350 pp. $7.95.

1567. * Honigmann, John J. *The Kaska Indians: An Ethnographic Reconstruction.* Yale University Publications in Anthropology Reprints Series. New York: Human Relations Area File Press, 1964. $4.00.

1568. Hood, Flora M. *Living in Navajoland.* See and Read Storybook Series. New York: G. P. Putnam's Sons, 1970. (Grades K-3) $3.29.

1569. ———. *Something for the Medicine Man.* Chicago: Melmont Publishers, Inc., 1962. (Grades 2-6) $3.25.

1570. Hooper, Lucille. See No. 4016.

1571. Hoopes, Alban W. *Indian Affairs and Their Administration, With Special Reference to the Far West.* 1932; rpt. New York: Kraus Reprint Co., 1971. $13.50.

1572. * Hooten, E. A. *Indian Village Site and Cemetery Near Madisonville, Ohio.* 1920; rpt. New York: Kraus Reprint Co., 1971. $5.50.

1573. Hopkins, Samuel. *Historical Memoires Relating to the Housatunnuk Indians.* 1753; rpt. New York: Johnson Reprint Corp., 1971. $9.00.

1574. Hopkins, William John. *The Indian Book.* Boston: Houghton-Mifflin, 1911. 239 pp.

1575. Horan, James D. *The McKenney-Hill Portrait Gallery of American Indians.* New York: Crown Publishers, 1972. $29.95.

1576. Horgan, Paul. *Heroic Triad.* New York: Holt, Rinehart and Winston, 1970. $7.95.

1577. Horn, Tom. *The Life of Tom Horn, Government Scout and Interpreter, Written by Himself, Together with His Letters and Statements by His Friends: A Vindication.* Rpt. Western Frontier Library, No. 26. Norman: University of Oklahoma Press, 1964. $2.95.

1578. Horsman, Reginald. *Expansion and American Indian Policy, 1783-1812.* East Lansing: Michigan State University Press, 1967. 209 pp. $5.75.

1579. ——. *Matthew Elliott, British Indian Agent: A Study of British Indian Policy in the Old Northwest.* Detroit: Wayne State University Press, 1964. $9.95.

1580. Hotz, Gottfried. *Indian Skin Paintings from the American Southwest.* Trans. Johannes Malthaner. Norman: University of Oklahoma Press, 1970. 248 pp. $9.95.

1581. Hough, Franklin B., ed. *The Proceedings of the Commissioners of Indian Affairs.* Vols. 1-2. 1861; rpt. Munsell's History Series. New York: Burt Franklin, Publishers, 1970. $28.50.

1582. * Hough, Henry W. *Development of Indian Resources.* Denver, Colorado: World Press, Inc., 1967. (In loose leaf binder.) 285 pp. $4.50. In paper: $2.50.

1583. Hough, Walter. *The Hopi Indians.* 1915; rpt. Seattle: Shorey Publications, 1970. $12.50.

1584. ——. *The Lamp of the Eskimo.* 1898; rpt. Seattle: Shorey Publications, 1971. $5.00.

1585. ——. *Primitive American Armor.* 1893; rpt. Seattle: Shorey Publications, 1970. $3.00.

1586. Houston, James A. *Akavak: An Eskimo Journey.* New York: Harcourt, Brace and World, 1968. (Grades 3-5) $3.80.

1587. ——. *Eskimo Prints.* Barre, Mass.: Barre Publishers, 1966. $12.50.

1588. Howard, Harold F. *Sacajawea.* Norman: University of Oklahoma Press, 1968. $4.95.

1589. Howard, Helen A. *Saga of Chief Joseph*. Caldwell, Idaho: Caxton Printers, Ltd., 1965. 395 pp.

1590. * Howard, Helen Addison, and Dan L. McGrath. *War Chief Joseph*. 1941; rpt. Lincoln: University of Nebraska Press, 1964. 368 pp. $2.25.

1591. Howard, Oliver O. *Famous Indian Chiefs I Have Known*. New York: The Century Company, 1907.

1592. ——. *My Life Among Our Hostile Indians*. 1907; rpt. American Scene, Comments, and Commentators Series. New York: Plenum Publishing Company, 1969. $19.50.

1593. *Howard's Campaign Against the Nez Perce Indians, 1877.* 1878; rpt. Facsimile Edition. Seattle: Shorey Publications, 1970. $3.50.

1594. Howbert, Irving. *The Indians of the Pike's Peak Region*. Glorietta, New Mexico: Rio Grande Press, 1970. 230 pp. $7.50.

1595. Howe, Carrol B. *Ancient Tribes of the Klamath Country*. Portland, Oregon: Binfords and Mort Publishers, 1968. 252 pp. $4.95.

1596. Howitt, William. *Colonization and Christianity: A Popular History of the Treatment of the Natives By the Europeans in All Their Colonies.* 1838; rpt. Westport, Connecticut: Negro Universities Press, 1970. $15.75.

1597. Howling Wolf and Zo-Tom. *Eighteen Seventy Seven: Plains Indians Sketchbooks*. Ed. with Introduction by Dorothy Dunn. Flagstaff, Arizona: Northland Press, 1969. $35.00.

1598. Hoyland, John S. *Indian Crisis: The Background*. 1943; rpt. Select Bibliographies Series. Facsimile Edition. Freeport, New York: Books for Libraries, Inc., 1970. $9.00.

1599. Hoyt, Olga. *American Indians Today*. New York: Abelard-Schuman Ltd., 1972. (Grades 7 up) $5.95.

1600. Hrdlicka, Ales. See No. 4004.

1601. Hubbard, John N. *An Account of Sa-Go-Ye-Wat-Ha, or Red Jacket and His People*. 1886; rpt. New York: Burt Franklin, Publisher, 1969. $21.50.

1602. Hubbard, William. *The History of the Indian Wars in New England*. Rev. Samuel G. Drake. 1865; rpt. New York: Kraus Reprint, Co., 1969. In Two Parts in one vol. 292 pp. and 303 pp. $25.00. Also: 2 vols. New York: Burt Franklin, Publisher, 1968. $25.00.

1603. Huddleston, Lee E. *Origins of the American Indians. European Concepts, 1492-1729*. Latin American Monographs, No. 11. Published for the Institute of Latin American Studies. Austin: University of Texas Press, 1967. 179 pp. $6.00.

1604. * Hudson, Charles M. *The Catawba Nation*. Athens: University of Georgia Press, 1970. $4.00.

1605. * ——, ed. *Red, White, and Black*. Symposium on Indians in the Old South. Athens: University of Georgia Press, 1972. 143 pp. $3.75.

1606. * Huffaker, Clair. *Nobody Loves a Drunken Indian*. New York: Paperback Library, 1969. (1967) 222 pp. Also published under title *Flap*. New York: Philosophical Library, 1969.

1607. Hughes, Charles C., and Jane M. Hughes. *An Eskimo Village in the Modern World*. Ithaca: Cornell University Press, 1960. 419 pp. $11.50.

1608. Hughes, Charles C., et al. *People of the Cove and Woodlot*. New York: Basic Books, Inc., 1960. $10.00.

1609. Hughes, Thomas. *Indian Chiefs of Southern Minnesota*. Containing Sketches of the Prominant Chieftains of the Dakota and Winnebago Tribes from 1825 to 1865. Mankato, Minnesota: Free Press Company, 1927; rpt. Minneapolis: Ross and Haines, 1969. 133 pp. $8.75.

1610. Hulbert, Archer. *Historic Highways*. Vol. II: *Indian Thoroughfares*. 1905; rpt. New York: AMS Press, 1971. $11.50.

1611. * ——. *The Paths of the Mound-Building Indians and Great Games Animals*. Columbus, Ohio: Frontier Press Company, 1970. $2.00.

1612. Humphrey, Seth K. *The Indian Dispossessed*. Boston: Little, Brown and Company, 1905.

1613. * Hungry Wolf, Adolph. *Good Medicine. Traditional Dress Issue*. Knowledge and Methods of Old-Time Clothings. Golden, British Columbia: Good Medicine Books, 1971. 64 pp.

1614. * Hunt, George T. *The Wars of the Iroquois: A Study in Intertribal Trade Relations*. Madison: University of Wisconsin Press, 1960. $2.95.

1615. Hunt, W. Ben and J. F. "Buck" Burshears. *American Indian Beadwork*. Milwaukee, Wisconsin: Bruce Publishing Company, 1951.

1616. Hunt, W. Ben. *Ben Hunt's Big Indiancraft Book*. New York: Bruce Publishing Company, 1969. $7.95.

1617. ——. *The Complete Book of Indian Crafts and Lore*. New York: Golden Press, 1970; rpt. of 1954 edition published by Western Publishing Company. 104 pp.

1618. ——. *The Golden Book of Indian Crafts and Lore*. New York: Simon and Shuster, 1954.

1619. ——. *Indiancraft*. Milwaukee, Wisconsin: The Bruce Publishing Company, 1942. 124 pp.

1620. ——. *Indian Leathercraft*. New York: Macmillan, 1972. $2.95.

1621. ——. *Indian Silversmithing*. New York: Crowell, Collier, and Macmillan, Inc., 1960. $4.50.

1622. Hunter, John D. *The Manners and Customs of Several Indian Tribes West of the Mississippi.* 1823; rpt. Facsimile Edition. Minneapolis: Ross and Haines, Inc., 1970. $8.75.

1623. ——. *Memoirs of a Captivity Among the Indians of North America, From Childhood to the Age of Nineteen.* 1823; rpt. American Studies Series. New York: Johnson Reprint Corp., 1970. $15.00.

1624. Hunter, Lois Marie. *The Shinnecock Indians.* New York: Buys Bros., 1952. 90 pp. Author is Shinnecock Indian.

1625. Hunter, Milton R. *Christ in Ancient America.* Salt Lake City: Deseret Book Company, 1970. $5.95.

1626. Huntington, Ellsworth. *Red Man's Continent.* Yale Chronicles of America Series, Vol. I. New York: United States Publishers Association, Inc., 1970. $3.95.

1627. * Hurdy, John M. *American Indian Religions.* Los Angeles: Sherbourne Press, 1971. $2.50.

1628. Hyde, George E. *Indians of the High Plains From the Prehistoric Period to the Coming of Europeans.* Civilization of the American Indian Series, No. 54. Norman: University of Oklahoma Press, 1959; rpt. 1970. 228 pp. $6.50.

1629. ——. *Indians of the Woodlands. From Prehistoric Times to 1725.* Civilization of the American Indian Series, No. 64. Norman: University of Oklahoma Press, 1962; rpt. 1970. 292 pp. $8.95.

1630. ——. *Life of George Bent. Written From His Letters.* Ed. Savoie Lottinville. Norman: University of Oklahoma Press, 1968. 389 pp. $8.95.

1631. ——. *The Pawnee Indians.* Denver: University of Denver Press, 1951. 304 pp.

1632. ——. *Red Cloud's Folk.* A History of the Oglala Sioux Indians. Civilization of the American Indian Series, No. 15. Norman: University of Oklahoma Press, 1967. 331 pp. $7.95.

1633. ——. *A Sioux Chronicle.* Civilization of the American Indian Series, No. 45. Norman: University of Oklahoma Press, 1956. 334 pp. $5.00.

1634. ——. *Spotted Tail's Folk: A History of the Brule Sioux.* Civilization of the American Indian Series, No. 57. Norman: University of Oklahoma Press, 1961. 325 pp. $7.95.

1635. Hymes, D. H., and W. E. Bittle, eds. *Studies in Southwestern Ethnolinguistics: Meaning and History in the Languages of the American Southwest.* Studies in General Anthropology, Vol. X. Rpt. The Hague: Mouton Publishers, 1967. 464 pp. $26.00. Also: New York: The Humanities Press, Inc., 1968. $23.00.

1636. *Indian and Eskimo Children*. Washington, D.C.: Government Printing Office, 1969. 48 pp. $ .50. Pictorial account of how the children live today.

1637. *Indian Education: A National Tragedy—A National Challenge*. 1969 Report of the Committee on Labor and Public Welfare. United States Senate Special Subcommittee on Indian Education. Washington, D.C.: U.S. Government Printing Office, 1969. Report No. 91-501. 220 pp. $1.00.

1638. Indian Tribes. For Indian Tribes within various states, write to Government Printing Office, Washington, D.C. 20402.

1639. *Indians, Eskimos and Aleuts of Alaska*. Rev. ed. Washington, D.C.: Government Printing Office, 1968. 16 pp. $ .15.

1640. *Indians in Minnesota*. Compiled by League of Women Voters. 1971. 165 pp. $2.00. Order from Minnesota Historical Society.

1641. *Indians in Washington*. Seattle: Shorey Publications, 1972. $3.00.

1642. Inman, H., and W. F. Cody. *The Great Salt Lake Trail*. 1897; rpt. Minneapolis: Ross and Haines, 1970. $10.00.

1643. *Institute of American Indian Arts*. Washington, D.C.: Government Printing Office, 1968. 60 pp. $ .65.

1644. *Inverarity, Robert B. *The Art of the Northwest Coast Indians*. 2nd ed. Berkeley: University of California Press, 1967. $12.75. In paper: University of California Press, 1967. $6.95.

1645. Irving, John T. *Indian Sketches: Taken During an Expedition to the Pawnee Tribes*. 1833; rpt. Ed. John F. McDermott. American Exploration and Travel Series, No. 18. Norman: University of Oklahoma Press, 1955. 275 pp. $7.50.

1646. Irving, Washington. *A Tour on the Prairies*. Ed. John F. McDermott. 1956; rpt. Western Frontier Library, No. 7. Norman: University of Oklahoma Press, 1971. $2.95. Also: New York: Pantheon Books, 1967. (Grades 6-8) $4.95.

1647. ———. *The Western Journals of Washington Irving*. Ed. John F. McDermott. 1944; rpt. Norman: University of Oklahoma Press, 1966. $7.50.

1648. Irwin, Constance. *Fair Gods and Stone Faces: Ancient Seafarers and the New World's Most Intriguing Riddle*. New York: St. Martin's Press, 1963. $8.50.

1649. Isreal, Marion L. *Apaches*. Chicago: Melmont Publishers, Inc., 1959. (Grades 1-6) $3.25.

1650. ———. *Cherokees*. Chicago: Melmont Publishers, Inc., 1961. (Grades 2-6) $3.25.

1651. ———. *Dakotas*. Chicago: Melmont Publishers, Inc., 1959. (Grades 1-6) $3.25.

1652. ——. *The Ojibway*. Chicago: Melmont Publishers, Inc., 1962. (Grades 2-6) 32 pp. $3.25.

1653. Jablow, Joseph. *The Cheyenne in Plains Indian Trade Relations, 1795-1840*. 1951; rpt. American Ethnological Society Monographs. Seattle: University of Washington Press, 1966. 100 pp. $5.00.

1654. Jackson, Donald. *Custer's Gold: The United States Cavalry Expedition of 1874*. New Haven: Yale University Press, 1966. $6.50.

1655. Jackson, Halliday. *The Civilization of the Indian Natives*. 1830; rpt. St. Clair Shores, Michigan: Scholarly Press, 1970. $8.50.

1656. * Jackson, Helen Hunt. *A Century of Dishonor: A Sketch of the United States Government's Dealings with Some of the Indian Tribes*. 1881; rpt. St. Clair Shores, Michigan: Scholarly Press, 1970. $16.50. Also: Ed. Andrew F. Rolle, Gloucester, Mass.: Peter Smith, 1971. $5.25. In paper: New York: Harper and Row, 1971. 342 pp. $3.75.

1657. * Jacobs, Melville. *A Sketch of Northern Sahaptin Grammar*. Seattle: University of Washington Press, 1931. $4.00.

1658. Jacobs, Melville, and John Greenway, eds. *An Anthropologist Looks at Myth*. Bibliographic and Special Series, Vol. 17. American Folklore Society Publications. Austin: University of Texas Press, 1966. $6.00.

1659. * Jacobs, Wilbur R. *Dispossessing the American Indian*. New York: Charles Scribner's Sons, 1972. $7.95. In paper: $3.95.

1660. * ——. *Wilderness Politics and Indian Gifts: The Northern Colonial Frontier, 1748-1673*. Originally titled: *Anglo-French Rivalry Along the Ohio and Northwest Frontier, 1748-1763*. Gloucester, Mass.: Peter Smith, 1970. $4.00. In paper: Lincoln: University of Nebraska Press, 1971. $1.65.

1661. Jacobsen, Daniel. *Great Indian Tribes*. Maplewood, New Jersey: Hammond, Inc., 1970. (Grades 7 up) 93 pp. $4.39.

1662. Jakes, John W. *Mohawk: The Life of Joseph Brant*. New York: Macmillan Company, 1969. (Grades 5 up) 136 pp. $3.95.

1663. James, Edwin. *The Narrative of the Captivity and Adventures of John Tanner During Thirty Years' Residence Among the Chippewa, Ottawa, and Ojibwa Tribes*. Ed. Noel Loomis. Minneapolis: Ross and Haines, Inc., 1970. $10.00.

1664. ——, ed. *An Account of an Expedition from Pittsburgh to the Rocky Mountains, Performed in the Years 1819 to 1820*. 2 vols. March of America Series. 1822-1823; rpt. Ann Arbor, Michigan: University Microfilms, 1966. $18.95. Also: Westport, Connecticut: Greenwood Press, Inc., 1968. $18.95.

1665. James, George W. *Indian Basketry and How to Make Baskets.* 1903; rpt. Glorieta, New Mexico: Rio Grande Press, Inc., 1970. $10.00.

1666. ———. *Indian Blankets and Their Makers.* Rpt. New York: Hacker Art Books, 1971. Also: Glorieta, New Mexico: Rio Grande Press, Inc., 1970. 213 pp. $25.00.

1667. ———. *Lake of the Sky.* 1928; rpt. Chicago: Charles T. Powner Company, 1971. $4.95.

1668. James, Harry C. *A Day with Honau—A Hopi Indian Boy.* Chicago: Melmont Publishers, Inc., 1957. (Grades 2-5) $2.75.

1669. ———. *A Day in Oraibi, a Hopi Indian Village.* Chicago: Melmont Publishers, Inc., 1959. (Grades 2-5) $3.25.

1670. ———. *An Indian Boy of the Grand Canyon.* Los Angeles: Ward Ritchie Press, Inc., 1969. (Grades 3-6) $3.95.

1671. ———. *Pages From Hopi History.* Tucson: University of Arizona Press, 1971.

1672. ———. *Red Man—White Man.* San Antonio, Texas: Naylor Company, 1957. (Grades 6 up) $5.95.

1673. James H. L. *Acoma, People of the White Rock.* Glorieta, New Mexico: Rio Grande Press, 1970. $10.00.

1674. Jayne, Mitchell, F. *Old Fish Hawk.* Pocket Book. New York: Pocket Books, 1970. 216 pp. $ .95.

1675. Jenkins, Mildred. *Before the White Man Came.* Portland, Oregon: Binfords and Mort, Publishers, 1970. (Grades 5-6) $3.00.

1676. * Jenks, A. E. *Minnesota's Browns Valley Man and Associated Burial Artifacts.* 1937; rpt. New York: Kraus Reprint Corp., 1970. $3.00.

1677. Jenness, Aylette. *Dwellers of the Tundra: Life in an Alaskan Eskimo Village.* New York: Macmillan, 1970. (Grades 7 up) 112 pp. $5.95.

1678. ———. *Gussuk Boy.* Chicago: Follett Publishing Company, 1967. (Grades 4-6) $2.95.

1679. Jenness, Diamond. *Dawn in Arctic Alaska.* Minneapolis: University of Minnesota Press, 1957. $4.75.

1680. ———. *The Life of the Copper Eskimos.* Part A of Vol. XII. A Report of the Canadian Arctic Expedition, 1913-18. 1922; rpt. New York: Johnson Reprint, 1970. 277 pp.

1681. ———. *The People of the Twilight.* Chicago: The University of Chicago Press, 1928 (rptd. 1959). 251 pp.

1682. ———, ed. *The American Aborigines: Their Origin and Antiquity.* A Collection of Papers by Ten Authors . . . 1933; rpt. New York: Russell and Russell, 1972. $19.00.

1683. * Jennings, Jesse D. *Danger Cave*. With a Chapter on Textiles by Sara Sue Rudy. 1957; rpt. New York: Kraus Reprint Co., 1971. $25.00.

1684. ——. *Prehistory of North America*. New York: McGraw-Hill, 1968. $11.30.

1685. Jennings, Jesse D., and Edward Norbeck, eds. *Prehistoric Man in the New World*. Chicago: University of Chicago Press, 1964. Papers delivered at Rice University, November 9-10, 1962. 633 pp.

1686. * Jessett, Thomas E. *The Indian Side of the Whitman Massacre*. Rpt. Fairfield, Washington: Ye Galleon Press, 1970. $2.00.

1687. Jett, Stephen. *Navajo Wildlands: As Long As the Rivers Shall Run*. San Francisco: Sierra Club Books, 1971. $25.00.

1688. * Johnson, Clifton. *Unredeemed Captive*. Rpt. Fairfield, Washington: Ye Galleon Press, 1970. $3.50.

1689. * Johnson, Dorothy M. *A Man Called Horse and Other Stories*. New York: Ballantine Books, Inc., 1970. $ .75. Originally titled *Indian Country*.

1690. * Johnson, Elden. *Prehistoric Peoples of Minnesota*. St. Paul: Minnesota Historical Society, 1970. 26 pp. $1.50.

1691. Johnson, Enid. *Cochise: Great Apache Chief*. New York: Julian Messner, Inc., 1953. (Grades 6 up) $3.50.

1692. Johnson, F. Roy. *The Algonquians: Indians of the Part of the New World First Visited by the English*. Vol. I: Prehistory and Culture. Vol. II: History and Traditions. Murfreesboro, North Carolina: Johnson Publishing Company, 1972. $6.50 / $8.50.

1693. Johnson, Kenneth M. *K-Three Hundred Forty Four (Or, The Indians of California Versus the United States)*. Los Angeles: Dawson's Book Shop, 1966. $7.50.

1694. Johnson, Olga W. *The Flathead and the Kootenuy*. Glendale, California: Arthur H. Clark, 1969. $13.50.

1695. * Johnston, Bernice. *Speaking of Indians: with an Accent on the Southwest*. Tucson: University of Arizona Press, 1970. 112 pp. $2.50.

1696. Johnston, Charles H. *Famous Indian Chiefs*. 1909; rpt. Facsimile ed. Essay Index Reprint Series. Freeport, New York: Books for Libraries, 1972. $16.75.

1697. Johnston, Charles M. *The Valley of the Six Nations: A Collection of Documents on the Indian Lands of the Grand River*. Toronto: University of Toronto Press, 1965. $12.50.

1698. Johnston, Johanna. *The Indians and the Strangers*. New York: Dodd, Mead, 1972. (Grades 2 up) $4.50.

1699. Jones, Charles, ed. *Look to the Mountain Top*. San Jose, Calif.: H. M. Gousha, 1972. $6.95. In paper: $3.95.

1700. Jones, Charles G. *Antiquities of the Southern Indians, Particularly of the Georgia Tribes.* 1873; rpt. Spartanburg, North Carolina: Reprint Co., 1972. $21.00.

1701. Jones, David. *The Journal of Two Visits Made to Some Nations of Indians on the West Side of the River Ohio in the Years 1772 and 1773 by the Rev. David Jones.* 1774; rpt. First American Frontier Series. New York: Arno Press, 1971. $6.00.

1702. Jones, David Earle. *Sanapia: Comanche Medicine Woman.* New York: Holt, Rinehart and Winston, Inc., 1972. 128 pp.

1703. Jones, Douglas C. *The Treaty of Medicine Lodge: the Story of the Great Treaty Council as Told by Eyewitnesses.* Norman: University of Oklahoma Press, 1966. (Council in fall, 1867 with leaders of Southern plains Indians, in Kansas, near Medicine Lodge.) 237 pp. $6.95.

1704. Jones, Gene. *Where the Wing Blew Free.* New York: Grosset and Dunlap, 1970. $4.95. Jones was an Indian captive.

1705. * Jones, J., ed. *Precolumbian Art in New York Private Collections.* Greenwich, Connecticut: New York Graphic Society, Ltd., 1970. $6.00.

1706. Jones, Jayne C. *The American Indian in America.* Minneapolis: Lerner Publications, 1972. (Grades 5-11) $3.95.

1707. Jones, Livingston F. *A Study of the Talingets of Alaska.* 1914; rpt. New York: Johnson Reprint Corp., 1970. $12.50.

1708. Jones, Louis T. *Amerindian Education.* San Antonio, Texas: Naylor Company, 1972. $5.95.

1709. ———. *Aboriginal American Oratory.* Los Angeles: Southwest Museum, 1965. 136 pp.

1710. ———. *Highlights of Puebloland.* San Antonio, Texas: Naylor Company, 1968. (Grades 6-9) 107 pp. $4.95.

1711. ———. *The Indian Cultures of the Southwest.* San Antonio, Texas: Naylor Company, 1967. (Grades 8 up) 77 pp. $3.95.

1712. ———. *Indians at Work and Play.* San Antonio, Texas: Naylor Company, 1971. (Grades 7 up) $6.95.

1713. ———. *Red Man's Trail.* San Antonio, Texas: Naylor Company, 1967. (Grades 8 up) 83 pp. $3.95.

1714. ———. *So Say The Indians.* San Antonio, Texas: Naylor Company, 1970. 191 pp. $6.95.

1715. Jones, Oakah L. *Pueblo Warriors and the Spanish Conquest.* Norman: University of Oklahoma Press, 1966. $6.95.

1716. Jones, Peter. *History of the Ojbway Indians: With Especial Reference to their Conversion to Christianity.* 1861; rpt. Select Bibliographies Reprint Series. Freeport, New York: Books for Libraries Press, 1970. 278 pp. $12.50.

1717. Jones, Philip M. See No. 4020.

1718. Jones, Robert H. *The Civil War in the Northwest*. Norman: University of Oklahoma Press, 1961. $6.95.

1719. * Jorgensen, Joseph G. *Salish Language and Culture: A Statistical Analysis of Internal Relationships, History and Evolution*. Language Science Monographs, Vol. XI. Rpt. The Hague: Mouton Publishers, 1969. 173 pp. $10.50. Also: Rpt. Language Science Monographs, Vol. 3. Bloomington: Indiana Research Center for the Language Sciences, 1969. $9.00.

1720. * Josephy, Alvin M. *The Indian Heritage of America*. New York: Bantam Books, 1969. 397 pp. $1.65. Also: New York: Alfred Knopf, 1968. $10.00.

1721. ———. *Indian Resistance: The Patriot Chiefs*. New York: Grossman Publishers, 1970. $3.95.

1722. * ———. *The Nez Perce Indians and the Opening of the Northwest*. New Haven: Yale University Press, 1965. 705 pp. $20.00. In paper: Abridged edition. New Haven: Yale University Press, 1971. $5.95.

1723. * Josephy, Alvin M. *Patriotic Chiefs: A Chronicle of American Indian Leadership*. New York: Viking Press, 1961. Book of biographies. 364 pp. $5.75. In paper: Viking Compass edition, 1969. $1.75.

1724. * ———. *Red Power: The American Indians' Fight for Freedom*. New York: McGraw-Hill, 1970. $13.50. In paper: $2.95.

1725. Judson, Katherine B. *Early Days in Old Oregon*. Seattle: Binfords and Mort, 1970. (Grades 7-9) $4.50.

1726. * Judge, W. James. *The Paleoindians of the Central Rio Grande Valley*. Albuquerque: University of New Mexico Press, 1972. 368 pp. $7.00.

1727. * Kahlenberg, Mary, and Tony Berlant. *The Navaho Blankets. 1800-1899*. Los Angeles: Los Angeles County Museum of Art Bookshop, 1972. Also: New York: Praeger Publishers, 1972. $10.00.

1728. Kappler, Charles J., ed. *Indian Affairs, Laws and Treaties*. 4 vols. Washington, D.C.: Government Printing Office, 1904-1909; rpt. 2 vols. New York: Burt Franklin, Publishers, 1967. $50.00. Also: Rpt. 5 vols. 1904-1941. New York: AMS Press, 1971. $475.00.

1729. ———. *Indian Treaties 1778-1883*. New York: Interland Publishing Company, 1971. 1110 pp. $67.50.

1730. Kastner, George C. *Riders from the West*. Portland Oregon: Binfords and Mort, Pub., 1970. $3.00.

1731. Keating, William H. *A Narrative of the Expedition to the Source of St. Peter's River*. 1825; rpt. Facsimile edition. Minneapolis: Ross and Haines, Inc., 1970. $10.00.

1732. Keegan, Marcia. *The Taos Indians and Their Sacred Blue Lake*. New York: Julian Messner, Inc., 1972. (Grades 3-5) $4.95.

1733. Keesing, Felix M. *The Menominee Indians of Wisconsin: A Study of Three Centuries of Cultural Contact and Changes*. 1939; rpt. New York: Johnson Reprint Corp., 1971. $13.00.

1734. Keiser, Albert. *The Indian in American Literature*. New York: Oxford Press, 1933; rpt. Octagon Books, 1970. 312 pp. $10.00. Also: New York: Gordon Publishers, 1972. $11.25.

1735. Keith, Harold. *Komantcia*. New York: Thomas Y. Crowell, 1965. (Grades 7 up) $4.50.

1736. Keithan, Edward L. *Alaska for the Curious*. Seattle: Superior Publishing Company, 1967. $1.95.

1737. ———. *Eskimo Adventure*. Seattle, Washington: Superior Publishing Company, 1963. $5.95.

1738. ———. *Monuments in Cedar*. Seattle, Washington: Superior Publishing Company, 1963. 160 pp. $12.95.

1739. * Kelemen, Pal. *Medieval American Art: Masterpieces of the New World Before Columbus*. 2 vols. New York: Dover Publications, 1969. $4.50; $3.75. Also: 3rd ed. rev. Gloucester, Mass.: Peter Smith, 1972. $15.00.

1740. * Kelly, Fanny. *My Captivity Among the Sioux Indians*. New York: Corinth Books, 1962. $1.75. Also: Gloucester, Mass.: Peter Smith, 1971. $4.00.

1741. Kelly, Isabel T. See Nos. 4024 and 4031.

1742. Kelly, Lawrence C. *The Navajo Indians and Federal Indian Policy, 1900-1935*. Tucson: University of Arizona Press, 1968. 221 pp. $7.50.

1743. ———. *Navajo Roundup*. Boulder, Colorado: Pruet Publishing Company, 1970. $8.95.

1744. Kelley, LeRoy V. *Range Men: The Story of the Ranchers and Indians of Alberta*. 1913; rpt. Ann Arbor, Michigan: University of Microfilms, 1965. $22.50.

1745. Kelly, William H. *Cocopa Ethnography: Study of the Indian Tribes of the Colorado River Delta*. Tucson: University of Arizona Press, 1972.

1746. Kendall, Lace. *Mud Ponies*. New York: Coward-McCann, Inc., 1963. (Grades 2-5) $3.49.

1747. * Kennard, Edward. *Field Mouse Goes to War*. Illustrated by Fred Kabotie. Pueblo Series. Washington, D.C.: Division of Education, Bureau of Indian Affairs, [c. 1950]. (Grades 3-7) $ .55.

1748. * ———. *Little Hopi*. Illustrated by Charles Laloma. Pueblo Series. Washington, D.C.: Division of Education, Bureau of Indian Affairs, 1948. (Grades 3-7) 100 pp. $ .50.

1749. Kennedy, John H. *Jesuit and Savage in New France*. 1950; rpt. Hamden, Conn.: Shoe String Press, 1971. $7.50.

1750. Kennedy, Michael S., ed. *The Red Man's West*. True Stories of the Frontier Indians from *Montana*, The Magazine of Western History. New York: Hastings House, 1965. 342 pp. $10.00.

1751. * Kennedy Paul E. *North American Indian Design Coloring Book*. New York: Dover Publications, 1971. 46 pp.

1752. Kenner, Charles L. *A History of New Mexican-Plains Indian Relations*. Norman: University of Oklahoma Press, 1969. 250 pp. $6.95.

1753. Kenton, Edna. *With Hearts Courageous*. Black and Gold Library Book. New York: Liveright, 1971. $5.95.

1754. ——, ed. *Jesuit Relations*. New York: Vanguard Press, 1970. $10.00.

1755. Ketchum, William. *The Authentic and Comprehensive History of the Buffalo*. 2 vols. 1864-1865; rpt. St. Clair Shores, Michigan: Scholarly Press, 1971. $21.00.

1756. * Keur, Dorothy L. *Big Bead Mesa: An Archaeological Study of Navaho Acculturation, 1745-1812*. 1941; rpt. New York: Kraus Reprint Co., 1971. $7.00.

1757. Kidder, Alfred V. *Explorations in Southeastern Utah in 1908*. Rpt. Sante Fe: Southwest Book Service, 1969. $4.50.

1758. * ——. *Introduction to the Study of Southwestern Archaeology*. New Haven: Yale University Press, 1962. $10.00. In paper: Yale University Press, 1970. $3.25.

1759. * ——. *The Pottery of the Pajarito Plateau and of Some Adjacent Regions in New Mexico*. 1915; rpt. New York: Kraus Reprint Co., 1971. $5.00.

1760. Kilpatrick, Jack F., and Anne G. Kilpatrick, eds. *New Echota Letters: Contributions of Samuel A. Worcester to the Cherokee Phoenix*. Dallas: Southern Methodist University Press, 1968. 140 pp. $5.00. Authors are Cherokee.

1761. ——, eds. *Run Toward the Nightland: Magic of the Oklahoma Cherokees*. Dallas: Southern Methodist University Press, 1967. $5.00.

1762. ——, eds. *The Shadow of Sequoyah, Social Documents of the Cherokees 1862 - 1964*. Civilization of the American Indian Series, No. 81. Norman: University of Oklahoma Press, 1965. 129 pp.

1763. ——, eds. *Walk in Your Soul: Love Incantations of the Oklahoma Cherokees*. Dallas: Southern Methodist University Press, 1965. 164 pp. $5.00.

1764. * Kimbal, Yeffe, and Jean Anderson. *The Art of American Indian Cooking*. Garden City, New York: Doubleday and Company, 1965. 215 pp. Author is Osage. In paper: New York: Avon Books, Inc., 1970.

1765. * King, A. Richard. *The School of Mopass: A Problem of Identity*. Case Studies in Education and Culture Series. New York: Holt, Rinehart and Winston, 1967. $2.75.

1766. * King, Cecil S. *Navajo New World Readers* (No. 1: "Away to School"; No. 2.: "The Flag of My Country"). Lawrence, Kansas: Haskell Press, 1970. .15 / .30. English and Navajo Texts.

1767. King, Charles. *Campaigning with Crook*. Western Frontier Library, No. 25. Norman: University of Oklahoma Press, 1964. $2.95.

1768. ——. *Campaigning with Crook and Stories of Army Life*. March of American Series. 1890; rpt. Ann Arbor, Michigan: University Microfilms, 1966. $7.75.

1769. ——. *Starlight Ranch and Other Stories of Army Life on the Frontier*. 1890; rpt. Short Story Index Reprint Series, Vol. I. Freeport: New York: Books for Libraries, Inc., 1970. $8.00.

1770. * King, Dale S. *Nalakihu: Excavations at a Pueblo Three Site on Wupatki National Monument*. Globe, Arizona: Southwest Parks and Monuments Association, 1949. $4.00.

1771. King, James T. *War Eagle: A Life of General Eugene A. Carr*. Lincoln: University of Nebraska Press, 1963. $6.00.

1772. King, Jeff, and Maud Oakes. *Where the Two Came to Their Father: A Navaho War Ceremonial*. Rev. ed. Bollingen Series, No. 1. Princeton: Princeton University Press, 1969. $17.50.

1773. * Kinietz, W. Vernon. *The Indian of the Western Great Lakes 1615-1760*. 1940; rpt. Ann Arbor Paperback. Ann Arbor: University of Michigan Press, 1965. 427 pp. $5.95. In paper: $2.95.

1774. Kirk, Ruth. *David, Young Chief of the Quileutes: An American Indian Today*. New York: Harcourt Brace Jovanovich, 1967. (Grades 3-5) $3.50.

1775. ——. *The Oldest Man in America: An Adventure in Archaeology*. New York: Harcourt Brace Jovanovich, 1970. (Grades 4-6) $4.75.

1776. Kirkland, Forrest, and W. W. Newcomb. *Rock Art of the Texas Indians*. Austin: University of Texas Press, 1966. $12.50.

1777. Kirkwood, Charlotte M. *The Nez Perce Indian War Under Chiefs Joseph and Whitebird*. Grangeville, Idaho: Idaho County Free Press, 1928.

1778. * Kleivan, Helge. *The Eskimos of Northwest Labrador*. Boston, Mass.: Universitetsforlaget, 1966. $5.85.

1779. Klimek, Stanislaw. See No. 4037.

1780. * Kluckhohn, Clyde. *Navaho Witchcraft.* Rpt. Boston: Beacon Press, 1962. $4.95. In paper: $2.95.

1781. ——. *To the Foot of the Rainbow.* Rpt. Glorieta, New Mexico: Rio Grande Press, Inc., 1967. $7.00.

1782. * Kluckhohn, Clyde, and Dorothea Leighton. *The Navaho.* 1946 Rev. ed. by Lucy H. Wales and Richard Kluckhohn. Anchor Books. The Natural History Library. Garden City, New York: Doubleday and Company, 1962. 355 pp. $1.95. Also: Cambridge: Harvard University Press, 1946. $5.00.

1783. * Kluckhohn, Clyde, and Leland C. Wyman. *An Introduction :ɔ Navajo: Chant Practice.* The American Anthropological Association Memoirs Vol. 35, 1940; rpt. New York: Kraus Reprint Co., 1970. $10.00.

1784. Kluckhohn, Clyde, et al. *Navaho Material Culture.* Cambridge: Harvard University Press, 1971. $25.00.

1785. * Kniffen, Fred B. See Nos. 4023 and 4036.

1786. Knight, Oliver. *Following the Indian Wars.* Norman: University of Oklahoma Press, 1960. 348 pp. $8.95.

1787. Kohl, Johann G. *The Kitchi Gami.* Minneapolis: Ross and Haines, Inc., 1970. $10.00.

1788. Kohn, Bernice. *Talking Leaves: The Story of Sequoyah.* New York: Hawthorn Books, Inc., 1969. (Grades 1-4) 32 pp. $4.95.

1789. * Kopit, Arthur. *Indians: A Play.* New York: Hill and Wang, 1969. 94 pp.

1790. * ——. *Indians.* A Play. With a Dialogue Between Arthur Kopit and John Lahr. New York: Bantam Books, 1971. 114 pp. $1.65.

1791. * Kowta, Makoto. *The Sayles Complex: A Late Milling Stone Horizon Assemblage from Cajon Pass, California, and The Ecological Implications of its Scraper Planes.* University of California Publications in Anthropology Series, Vol. 6. Berkeley: University of California Press, 1969. $2.50.

1792. * Krause, Aurel. *The Tlingit Indians: Results of a Trip to the Northwest Coast of America and the Bering Straits.* Trans. Erna Gunther. American Ethnological Society Monographs. Seattle: University of Washington Press, 1970. $5.95. In paper: $2.95.

1793. Krickerberg, Walter, et al. *Pre-Columbian Religions.* Ed. E. O. James. Trans. Stanley Davis. History of Religion Series, Vol. 6. New York: Holt, Rinehart and Winston, Inc., 1969. $8.95.

1794. * Krieger, Alex D. See No. 4047.

1795. * Krieger, Herbert W. *The Indian Villages of Southeast Alaska.* 1927; rpt. Facsimile Edition Extracts. Seattle: Shorey Publications, 1970. $2.50.

1796. Kroeber, Alfred L. *Native Tribes Map*. Berkeley: University of California Press, 1971. $ .50. Also See Nos. 4002-4047, many of which contain works by Kroeber as sole or joint author.

1797. *——. *Walapai Ethnography*. 1935; rpt. Sante Fe, New Mexico: William Gannon, 1971. $12.50. In paper: New York: Kraus Reprint Co., 1971. $15.00.

1798. * Kroeber, Theodora. *Ishi In Two Worlds*. A Biography of the Last Wild Indian in North America. Berkeley: University of California Press, 1969. 258 pp. In paper: $2.25.

1799. ——. *Ishi, Last of His Tribe*. Berkeley: Parnasus Press, 1964. (Grades 4-10) $4.50.

1800. * Kroeber, Theodora, and Robert F. Heizer. *Almost Ancestors: First Californians*. New York: Ballantine Books, Inc., 1970. 168 pp. $3.95. Also: San Francisco: Sierra Club Books, 1968. $15.00.

1801. Kubiac, William. *The Great Lakes Indians*. Grand Rapids, Michigan: Baker Book House, 1970. 255 pp. $14.95.

1802. Kubler, George. *Art and Architecture of Ancient America*. Baltimore: Penquin Books, Inc., 1961. $18.50.

1803. Kubler, George. *Santos: The Religious Folk Art of New Mexico*. Amon Carter Museum of Western Art Publications. Austin: University of Texas Press, 1971. $2.00.

1804. Kuipers, A. H. *The Squamish Language: Grammar, Texts, Dictionary*. 2 vols. Rpt. Vol. 1967; Vol. II, 1969. Rpt. The Hague: Mouton Publishers. 470 pp / 98 pp. $36.00 / $7.50.

1805. * Kurz, Rudolph F. *The Journal of Rudolph Friederick Kurz: An Account of His Experiences Among Fur Traders on the Upper Mississippi and the Upper Missouri Rivers During the Years 1846 to 1852*. Ed. J. N. Newitt. Trans. Myrtis Jarrell. 1937; rpt. Lincoln: University of Nebraksa Press, 1970. $2.75.

1806. * La Barre, Weston. *The Peyote Cult*. Rev. ed. Archon Books. Hamden, Connecticut: Shoe String Press, 1964. $7.50. In paper: New York: Schocken Books, 1969. 260 pp. $2.45.

1807. Lacher, Hermann J., trans. *Detailed Reports on the Saltzburger Emigrants Who Settled in America, 1733-1734*. Vol. I. Wormsloe Foundation Publications, No. 9. Athens: University of Georgia Press, 1968. $7.50.

1808. LaFarge, Oliver. *The American Indian*. Deluxe Golden Book. Racine, Wisconsin: Western Publishing Company, Inc., 1960. (Grades 7 up) 215 pp. $5.95.

1809. ——. *Behind the Mountains*. Boston: Houghton Mifflin Company, 1956. $4.00.

1810. ——. *Cochise of Arizona: The Pipe of Peace is Broken*. New York: E. P. Dutton and Company, 1953. (Grades 5-9) $4.50.

1811. *——. *Laughing Boy*. Signet Book. New York: New American Library, Inc., 1971. Reprint of the novel which won the Pulitzer Prize in 1929. 192 pp. $ .95.

1812. ——. *The Man with the Calabash*. Boston: Houghton Mifflin Company, 1966, $4.95.

1813. ——. *A Pictorial History of the American Indian*. New York: Crown Publishers, 1956. 272 pp.

1814. ——, et al., eds. *An Introduction to American Indian Art*. 2 vols. in 1. Rpt. Glorieta, New Mexico: Rio Grande Press, Inc., 1971. $10.00.

1815. LaFlesche, Francis. *A Dictionary of the Osage Language*. U.S. Government Ethnology Bureau Bulletin No. 109. Washington, D.C.: Government Printing Office, 1932. 406 pp. Author is Omaha.

1816. *——. *The Middle Five: Indian Schoolboys of the Omaha Tribe*. Madison: University of Wisconsin Press, 1963. 152 pp. $2.50.

1817. ——. *The Osage Tribe*. Part I : Rite of the Chiefs; Sayings of the Ancient Men. Bureau of American Ethnology. *36th Annual Report*. Washington, D.C., 1921, pp. 37-597.

1818. ——. *The Osage Tribe*. Part II: The Rite of Vigil. Bureau of American Ethnology. *39th Annual Report*. Washington, D.C., 1925, pp. 1-630.

1819. ——. *The Osage Tribe*. Part III: Two Versions of the Child-Naming Rite. Bureau of American Ethnology. *43rd Annual Report*. Washington, D.C., 1928, pp. 23-164.

1820. ——. *The Osage Tribe*. Part IV: Songs of Wa-xo-be. Bureau of American Ethnology. *45th Annual Report*. Washington, D.C., 1930, pp. 523-833.

1821. ——. *The Osage Tribe*. Landmarks in Anthropology. New York: Johnson Reprint Corp., 1970.

1822. ——. *The War Ceremony and Peace Ceremony of the Osage Indians*. U.S. Government Ethnology Bureau Bulletin No. 101. Washington, D.C.: Government Printing Office, 1939. 280 pp.

1823. LaFlesche, Francis, and Alice Cunninghan Fletcher. *The Omaha Tribe*. Washington, D.C.: Government Printing Office, 1911; rpt. New York: Johnson Reprint Corp., 1970. 672 pp.

1824. *——. *A Study of Omaha Indian Music*. Harvard University Peabody Museum of Archaeology and Ethnology Papers Series. 1893; rpt. New York: Kraus Reprint Co., 1971. $6.00.

1825. * Laguna, Frederica De. *The Prehistory of North America as Seen From the Yukon*. 1947; rpt. New York: Kraus Reprint Co., 1971. $28.00.

111

1826. * Lambert, Marjorie F., and J. Richard Ambler. *Survey and Excavation of Caves in Hidalgo County, New Mexico.* School of American Research Monographs, No. 25. Albuquerque: University of New Mexico Press, 1961. $ .80.

1827. * Lambert, Marjorie F., and Spencer L. Rogers. *PAA-KO, Archaeological Chronicle of an Indian Village in North Central New Mexico.* School of American Research Monograph No. 19. 2 vols. Albuquerque: University of New Mexico Press, 1954. 183 pp. / 48 pp.

1828. Lamphere, Marjorie F. *To Run After Them: The Cultural Bases of Cooperation in a Navajo Community.* Tucson: University of Arizona Press, 1972.

1829. Lampman, Evelyn S. *Half-Breed.* New York: Doubleday Doran, 1970. (Grades 4-6) $3.95.

1830. ———. *Once Upon the Little Big Horn.* New York: Thomas Y. Crowell, 1971. (Grades 5-8) 160 pp. $4.50.

1831. ———. *Navaho Sister.* New York: Doubleday Doran, 1956. (Grades 4-7) $3.95.

1832. Lancaster, Richard. *Piegan: A Look from Within at the Life, Times, and Legacy of an American Indian Tribe.* Garden City, New York: Doubleday and Company, 1966. 359 pp. $4.95.

1833. Landes, Ruth. *The Mystic Lake Sioux.* Sociology of the Mdewakantonwan Santee. Madison: University of Wisconsin Press, 1968. 224 pp. $10.00.

1834. ———. *Ojibwa Religion and the Midewiwin.* Madison: University of Wisconsin Press, 1968. 250 pp. $10.00.

1835. ———. *Ojibwa Sociology.* Columbia University Contributions to Anthropology, Vol. 29. 1937; rpt. New York: AMS Press, Inc., 1969. 144 pp. $7.50.

1836. ———. *Ojibwa Woman.* Columbia University Contributions to Anthropology Series, Vol. 31. 1938; rpt. New York: AMS Press, 1969. $12.50. In paper: New York: W. W. Norton and Company, 1971. $2.25.

1837. ———. *The Prairie Potawatomi: Tradition and Ritual in the Twentieth Century.* Madison: University of Wisconsin Press, 1970. 420 pp. $12.50.

1838. * Landgraf, John L. *Land-Use in the Ramah Area of New Mexico: An Anthropological Approach to Area Study.* 1954; rpt. New York: Kraus Reprint Co., 1971. $10.00.

1839. Lane, Jack C., ed. *Chasing Geronimo: The Journal of Leonard Wood, May-September, 1886.* Albuquerque: University of New Mexico Press, 1970. 160 pp. $6.95.

1840. * Langdon, Margaret. *The Grammar of Diegueno: The Mesa Grande Dialect.* University of California Publications in Linguistics Series, Vol. 66. Berkeley: University of California Press, 1970. $3.50.

1841. * Lange, Charles H. *Cochiti A New Mexico Pueblo, Past and Present.* Austin: University of Texas Press, 1959; rpt. Carbondale: Southern Illinois University Press, 1968. 618 pp. $10.00. In paper: SIU Press. $4.95.

1842. Lange, Charles H., and Carroll L. Riley. *The Southwestern Journals of Adolph F. Bandelier, 1880-1882.* See Bandelier, Adolph F., No. 612.

1843. * Lankford, John, ed. *Captain John Smith's America: Selections from his Writings.* New York: Harcourt Brace and World, 1970. $2.25.

1844. * Lanning, Edward P. See No. 4049.

1845. Lantis, Margaret. *Alaskan Eskimo Ceremonialism.* American Ethnological Society Monographs. Seattle: University of Washington Press, 1947. $5.95.

1846. ——. *Eskimo Childhood and Interpersonal Relationships: Nunivak Biographies and Genealogies.* American Ethnological Society Monographs. Seattle: University of Washington Press, 1960. $5.95.

1847. ——, ed. *Ethnohistory in Southwestern Alaska and the Southern Yukon: Method and Content.* Rpt. Studies in Anthropology, No. 7. Lexington: University Press of Kentucky, 1970. $9.75.

1848. La Pointe, Frank. *The Sioux Today.* New York: Crowell-Collier Press, 1972. 132 pp. $4.95.

1849. Larpenteur, Charles. *Forty Years a Fur Trader on the Upper Missouri.* 1898; rpt. Minneapolis: Ross and Haines, 1970. $10.00.

1850. Lauber, Almon W. *Indian Slavery in Colonial Times Within the Present Limits of the United States.* Columbia University Studies in the Social Sciences Series No. 134. 1913; rpt. New York: AMS Press, 1968. $12.50.

1851. * Laubin, Reginald, and Gladys Laubin. *The Indian Tipi: Its History, Construction, and Use.* Norman: University of Oklahoma Press, 1957; rpt. 1969. 208 pp. $6.95. In paper: New York: Ballantine Books, 1971. 270 pp. $1.65.

1852. Laumer, Frank. *Massacre.* Gainesville: University of Florida Press, 1968. $7.50.

1853. * La Violette, Forrest E. *Struggle for Survival: British Columbia and the Coastal Indians.* 1961; rpt. Toronto: University of Toronto Press, 1972.

1854. * Lawlor, Florine. *Southern Nevada Indian Trails.* Glendale, California: La Siesta Press, 1970. $1.95.

1855. Lawson, John. *New Voyage to Carolina.* 1709; rpt. March of America Series. Ann Arbor, Michigan: University Microfilms, 1966. $6.75. Also: Ed. Hugh T. Lefler. Limited edition. Chapel Hill: University of North Carolina Press, 1967. $25.00.

1856. Lawson, Marie. *Pocahontas and Captain John Smith.* New York: Random House, 1971. $2.95.

1857. Lawson, Marion. *Proud Warrior: The Story of Black Hawk.* New York: Hawthorn Books, Inc., 1968. (Grades 5-9) 175 pp. $3.95.

1858. * Leach, Douglas E. *Flintlock and Tomahawk: New England in King Philip's War.* New York: W. W. Norton and Company, 1958. 304 pp. In paper: Norton Library. New York: W. W. Norton and Company, Inc., 1966. $2.25.

1859. ——. *The Northern Colonial Frontier, 1607-1763.* Histories of the American Frontier Series. New York: Holt, Rinehart and Winston, 1966. $7.95.

1860. Leacock, Eleanor B., and Nancy O. Lurie, eds. *North American Indians in Historical Perspective.* New York: Random House, 1971. 512 pp. $9.95.

1861. Leavitt, Jerome E. *America and Its Indians.* Chicago: Children's Press, Inc., 1963. (Grades 4-8) 220 pp. $5.50.

1862. Le Beau, Claude. *Adventures Du Sr. C. Le Beau, Avocat En Parlement, Ou Voyage Curieux et Nouveau, Parmi les Sauvages De l'Amerique Septentrionale.* 1738; rpt. 2 vols. New York: Johnson Reprint Corp., 1970. $25.00.

1863. Leckie, William H. *The Military Conquest of the Southern Plains.* Norman: University of Oklahoma Press, 1963. 269 pp. $7.95.

1864. Le Clercq, Chretien. *First Establishment of the Faith in New France.* 2 vols. 1881; rpt. New York: AMS Press, 1970. $28.00 / $55.00.

1865. ——. *New Relation of Gaspesia, with the Customs and Religion of the Gaspesian.* 1910; rpt. Ed. William F. Ganong. Westport, Connecticut: Greenwood Press, Inc., 1968. $29.25.

1866. Lederer, John. *The Discoveries of John Lederer, in Three Small Marches from Virginia to the West of Carolina.* 1672; rpt. March of America Series. Ann Arbor: University Microfilms, 1966. $3.55.

1867. * Lee, E. Lawrence. *The Indian Wars in North Carolina, 1663-1763.* Rpt. Raleigh: North Carolina State Department of Archives and History, 1968. $ .50.

1868. Lee, L. P. *History of the Spirit Lake Massacre!* Fairfield, Washington: Ye Galleon Press. 489 copies printed. Originally published as: *History of the Spirit Lake Massacre! 8th March, 1857, and of Miss Abigail Gardiner's Three Month's* (sic) *Captivity Among the Indians. According to Her Own Account as Given to L. P. Lee.* New Britain, Connecticut: L. P. Lee, Publisher, 1857. 47 pp.

1869. Lee, Nelson. *Three Years Among the Comanches: The Narrative of Nelson Lee, the Texas Ranger.* Western Frontier Library, No. 9. 1957; rpt. Norman: University of Oklahoma Press, 1967. $2.95.

1870. * Left-Handed Mexican Clansmen, et al. *The Trouble at Round Rock.* Lawrence, Kansas: Haskell Press, 1970. $ .55.

1871. Leigh, Rufus W. See No. 4023 and 4034.

1872. * Leighton, Alexander H., and Dorothea C. Leighton. *Gregorio, the Hand-Trembler: A Psychobiological Personality Study of a Navaho Indian.* 1949; rpt. New York: Kraus Reprint Co., 1971. $13.00.

1873. ——. *Navaho Door: An Introduction to Navaho Life.* 1944; rpt. New York: Russell and Russell, 1967. 149 pp. $12.50.

1874. * Leighton, Dorothea C., and John Adair. *People of the Middle Place. A Study of the Zuni Indians.* New Haven: Human Relations Area Files, Inc., 1966. 171 pp. $6.00.

1875. Leighton, Dorothea, and Clyde Kluckhohn. *Children of the People.* 1947; rpt. New York: Octagon Books, 1970. 277 pp. $9.50.

1876. Lemert, Edwin M. See No. 4044.

1877. Lenski, Lois. *Indian Captive: The Story of Mary Jemison.* Philadelphia: J. P. Lippincott Company, 1941. (Grades 7-9) $5.19.

1878. ——. *The Little Sioux Girl.* Philadelphia: J. B. Lippincott Company, 1958. (Grades K-3) $3.39.

1879. Leonard, Jonathan. *Ancient America.* Great Ages of Man Series. Published by Time-Life. Morristown, New Jersey: Silver Burdett Company, 1967. (Grades 7 up) $6.95.

1880. Lescarbot, Marc. *A History of New France.* 3 vols. 1907; rpt. Westport, Connecticut: Greenwood Press, Inc., 1968. $24.00 / $33.00 / $30.75.

1881. Lesser, Alexander. *The Pawnee Ghost Dance Hand Game.* Columbia University Contributions to Anthropology Series, Vol. 16. 1933; rpt. New York: AMS Press, 1969. $17.00.

1882. Letterman, Ed. *From Whole Log to No Log.* Minneapolis: Dillon Press, 1969. $8.50.

1883. Leupp, Francis E. *The Indian and His Problems.* 1910; rpt. Series in American Studies. New York: Johnson Reprint Corp., 1970. $12.00. Also: Poverty U.S.A. Historical Records Series: New York: Arno Press, 1971. $17.00.

1884. * Levine, Stuart, and Nancy O. Lurie, eds. See *The American Indian Today,* No. 531.

1885. * Lewis, Albert B. *The Tribes of the Columbia Valley and the Coast of Washington and Oregon.* 1905; rpt. New York: Kraus Reprint Co., 1970. $3.50.

1886. Lewis, Anna. *Chief Pushmataha: American Patriot: The Story of the Choctaws' Struggle for Survival.* New York: Exposition Press, 1959. 204 pp.

1887. Lewis, Claudia. *American Indian Families: The Impact of Change.* Chicago: University of Chicago Press, 1970. $8.75.

1888. ———. *Indian Families of the Northwest Coast. The Impact of Change.* Chicago: University of Chicago Press, 1970. 224 pp. $8.75.

1889. Lewis, Henry. *The Valley of the Mississippi Illustrated.* Ed. Bertha L. Heilbron. Trans. A. H. Postgieter. St. Paul: Minnesota Historical Society, 1967. $39.50.

1890. Lewis, Oscar. *The Effects of White Contact Upon Blackfoot Culture, With Special Reference to the Role of the Fur Trade.* Monographs of the American Ethnological Society, VI. New York: J. J. Augustin, Publisher, 1942; rpt. Seattle: University of Washington Press, 1966. 73 pp. $5.00.

1891. Lewis, Thomas M. and Madeline Kneberg. *Hiwassee Island: An Archaeological Account of Four Tennessee Indian Peoples.* 1946; rpt. Nashville: University of Tennessee Press, 1972. $8.95.

1892. * Lewis, Thomas M., and Madeline K. Lewis. *Eva: An Archaic Site.* Nashville: University of Tennessee Press, 1962. $3.00.

1893. * ———. *Tribes that Slumber: The Indians of the Tennessee Region.* Nashville: University of Tennessee Press, 1966. 196 pp. $7.50. In paper: $4.95.

1894. * Lighthall, J. L. *The Indian Folk Medicine Guide.* Eagle Books. New York: Popular Library Inc., 1972. $1.25.

1895. Lincke, Jack R. *Where the Sun Now Stands: The Nez Perce War with the United States.* New York: W. W. Norton and Company, 1972. $7.50.

1896. Lincoln, Charles H., ed. *Narratives of the Indian Wars, 1675-1699.* 1913; rpt. New York: Harper and Row, 1959. 312 pp. $5.75.

1897. Lindermann, Frank B. *Red Mother.* New York: John Day Company, 1932; rpt. as: *Pretty Shield, Medicine Woman of the Crows.* New York: John Day Company, 1972. $6.95.

1898. Lindquist, G. E. E. *The Red Man in the United States.* An Intimate Study of the Social, Economic, and Religious Life of the American Indian. New York: George H. Doran Company, 1921. 461 pp. Rpt. New York: Augustus M. Kelley, Pub., 1969. $15.00. Also: New York: Burt Franklin, Inc., $25.00.

1899. Linton, Ralph, ed. *Acculturation in Seven American Indian Tribes.* New York: Appleton-Century-Crofts, 1940; rpt. Gloucester, Mass.: Peter Smith, 1970. 526 pp. $7.50.

1900. * Lisitzky, Gene. *Four Ways of Being Human.* New York: Viking Press, 1956. (Grades 7 up) $4.53. In paper: $1.65.

1901. Lister, Florence, and Robert Lister. *Earl Morris and Southwestern Archaeology.* Albuquerque: University of New Mexico Press, 1968. $7.95.

1902. Llewellyn, Karl N., and E. Adamson Hoebel. *The Cheyenne Way: Conflict and Case Law in Primitive Jurisprudence.* Civilization of the American Indian Series, No. 21. 1953; rpt. Norman: University of Oklahoma Press, 1967. 360 pp. $8.95.

1903. * Lloyd, J. P. *The Message of an Indian Relic: Seattle's Own Totem Pole.* 1909; rpt. Facsimile ed. Seattle: Shorey Publications, 1972. $2.00.

1904. * Locke, Raymond F., ed. *The American Indian.* 1967; rpt. New York: Hawthorn Books, 1970. $5.95. Also: Los Angeles: Mankind Publishing Co., 1970. In paper: $1.75.

1905. Lockwood, Frank C. *The Apache Indians.* New York: The Macmillan Company, 1938.

1906. * Loeb, Edwin M. See Nos. 4019, 4025, and 4033.

1907. *Logan, The Last of the Race of Shikellemus, Chief of the Cayuga Nation.* 1868; rpt. Parsons, West Virginia: McClain Printing Company, 1972.

1908. Loh, Jules. *Lords of the Earth: A History of the Navajo Indians.* New York: Macmillan and Company, 1971. (Grades 7-12) $4.95.

1909. Long, John. *Voyages and Travels of an Indian Interpreter and Trader.* 1791; rpt. American Studies Series. New York: Johnson Reprint Corp., 1969. $9.00. Also: 1910 edition; rpt. New York: Plenum Publishing Company, 1969. $15.00.

1910. Longacre, William A. *Archaeology as Anthropology: A Case Study.* Anthropological Papers Series. Tucson: University of Arizona Press, 1969. $4.00.

1911. * ——, ed. *Reconstructing Prehistoric Pueblo Societies.* Albuquerque: University of New Mexico Press, 1970. Grew out of seminar held in 1968. 256 pp. $8.50. In paper: University of New Mexico Paperbacks. $3.95.

1912. * Longstreet, Stephen. *War Cries on Horseback: The Story of the Indian Wars of the Great Plains.* Garden City, New York: Doubleday and Company, 1970. 337 pp. $7.95. In paper: New York: Modern Literary Editions Pub. Co., 1970. 414 pp.

1913. Lorant, Stephen. *The New World.* New York: Hawthorn Books, Inc., 1965. $20.00.

1914. Loskiel, George H. *The History of the Missions of the United Brethren Among the Indians in North America.* 3 parts. Trans. Christian Latrobe. 1794; rpt. St. Clair Shores, Michigan: Scholarly Press, 1970. $13.00.

1915. Lothrop, Samuel K., et al. *Essays in Pre-Columbian Art and Archaeology.* Cambridge: Harvard University Press, 1961. $14.00.

1916. * Lott, Milton. *Dance Back the Buffalo.* New York: Pocketbooks, Inc., 1968. $ .75.

1917. Loudon, Archibald. *A Selection of Some of the Most Interesting Narratives of Outrages Committed by the Indians in Their Wars with the White People.* 2 vols. 1808; rpt. First American Frontier Series. New York: Arno Press, 1970. $30.00.

1918. Lowie, Robert H. *The Assiniboine.* Anthropological Papers of the American Museum of Natural History, Vol. IV, Part I. New York: Published by order of The Trustees, 1909. 270 pp. See also Nos. 4016, 4020, 4023, 4029, 4036, 4039, and 4040.

1919. * ——. *The Crow Indians.* New York: Farrar and Rinehart, 1935; rpt. 1956. $6.75. In paper: New York: Holt, Rinehart and Winston, 1970.

1920. * ——. *Indians of the Plains.* Garden City, New York: The Natural History Press, 1965. An American Museum Science Books Edition. Originally published by McGraw-Hill, 1954. In paper: 258 pp. $1.95.

1921. ——. *Plains Indian Age-Societies.* Historical and Comparative Summary. Anthropological Papers of the American Museum of Natural History. Vol. XI, Part XIII. New York: Published by Order of the Trustees, 1916.

1922. ——. *Primitive Society.* Rev. ed. Black and Gold Library. 1947; rpt. New York: Liveright, 1970. $6.95.

1923. Lummis, Charles F. *General Crook and the Apache Wars.* Rpt. Flagstaff, Arizona: Northland Press, 1966. $7.50.

1924. * ——. *The Land of Poco Tiempo.* Rpt. Albuquerque: University of New Mexico Press, 1969. 328 pp. $5.00. In paper: $2.45.

1925. ——. *New Mexico David, and Other Stories and Sketches of the Southwest.* 1891; rpt. Vol. I. Facsimile edition. New York: Books for Libraries, 1970. $7.75.

1926. Lumpkin, Wilson. *The Removal of the Cherokee Indians From Georgia*. 1907; rpt. 2 vols. in One. New York: Augustus M. Kelley, Publisher, 1971. $17.50. Also: Mass Violence in America Series. New York: Arno Press, 1970. $25.00.

1927. * Lurie, Nancy O. *The Wisconsin Indians: Lives and Lands*. Madison, Wisconsin: Society Press, 1970. $ .50.

1928. Lydekker, John W. *The Faithful Mohawks*. 1938; rpt. Empire State Historical Publications Series, No. 50. Port Washington, New York: Ira J. Friedman, Inc., 1968. $8.00.

1929. * Lyford, Carrie A. *Iroquois Crafts*. Ed. Willard W. Beatty. Washington, D.C.: Division of Education, Bureau of Indian Affairs, 1945. 98 pp. $ .50.

1930. * ———. *Ojibwa Crafts (Chippewa)*. Ed. Willard W. Beatty. Washington, D.C.: Publication on the Branch of Education, Bureau of Indian Affairs, 1943. 216 pp. $1.10.

1931. * ———. *Quill and Beadwork of the Western Sioux*. Lawrence, Kansas: Haskell Press, 1970. $ .50.

1932. Lyman, Albert R. *Native Blood*. Salt Lake City: Deseret Book Company, 1970. $1.95.

1933. * MacDowell, L. W. *Alaska Indian Basketry*. 1904; rpt. Facsimile Ed. Seattle: Shorey Publications, 1970. $1.00.

1934. Macfarlan, Allan A. *The Boy's Book of Indian Skills*. World of Boyhood Library. Harrisburg, Pennsylvania: Stackpole Books, 1969. (Grades 5 up) 159 pp. $4.50.

1935. ———. *The Hunting Secrets of the Indians*. Harrisburg, Pennsylvania: Stackpole Books, 1970. $5.95.

1936. * Macgowan, Kenneth, and Joseph A. Hester, Jr. *Early Man in the New World*. Rev. ed. Anchor Book. Garden City, New York: Doubleday, 1962. A Natural History Library Edition. 333 pp. $1.45.

1937. Macgregor, Gordon. *Warriors Without Weapons*. A Study of the Society and Personality Development of the Pine Ridge Sioux. Chicago: University of Chicago Press, 1946. 228 pp.

1938. Mackenzie, Alexander. *Exploring the Northwest Territory*. Sir Alexander Mackenzie's Journal of a Voyage by Bark Canoe from Lake Athabasca to the Pacific Ocean in the Summer of 1789. Ed. T. H. McDonald. American Exploration and Travel Series, No. 50. Norman: University of Oklahoma Press, 1966. $5.95.

1939. * ———. *Voyages from Montreal, on the River St. Lawrence*. 1801; rpt. March of America Series. Ann Arbor: University Microfilms, 1966. $11.95. In paper: Facsimile Reprint. Extracts. Seattle: Shorey Publications, 1971. $2.50.

1940. Macleod, Willaim C. *The American Indian Frontier*. New York: Alfred A. Knopf, 1928.

1941. Madsen, Brigham D. *The Bannock of Idaho*. Caldwell, Idaho: The Caxton Printers, 1958. 382 pp.

1942. Mahon, John K. *A History of the Second Seminole War, 1835-1842*. Gainesville: University of Florida Press, 1967. 387 pp. $10.00.

1943. ——, ed. *Reminiscences of the Second Seminole War*. By John Bemrose. Gainesville: University of Florida Press, 1966. 115 pp. $10.00.

1944. Mails, Thomas E. *The Mystic Warriors of the Plains*. New York: Doubleday and Company, 1972. $25.00.

1945. * Mallery, Garrick. *Picture-Writing of the American Indians*. American Ethnology Bureau Annual Report, Vol. 10, 1888-1889. Washington, D.C.: Government Printing Office, 1893. 822 pp. Rpt. 2 vols. New York: Dover Publications, 1972. $5.00. each.

1946. ——. *Sign Language Among North American Indians Compared with that Among Other Peoples and Deaf-Mutes*. 1881; rpt. The Hague: Mouton Publishers, 1972. $18.50.

1947. Malone, Henry T. *The Cherokees of the Old South: A People in Transition*. Athens: University of Georgia Press, 1966. $5.50.

1948. Malone, P. V. *Sam Houston's Indians: The Alabama-Coushatti*. San Antonio, Texas: Naylor Company, 1960. (Grades 7 up) $3.95.

1949. * Manfred, Frederick. *Conquering Horse*. 1959; rpt. New York: The New American Library, 1965. 276 pp. $ .60.

1950. * ——. *Scarlet Plume*. A Pocket Cardinal Edition. New York: Pocket Books, 1968. 328 pp. $ .75.

1951. ——. *Winter Count*. Limited edition. Minneapolis: J. D. Thueson, 1966. $7.00.

1952. Manring, Benjamin F. *The Conquest of the Coeur d'Alenes, Spokanes, and Palouses*. Spokane, Washington: The Inland Printing Company, 1912.

1953. Manypenny, George W. *Our Indian Wards*. 2nd edition. American Scene Series. New York: Plenum Publishing Company, 1968. $14.50.

1954. Mardock, Robert W. *Reformers and the American Indian*. Columbia: University of Missouri Press, 1971. 240 pp. $9.00.

1955. * Marquis, Thomas B. *Custer on the Little Bighorn*. Ed. Anna R. Heil. Lodi, California: Dr. Marquis Custer, Pub., 1969. $2.50.

1956. ——. See Wooden Leg, No. 206.

1957. * Marriott, Alice. *The Black Stone Knife*. Rpt. New York: Washington Square Press, Inc., 1968. $ .60.

1958. ——. *First Comers: Indians of America's Dawn*. New York: David McKay Co., Inc., 1960. (Grades 4 up) $4.19.

1959. ——. *Greener Fields: Experiences Among the American Indians.* Westport, Connecticut: Greenwood Press, Inc., 1953. $12.00.

1960. Marriott, Alice. *Indian Annie: Kiowa Captive.* New York: David McKay Co., Inc., 1965. (Grades 6 up) $3.75. Also: Eau Claire, Wisconsin: E. M. Hale and Company, 1965. (Grades 6 up) $2.91.

1961. ——. *Indians on Horseback.* Rev. ed. New York: T. Y. Crowell Company, 1968. (Grades 4-8) 136 pp. $3.95.

1962. ——. *Maria: The Potter of San Ildefonso.* Civilization of the American Indian Series, No. 27. Rev. ed. Norman: University of Oklahoma Press, 1948; rpt. 1967. 294 pp. $5.95.

1963. ——. *Sequoyah: Leader of the Cherokees.* New York: Random House, 1956. (Grades 4-6) $2.95.

1964. ——. *These Are the People: Some Notes on the Southwestern Indians.* 1949; rpt. Sante Fe, New Mexico: William Gannon, 1970. $7.50. Also: Sante Fe, New Mexico: Southwest Book Service, 1969. $7.50.

1965. * Marriott, Alice, and Carol K. Rachlin. *American Epic: The Story of the American Indian.* New York: New American Library, 1969. $ .95. 207 pp. Also: New York: G. P. Putnam's Sons, 1969. $6.95.

1966. ——. *Peyote.* New York: T. Y. Crowell Company, 1971. $6.95.

1967. Marryat, Frederick. *Narratives of the Travels and Adventures of Monsieur Violet.* 3 vols. 1843; rpt. 3 vols. in one. Upper Saddle River, New Jersey: Gregg Press, Inc., 1970. $40.00.

1968. * Marsden, W. L. *The Northern Paiute Language of Oregon.* See No. 4020.

1969. Marshall, Orasmus H. *The Historical Writings of Orasmus Holmes Marshall Relating to the Early History of the West.* Munsell's History Series. 1887; New York: Burt Franklin, Pub. 1970. $28.50.

1970. Marshall, S. L. *Crimsoned Prairie.* New York: Charles Scribner's Sons, 1972. $8.95.

1971. Martin, Norella G. *Choctaw Little Folk.* San Antonio, Texas: Naylor Company, 1970. (Grades 4-7) $3.95.

1973. Martin, Patricia M. *Eskimos: People of Alaska.* New York: Parents Magazine Press, 1970. (Grades 1-4) $3.47.

1973. ——. *Indians: The First Americans.* New York: Parents Magazine Press, 1970. (Grades 1-4) $3.78.

1974. Martin, Patricia M. *Pocahantas.* See and Read Biography Series. New York: G. P. Putnam's Sons, 1964. (Grades 2-4) $2.68.

1975. *Martin, Paul S. *Lowry Ruin in Southwestern Colorado.* Archaeological Work in the Ackmen-Lowry Area. 1936-38; rpt. New York: Kraus Reprint Co., 1971. $30.00.

1976. *———. *The SU Site Excavations at a Mongollon Village, Western New Mexico.* First, Second, and Third Seasons. 1940-1947; rpt. New York: Kraus Reprint Co., 1971. $15.00.

1977. ———, et al. *Indians Before Columbus. Twenty Thousand Years of North American History Revealed by Archaeology.* Chicago: Univeristy of Chicago Press, 1947. 582 pp. $8.50.

1978. Martin, Paul S., and Elizabeth S. Willis. *Anasazi Painted Pottery in the Field Museum of Natural History.* Fieldiana Anthropology Memoirs, Vol. 5. 1940; rpt. New York: Kraus Reprint Co., 1968. $25.00.

1979. Martini, Teri. *The Treasure of the Mohawks.* Paterson, New Jersey: St. Anthony Guild Press, 1956. $2.00.

1980. ———. *The True Book of Indians.* Chicago: Children's Press, Inc., 1954. (Grades K-4) $3.50.

1981. Mary-Rousseliere, Guy. *Beyond the High Hills: A Book of Eskimo Poems.* Cleveland: World Publishing Company, 1961. (Grades 4 up) $4.95.

1982. Mason, Bernard S. *The Book of Indian-Crafts and Costumes.* New York: A. S. Barnes and Co., 1946. 118 pp. $5.50.

1983. Mason, John. *A Brief of the Pequot War.* 1736; rpt. Facsimile ed. Select Bibliographies Reprint Series. New York: Books for Libraries, $5.00. See also Nos. 4010, 4011, 4014, and 4020.

1984. Mason, Otis T. *Aboriginal American Harpoons.* 1902; rpt. Seattle: Shorey Publications, 1970. $7.50.

1985. ———. *Aboriginal Indian Basketry.* 1902; rpt. Beautiful Rio Grande Classic Series. Glorieta, New Mexico: Rio Grande Press, Inc., 1970. $25.00.

1986. ———. *Aboriginal Skin-Dressing.* 1889; rpt. Seattle: Shorey Publications, 1970. $5.00.

1987. ———. *Basket Work of the Aborigines.* 1884; rpt. Facsimile Ed. Seattle: Shorey Publications, 1971. $5.00.

1988. ———. *Cradles of the American Aborigines.* 1889; rpt. Seattle: Shorey Publications, 1970. $5.00.

1989. ———. *Man's Knife Among the North American Indians.* 1899; rpt. Seattle: Shorey Publications, 1970. $2.00.

1990. ———. *Pointed Bark Canoes of the Kutenai and Amur.* 1901; rpt. Seattle: Shorey Publications, 1971. $2.00.

1991. *———. *Throwing Sticks in the National Museum.* 1884; rpt. Facsimile ed. Extracts. Seattle: Shorey Publications, 1970.

1992. *———. *Traps of the American Indians.* 1901; rpt. Facsimile ed. Extracts. Seattle: Shorey Publications, 1970. $1.25.

1993. Mathews, John J. *Life and Death of an Oilman: The Career of E. W. Marland.* Norman: University of Oklahoma Press, 1952. 259 pp. Author is an Osage Indian.

1994. ———. *The Osages: Children of the Middle Waters.* Civilization of the American Indian Series, No. 60. Norman: University of Oklahoma Press, 1961. 832 pp. $12.50.

1995. ———. *Sundown.* New York: Longmans, Green, and Co., 1934. 312 pp.

1996. ———. *Talking to the Moon.* Chicago: University of Chicago Press, 1945. 234 pp.

1997. ———. *Wah'Kon-Tah: The Osage and the White Man's Road.* Civilization of the American Indian, No. 3. Norman: University of Oklahoma Press, 1932; rpt. 1968. 360 pp. $5.95.

1998. Mathur, L. P. *The Indian Revolutionary Movement in the United States of America.* Mystic, Connecticut: Lawrence Verry, Inc., 1970. $7.50.

1999. Matteson, E., et al. *Comparative Studies in Amerindian Languages.* Janua Linguarum No. 127. The Hague: Mouton Publishers, 1972. $26.00.

2000. * Matthews, G. H. *Hidatsa Syntax.* Papers on Formal Linguistics. The Hague: Mouton Publishers, 1965. 299 pp. $18.50.

2001. * Matthews, Mathew. *The Catlin Collection of Indian Paintings* 1890; rpt. Facsimile Edition. Seattle: Shorey Publications, 1970. $3.00.

2002. Matthews, Washington. *Ethnography and Philology of the Hidatsa Indians.* Washington: Government Printing Office, 1877; rpt. New York: Johnson Reprint Corp., 1971. $12.50. See also No. 4005.

2003. ———. *The Mountain Chant of the Navajo Indians: A Mystic Ceremony.* Glorieta, New Mexico: Rio Grande Press, Inc., 1971. 185 pp. $15.00.

2004. * ———. *Navajo Weavers.* Facsimile Ed. 1884; rpt. Seattle: Shorey Publications, 1970. $2.50.

2005. * ———. *Navajo Weavers and Navajo Silversmiths.* Wild and Wooly West Series. Palmer Lake, Colorado: Filter Press, 1968. 37 pp. $3.50. In paper: $1.00.

2006. Maurault, Joseph P. *Histoire Des Abenakis, Depuis 1605 Jusqu'a Nos Jours.* Rpt. Canadiana Before 1867 Series. New York: Johnson Reprint Corp., 1969. $25.00.

2007. Maxwell, Gilbert S. *Navajo Rugs—Past, Present and Future* Palm Desert, California: Best West Publications, 1963.

2008. May, Charles P. *The Early Indians: Their Natural and Imaginary Worlds.* Camden, New Jersey: Thomas Nelson, Inc., 1971. (Grades 5-7) $4.95.

123

2009. May, Julian. *Before the Indians.* New York: Holiday House, Inc., 1969. (Grades 1-4) 38 pp. $4.50.

2010. Mayberry, Genevieve. *The Eskimo of Little Diomede.* Chicago: Follett Publishing Co., 1961. (Grades 2-4) $1.25.

2011. Mayfield, Clara M. *The History of the Southern Ute Indians.* New York: Carlton Press, 1970. $2.50.

2012. Mayhall, Mildred P. *The Indian Wars of Texas.* Waco, Texas: Texian Press, 1970. $7.50.

2013. ———. *The Kiowas.* Civilization of the American Indian Series, No. 63. Norman: University of Oklahoma Press, 1962; rpt. 1971. 315 pp. $8.95.

2014. Maynard, Eileen, and Gayla Twiss. *Hechel Lena Oyate Kin Nipi Kte: That These People May Live.* Pine Ridge, South Dakota: U.S. Public Health Service, 1969. 183 pp.

2015. * McAllester, David P. *Enemy Way Music: A Study of Social and Esthetic Values as Seen in Navaho Music.* 1954; rpt. New York: Kraus Reprint Co., 1971. $12.00.

2016. * ———. *Peyote Music.* New York: Johnson Reprint Corp., 1949. $10.00.

2017. McCague, James. *Tecumseh: Shawnee Warrior-Statesman.* Champaign, Illinois: Garrard Publishing Company, 1970. (Grade 3) 80 pp. $2.59.

2018. McCall, Edith. *Pioneer Traders.* Chicago: Children's Press, Inc., 1964. (Grades 3-8) $3.00.

2019. McCallum, James D. *Letters of Eleazar Wheelock's Indians.* 1932; rpt. Hanover, New Hampshire: University Press of New England, 1972. $4.00.

2020. * McCary, Ben C. *Indians in Seventeenth Century Virginia.* Charlottesville: University Press of Virginia, 1957. $1.00.

2021. McChesney, et al. *The Rolls of Certain Indian Tribes.* Fairfield, Washington: Ye Galleon, 1971. $10.00.

2022. McClung, John A. *Sketches of Western Adventure.* 1832; rpt. Mass Violence in America Series. New York: Arno Press, 1970. $13.00.

2023. McConkey, H. E. *Dakota War Whoop.* 1864; rpt. Minneapolis: Ross and Haines, Inc., 1970. $12.50.

2024. * McConnell, Virginia. *Ute Pass: Route of the Blue Sky People.* Chicago: Swallow Press, 1971. $1.50.

2025. McCoy, Isaac. *History of Baptist Indian Missions.* 1840; rpt. New York: Johnson Reprint Corp., 1970. $20.00.

2026. McCracken, Harold. *The Charles M. Russell Book.* New York: Doubleday Doran, 1957. $16.95.

2027. ———. *Frederic Remington, Artist of the Old West.* New York: J. B. Lippincott Company, 1947. $17.50.

2028. ——. *George Catlin and the Old Frontier*. New York: Bonanza Books, 1959. 216 pp. $18.50.

2029. ——. *The Great White Buffalo*. New York: J. B. Lippincott Company, 1946. (Grades 7-9) $4.25.

2030. ——. *The Winning of the West*. New York: Doubleday and Co., 1970. (Grades 4-7) $3.50.

2031. McDermott, John Francis. *Seth Eastman, Pictorial Historian of the Indians*. Norman: University of Oklahoma Press, 1961. $15.00.

2032. ——, ed. *Tixier's Travels on the Osage Prairies*. Trans. Albert J. Salvan. American Exploration and Travel Series, No. 4. 1940; rpt. Norman: University of Oklahoma Press, 1968. 309 pp. $8.95.

2033. *——, ed. *The Western Journals of Doctor George Hunter, 1796-1805*. Philadelphia: American Philosophical Society, 1963. $3.00.

2034. McDowell, William L., ed. *Documents Relating to Indian Affairs, May 21, 1750-August 7, 1754*. Columbia: University of South Carolina Press, 1958. $20.00.

2035. ——, ed. *Documents Relating to Indian Affairs, Seventeen Fifty-Four to Seventeen Sixty-Five* Colonial Records of South Carolina Series. Columbia: University of South Carolina Press, 1970. $20.00.

2036. ——, ed. *The Journals of the Commissioners of the Indian Trade*. Colonial Records of South Carolina Series. Columbia: University of South Carolina Press, 1955. $20.00.

2037. *McFeat, Tom, ed. *Indians of the North Pacific Coast*. Washington Paperbacks. Seattle: University of Washington Press, 1967. 268 pp. $5.95. In paper: $2.95.

2038. McFee, Malcolm. *Modern Blackfeet: Montanans on a Reservation*. New York: Holt, Rinehart, and Winston, 1972. 144 pp.

2039. McGaa, Ed. *Red Cloud. The Story of an American Indian*. Minneapolis: Dillon Press, 1971. $3.95. Author is Sioux.

2040. *McGinnis, Duane. *After the Death of an Elder Klallam*. Phoenix: Baleen Press, 1970. 54 pp. $6.00. In paper: $1.95. Author is Klallan.

2041. *McGregor, James H. *The Wounded Knee Massacre: From the Viewpoint of the Sioux*. Minneapolis, Minnesota: The Lund Press, Inc., 1940. 140 pp. In paper: Seventh Ed. Rapid City, South Dakota: Fenwyn Press Books, 1972. 131 pp. $2.95.

2042. McGregor, John C. *Cohonina Culture of Mount Floyd, Arizona*. Lexington: University Press of Kentucky, 1967. $5.00.

2043. ——. *Southwestern Archaeology*. 2nd edition. Champaign-Urbana: University of Illinois Press, 1965. $10.00.

2044. McKenney, Thomas L. *Sketches of A Tour to the Lakes, of the Character and Customs of the Chippeway Indians . . .* 1827. Facsimile Reprint. Minneapolis: Ross and Haines, Inc., 1959. 494 pp. $10.00.

2045. ——. *Sketches of A Tour to the Lakes.* Rpt. Minneapolis: Ross and Haines, Inc., 1971. $10.00.

2046. McKenny, Thomas L., and James Hall. *The History of the Indian Tribes of North America: With Biographical Sketches and Anecdotes of the Principal Chiefs.* Ed. Frederick W. Hodge. 3 vols. 1933; rpt. St. Clair Shores, Michigan: Scholarly Press, 1970. $35.00. Also: Totowa, New Jersey: Bowman and Littlefield, Inc., 1972. $100.00.

2047. McKenzie, Fayette A. *The Indian in Relation to the White Population of the United States.* 1908; rpt. New York: Burt Franklin, Publisher, 1970. $11.00.

2048. *McKenzie, Parker, and John P. Harrington. *Popular Account of the Kiowa Indian Language.* School of American Research Publications No. 12. Albuquerque: University of New Mexico Press, 1948. 26 pp. $2.50.

2049. McKeown, Martha F. *Come to Our Salmon Feast.* Portland, Oregon: Binfords and Mort, Publishers, 1959. (Grades 5-6) 78 pp. $3.00.

2050 ——. *Linda's Indian Home.* Portland, Oregon: Binfords and Mort, Publishers, Inc., 1970. (Grades 3-4) $3.00.

2051. McKern, Will C. See Nos. 4013 and 4020.

2052. McKnight, Charles. *Our Western Border, Its Life, Combats, Adventures, Forays, Massacres, Captivities, Scouts, Red Chiefs, Pioneer, Women, One Hundred Years Ago, Carefully Written and Compiled.* 1876; rpt. Rediscovering America Series. New York: Johnson Reprint Corp., 1971. $27.50.

2053. McKusick, Marshall. *Men of Ancient Iowa.* Ames: Iowa State University Press, 1964. 260 pp.

2054. McLaughlin, James. *My Friend the Indian.* 1910; rpt. Deluxe Edition. Seattle, Washington: Superior Publishing Co., 1969. $19.95.

2055. McLean, John. *John McClean's Notes of a Twenty-Five Years' Service in the Hudson's Bay Territory.* Ed. W. S. Wallace. 1932; rpt. Westport, Connecticut: Greenwood Press, Inc., 1968. $26.00.

2056. McLean, John L., and Robert E. Squires. *American Indian Dances: Steps, Rhythms, Costumes, and Interpretations.* New York: Ronald Press, 1963. $4.50.

2057. McLuhan, T. C., ed. See *Touch the Earth*, No. 2789.

2058. McNeer, May. *American Indian Story.* New York: Farrar, Straus, and Giroux, Inc., 1963. (Grades 7-9) 95 pp. $5.95.

2059. ——. *War Chief of the Seminoles*. New York: Random House, 1954. (Grades 4-6) $2.95.

2060. McNichol, Donald M. *The Amerindians*. New York: Frederick A. Stokes Company, 1937.

2061. * McNichols, Charles L. *Crazy Weather*. 1938; rpt. Lincoln: University of Nebraska Press, 1967. 195 pp. $1.65.

2062. McNickle, D'Arcy. *Indian Man: A Life of Oliver La Farge*. Bloomington: Indiana University Press, 1971. 242 pp. $7.95. Author is Flathead Indian.

2063. * ——. *The Indian Tribes of the United States: Ethnic and Cultural Survival*. London: Oxford University Press, 1962. 79 pp. $1.20.

2064. McNitt, Frank. *The Indian Traders*. 1962; rpt. Norman: University of Oklahoma Press, 1972. 393 pp. $8.95.

2065. ——. *The Navajos. A Military History: 1540-1861*. Albuquerque: University of New Mexico Press, 1972. 328 pp. $12.00.

2066. ——. *Richard Wetherill: Anasazi*. Rev. ed. Albuquerque: University of New Mexico Press, 1966. 382 pp. $10.00.

2067. McReynolds, Edwin C. *Oklahoma: History of the Sooner State*. Rev. ed. 1964; rpt. Norman: University of Oklahoma Press, 1969. $6.95.

2068. ——. *The Seminoles*. Civilization of the American Indian Series, No. 47. Norman: University of Oklahoma Press, 1957. 394 pp. $5.95.

2069. McReynolds, Edwin C., et al. *Oklahoma: The Story of its Past and Present*. Rev. ed. Norman: University of Oklahoma Press, 1968. $3.95.

2070. McWhorter, Lucullus V. *The Crime Against the Yakimas*. 1931; rpt. Facsimile edition. Seattle: Shorey Publications, 1970. $4.50.

2071. ——. *Hear Me, My Chiefs*. Caldwell, Idaho: The Caxton Printers, 1952. 640 pp.

2072. * ——. *The Tragedy of the Wahk-Shum*. Rpt. Fairfield, Washington: Ye Galleon Press, 1971. $3.50.

2073 ——. See Yellow Wolf, No. 210.

2074. * Mead, Margaret. *The Changing Culture of an Indian Tribe*. New York: Columbia University Press, 1932; rpt. New York: AMS Press, 1971. 313 pp. $14.50. In paper: New York: G. P. Putnam's Sons, 1966. $2.75.

2075. Meadowcroft, Enid L. *Crazy Horse: Sioux Warrior*. Indian Books Series. Champaign, Illinois: Garrard Publishing Company, 1965. (Grades 2-5) $2.59.

2076. ——. *Story of Crazy Horse*. New York: Grosset and Dunlap, 1954. (Grades 4-6) 181 pp. $2.95.

127

2077. *Meany, Edmond S. *The Indian Geographic Names of Washington.* 1908; rpt. Facsimile Edition. Seattle: Shorey Publications, 1970. $1.00.

2078. Meares, John. *Voyages Made in the Years 1788 and 1789, from China to the North-West Coast of America.* Rpt. Bibliotheca Australiana Series 2. New York: Plenum Publishing Company, 1967. $35.00.

2079. Meggers, Betty J. *Prehistoric America.* Chicago: Aldine Publishing, 1972. $3.95.

2080. Meggers, Betty J., and Clifford Evans, eds. *New Interpretations of Aboriginal American Culture History.* 1955; rpt. New York: Cooper Square Publishers, 1972. $6.00.

2081. Menager, Francis M. *Kingdom of the Seal.* Chicago: Loyola University Press, 1962. $3.00.

2082. Mera, H. P. *Indian Silverwork of the Southwest: Band Bracelets.* Sante Fe, New Mexico: William Gannon, 1945. $4.00.

2083. *——. *Pueblo Designs: One Hundred Six Illustrations of the Red Bird.* New York: Dover Publications, 1970. $2.50.

2084. *——. *Rain Bird: A Study in Pueblo Design.* New York: Dover Publications, 1970. $2.50.

2085. ——. *Reconnaissance and Excavation in Southeastern New Mexico.* 1938; rpt. New York: Kraus Reprint Co., 1970. $5.00.

2086. Mercer, A. S. *The Banditti of the Plains* or *The Cattlemen's Invasion of Wyoming in 1892.* Norman: University of Oklahoma Press, 1968. $2.95.

2087. Merriam, Alan P. *Ethnomusicology of the Flathead Indians.* Chicago: Aldine Publishing Co., 1967. $10.00.

2088. Merriam, H. G. *Way Out West: Reminiscences and Tales.* Norman: University of Oklahoma Press, 1969. $5.95.

2089. *Merrill, Ruth E. See No. 4020.

2090. Merritt, Wesley. *Three Indian Campaigns.* 1890; rpt. Seattle: Shorey Publications, 1972. $1.50.

2091. Messiter, Charles A. *Sport and Adventures Among the North American Indians.* 1890; rpt. New York: Abercrombie and Fitch, 1966. 368 pp. $10.00. Also: Ann Arbor: University Microfilms, 1966.

2092. Meyer, Roy W. *History of the Santee Sioux. United States Indian Policy on Trial.* Lincoln: University of Nebraska Press, 1967. 434 pp. $7.50.

2093. *Meyer, William. *Native Americans: The New Indian Resistance.* New York: International Publishers Company, 1971. $1.25.

2094. Michael, Henry N., ed. *Lieutenant Zabkoskin's Travels in Russian America, 1842-1844: The First Ethnographic and Geographic Investigations in the Yukon and Kuskokwim Valleys of Alaska.* Toronto: University of Toronto Press, 1967. $12.50.

2095. Michaelson, Truman. *On the Fox Indians.* 40th Annual Report of the Bureau of American Ethnology. Bulletin 114. Washington, D.C., 1937.

2096. ——. *The Owl Sacred Pack of the Fox Indians.* Bureau of American Ethnology. Bulletin 72. Washington, D.C., 1921.

2097. Miles, Charles. *Indian and Eskimo Artifacts of North America.* Chicago: Henry Regnery Co., 1963. 244 pp. $25.00.

2098. Miles, Nelson K. *Personal Recollections and Observations of General Nelson A. Miles.* Rev. ed. 1896; rpt. New York: Plenum Publishing Company, 1971. $27.50.

2099. Miller, Joaquin. *Life Amongst the Modocs.* 1878; rpt. American Novels of Muckraking, Propaganda, and Social Protest Series, Vol. 12. Upper Saddle River, New Jersey: Gregg Press, Inc., 1969. $13.50.

2100. * Miller, Marjorie. *Indian Arts and Crafts.* Los Angeles: Nash Publication Company, 1970. $1.95.

2101. Miller, Mark. *The White Captive of the Sioux.* New York: Holt, Rinehart and Winston, 1953. (Grades 6-9) $2.50.

2102. * Milligan, Edward A. *Petroglyphs, Pictographs, and Prehistoric Art In the Upper Missouri River and The Red River of the North Valley Areas.* Privately Published. Bottineau, North Dakota, 1968. Unpaged. Approximately 20 pp. with photographs.

2103. Milling, Chapman J. *Red Carolinians.* Columbia: University of South Carolina Press, 1969. 438 pp. $10.00.

2104. Milton, John. *Oscar Howe.* The Story of An American Indian. Minneapolis: Dillon Press, Inc., 1971. 56 pp. $3.95.

2105. * ——, ed. *The American Indian. South Dakota Review,* VII (Summer, 1969). 194 pp. Reissued as *The American Indian Speaks.* 1969. $3.00.

2106. * ——, ed. *American Indian II. South Dakota Review,* IX (Summer, 1971). 199 pp. $3.50.

2107. * Minor, Marz N. *American Indian Craft Book.* New York: Popular Library Inc., 1972. $1.25.

2108. Mishkin, Bernard. *Rank and Warfare Among the Plains Indians.* American Ethnological Society Monographs. Seattle: University of Washington Press, 1966. 65 pp. $5.00.

2109. Mohr, Walter H. *The Federal Indian Relations, 1774-1788.* 1933; rpt. New York: AMS Press, 1970. 247 pp. $10.00.

2110. * Momaday, N. Scott. *House Made of Dawn.* New York: Harper Row, 1968. $4.95. In paper: New York: New American Library, 1969. $ .95. Author is Kiowa-Cherokee Indian.

2111. * Momaday, Natachee Scott. *American Indian Authors.* Boston: Houghton Mifflin Co., 1972. 151 pp. $3.95. Author is of Cherokee descent.

2112. Monaghan, Jay, ed. *The Book of the American West.* New York: Bonanza Books, 1963. 607 pp. $22.50.

2113. Montgomery, Elizabeth R. *Chief Joseph, Guardian of his People.* Indian Series. Champaign, Illinois: Garrard Publishing Company, 1969. (Grades 3 up) 80 pp. $2.59.

2114. ———. *Chief Seattle: Great Statesman.* Indian Series. Champaign, Illinois: Garrard Publishing Company, 1966. $2.59.

2115. * Montgomery, Ross G., et al. *Franciscan Awatovi: the Excavation and Conjectural Reconstruction of a 17th-Century Spanish Mission Establishment at a Hopi Town in Northeastern Arizona.* 1949; rpt. New York: Kraus Reprint Co., 1971. $12.00.

2116. Monture, Ethel Brant. *Famous Indians: Brant, Crowfoot, and Oronhyatekha.* Toronto: Clarke, Irwin, and Co., Ltd., 1960. 160 pp. Author is Mohawk.

2117. ———. *Joseph Brant, Mohawk.* with Harvey Chalmers. East Lansing: Michigan State University Press, 1955. 364 pp.

2118. ———. *West to the Setting Sun.* with Harvey Chalmers. New York: Macmillan Co., 1943. 362 pp.

2119. Moody, Ralph. *Geronimo: Wolf of the Warpath.* Landmark Book. New York: Random House, 1958. (Grades 4-6) $3.95.

2120. Moon, Grace. *The Arrows of Tee-May.* New York: A. L. Burt Company, 1951. 284 pp.

2121. ———. *Chi-Wee.* Garden City, New Jersey: Doubleday and Company, Inc., 1925. (Grades 4-6) $4.50.

2122. ———. *The Missing Katchina.* New York: Sun Dial Press, Inc., 1939. 386 pp.

2123. ———. *One Little Indian.* Rev. ed. Chicago: Albert Whitman and Company, 1967. $3.50.

2124. * Mooney, James. *The Cheyenne Indians.* Bound with R. Peter. *Sketch of the Cheyenne Grammar.* 1907; rpt. New York: Kraus Reprint Co., 1971. $3.50.

2125. ———. *The Siouan Tribes of the East.* 1894; rpt. American Indian History Series. St. Clair Shores, Michigan: Scholarly Press, 1970. $8.50. Also: New York: Johnson Reprint Corp., 1970. $5.00.

2126. * Mooney, James, and R. Peter. *The Cheyenne Indians and A Sketch of the Cheyenne Grammar.* 1907; rpt. New York: Kraus Reprint Co., 1970. $3.50.

2127. * Moore, William M., et al., eds. *Nutrition, Growth and Development of North American Indian Children.* Washington, D.C.: Government Printing Office, 1972. 246 pp. $1.25.

2128. Moorehead, Warren K. *American Indian in the United States, Period 1850-1914*. Facsimile Ed. Freeport, New York: Books for Libraries, Inc., 1970. $23.50.

2129. * ——. *Prehistoric Relics*. Rpt. Facsimile ed. Seattle: Shorey Publications, 1967. $7.50.

2130. Moorehead, Max L. *Apache Frontier: Jacobo Ligarte and the Spanish-Indian Relations in Northern New Spain, 1769-1791*. Civilization of the American Indian Series, No. 90. Norman: University of Oklahoma Press, 1968. $6.95.

2131. * Moquin, Wayne, and Charles Van Doren, eds. *Great Documents in American Indian History*. New York: Praeger Publishers, 1972. $13.50. In paper: $4.95.

2132. * Morey, Sylvester M., ed. *Can the Red Man Help the White Man?* A Denver Conference with the Indian Elders. New York: Gilbert Church, Publisher, 1970. 113 pp. of text and Addenda "To Indian Youth" and "To Indian Elders." $1.95.

2133. Morfi, Juan A. *History of Texas, 1673-1779*. Ed. Carlos F. Castaneda. Vol. 6, 2 pts. Quivira Society Publications. 1935; rpt. New York: Arno Press, 1967. $25.00.

2134. * Morgan, Lewis H. *Ancient Society*. Ed. L. A. White. John Harvard Library Series. Rpt. Facsimile ed. Belknap Press. Cambridge: Harvard University Press, 1964. $7.95. In paper: Meridian Books: New York: World Publishing Company, 1970. $3.95.

2135. * ——. *The Houses and House Life of the American Aborigine*. Rpt. Chicago: University of Chicago Press, 1966. $6.95. In paper: University of Chicago Press, 1966. $2.95.

2136. ——. *Indian Journals, 1859-1862*. Rpt. Ed. Clyde Walton. Ann Arbor: University of Michigan Press, 1959. $17.50.

2137. ——. *The League of the Ho-De-No-Sau-Nee or Iroquois*. 2 vols. 1902; rpt. Ed. U. M. Loyd. New York: Burt Franklin, Pub., 1966. $37.50.

2138. * ——. *The League of the Iroquois*. Rpt. Gloucester, Mass.: Peter Smith, 1971. $6.00. In paper: New York: Corinth Books, 1962. $3.95.

2139. ——. *Systems of Consanguinity and Affinity of the Human Family*. New York: Humanities Press, Inc., 1966. $35.00.

2140. Morgan, William. *Human-Wolves Among the Navajo*. Yale University Publications in Anthropology, No. 11. New Haven: Yale University Press, 1936. 43 pp. Author is Navaho.

2141. * ——. *Navajo-English Dictionary*. With Leon Wall. Window Rock, Arizona: Navajo Agency, Branch of Education, 1958. 65 pp. Also: Lawrence, Kansas: Haskell Press, 1970. $1.00. (paperbound)

2142. Morgan, William, and Robert W. Young. *Navajo Historical Selections.* Lawrence, Kansas: Haskell Press, 1954. 209 pp. $1.00.

2143. * Morrill, Sibley S. *The Texas Cannibals, Or, Why Father Serra Came to California.* Oakland, California: Holmes Book Company, 1964. $1.00.

2144. Morris, Laverne. *The American Indian as Farmer.* Chicago: Melmont Publishers, Inc., 1963. (Grades 3-6) 147 pp. $3.25.

2145. Morris, Richard B. *The First Book of the Indian Wars.* New York: Franklin Watts, Inc., 1959. (Grades 4-6) 83 pp. $3.75.

2146. * Morris, Richard B., and Jack M. Sosin, eds. *The Opening of the West.* Documentary History of the United States Series. Harper Torchbooks. New York: Harper Row, 1969. $2.95.

2147. Morris, Thomas. *The Journal of Captain Thomas Morris, from Miscellanies in Prose and Verse.* 1791; rpt. March of America Series. Ann Arbor: University Microfilms, 1966. $4.55.

2148. Morse, Jedidiah, ed. *A Report to the Secretary of War . . . On Indian Affairs,* etc., 1822. Rpt. New York: Augustus M. Kelley, 1968. $15.00. 496 pp. Also: St. Clair Shores, Michigan: Scholarly Press, 1970. $15.00. Also: New York: Kraus Reprint Co., 1971. $10.00.

2149. * Morss, Noel. *Ancient Culture of the Fremont River in Utah.* 1931; rpt. New York: Kraus Reprint Co., 1970. $4.75.

2150. * ———. *Archaeological Explorations on the Middle Chinlee.* 1927; rpt. New York: Kraus Reprint Co., 1970. $4.50.

2151. * ———. *Notes on the Archaeology of the Kaibito and Rainbow Plateaus in Arizona.* 1931; rpt. New York: Kraus Reprint Co., 1971. $1.25.

2152. Morton, Thomas. *New England Canaan.* Ed. Charles F. Adam. Rpt. New York: Burt Franklin, Pub., 1966. $20.00.

2153. Moss, Claude R., See Nos. 4015 and 4017.

2154. Motte, Jacob R. *The Journey Into Wilderness.* Gainesville: University of Florida Press, 1953. $9.00.

2155. *Mountain Wolf Woman.* See Lurie, Nancy O., No. 182.

2156. Mowat, Farley. *The Desperate People.* Boston: Little, Brown, and Company, 1959. 305 pp.

2157. ———. *People of the Deer.* Boston: Little, Brown and Company, 1951. 344 pp.

2158. Moyer, John W. *Famous Indian Chiefs.* Chicago: M. A. Donohue and Company, 1970. 86 pp. $3.95.

2159. Mozino, Jose M. *Noticias De Nutka: An Account of Nootka Sound.* Trans. Iris H. Wilson. American Ethnological Society Monographs. Seattle: University of Washington Press, 1970. $8.50.

2160. Murchison, Kenneth S., ed. *Digest of Decisions Relating to Indian Affairs.* 1901; rpt. New York: Kraus Reprint Co., 1971. $20.00.

2161. Murfree, Mary N. *The Story of Old Fort Loudon.* 1899; rpt. Upper Saddle River, New Jersey: Gregg Press, Inc., 1970. $14.00.

2162. Murie, James R. *Pawnee Indian Societies.* Anthropological Papers of the American Museum of Natural History. Vol. XI, Part VII. New York: Printed for the Trustees, 1914, pp. 543-644. Author was Pawnee.

2163. ———. *Traditions of the Skidi Pawnee.* Told to George A. Dorsey. Memoirs of the American Folklore Society. Vol. VIII. Boston, Mass.: Houghton Mifflin Co., 1904. 366 pp.

2164. Murray, C. A *Travels in North America, Including A Summer Residence with the Pawnees.* 2nd ed. Rpt. New York: Plenum Publishing Corp., 1968. $37.50.

2165. Murray, Keith A. *The Modocs and Their War.* Civilization of the American Indian Series, No. 52. Norman: University of Oklahoma Press, 1959. Rpt. in 1969. 343 pp.. $8.95.

2166. Murray, Robert A. *Military Posts in the Powder River Country of Wyoming, 1865-1894.* Lincoln: University of Nebraska Press, 1968. $5.50.

2167. * ———. *Pipes on the Plains.* Pipestone, Minnesota: Pipestone Indian Shrine Association, 1968. On the mining of catlinite, the making of the Indian pipe, legends about the pipe, with pictures of pipe-making. 40 pp. $1.00.

2168. Myers, Albert C., ed. *William Penn's Own Account of the Lenni Lanape or Delaware Indians.* Rev. ed. Somerset, New Jersey: Mid Atlantic Press, 1970. 96 pp. $6.50.

2169. Nabakov, Peter. See Two Leggings, No. 199.

2170. Nadeau, Remi. *Fort Laramie and the Sioux Indians.* New York: Prentice-Hall, 1967. 335 pp. $7.95.

2171. Naish, C. M. *A Syntactic Study of Tlingit.* Janua Linguarum, Series Practica, No. 117. The Hague: Mouton Publishers, 1972. $14.80.

2172. Nammack, Georgiana C. *Fraud, Politics, and the Dispossession of the Indians.* The Iroquois Land Frontier in the Colonial Period. Civilization of the American Indian Series, No. 97. Norman: University of Oklahoma Press, 1969. 128 pp.

2173. Natches, Gilbert. *Northern Paiute Verbs.* See No. 4020.

2174. *Navajo Political Process.* Smithsonian Institution Contributions to Anthropology, Vol. 9. Washington, D.C.: Government Printing Office, 1970. 75 pp. $3.75.

2175. * Navajo School of Indian Basketry. *Indian Basket Weaving.* 1903; rpt. New York: Dover Publications, 1971. 103 pp. $1.75.

2176. * Navajo Tribal Council. *Navajo Treaty*. Flagstaff, Arizona: Northland Press, 1968. $ .50.

2177. *Navajo Wildlands*. San Francisco: Sierra Club / Ballantine Books, 1970.

2178. Nee, Kay B. *Powhatan*. The Story of an American Indian. Minneapolis: Dillon Press, Inc., 1971. (Grades 4-7) $3.95.

2179. Neihardt, John. See Black Elk, No. 152.

2180. * ——. *A Cycle of the West*. 1943; rpt. Lincoln: University of Nebraska Press, 1961. In paper: $2.95.

2181. ——. *The Song of the Indian Wars*. New York: Macmillan, 1925. 231 pp. Reprinted in *A Cycle of the West* and *The Twilight of the Sioux*.

2182. * ——. *The Twilight of the Sioux*. A Bison Book. Lincoln: University of Nebraska Press, 1971. Contains *The Song of the Indian Wars* and *The Song of the Messiah*. 289 pp. $2.25.

2183. * ——. *When the Tree Flowered*. The Fictional Autobiography of Eagle Voice, A Sioux Indian. Lincoln: University of Nebraska Press, 1970. 248 pp.

2184. * Nelson, Bruce. *Land of the Dacotahs*. 1946; rpt. Lincoln: University of Nebraska Press, 1964. 354 pp. $1.60. Also: Gloucester, Mass.: Peter Smith, 1971. $3.75.

2185. Nelson, Edward W. *The Eskimo About Bering Strait*. 1899; rpt. New York: Johnson Reprint Corp., 1970. $30.00.

2186. Nelson, John Y., and Harrington O'Reilly. *Fifty Years on the Trail, a True Story of Western Life: The Adventures of John Young Nelson, As Told to Harrington O'Reilly*. 1963; rpt. Norman: University of Oklahoma Press, 1969. $2.95.

2187. Nelson, Mary C. *Annie Wauneka*. The Story of an American Indian Series. Minneapolis: Dillion Press, 1972. $3.95.

2188. ——. *Maria Martinez*. The Story of an American Indian. Minneapolis: Dillon Press, 1972. $3.95.

2189. ——. *Pablita Velarde*. The Story of an American Indian. Minneapolis: Dillon Press, Inc., 1971 (Grades 4-7) $3.95.

2190. * Nelson, Nels C. See No. 4007.

2191. Nelson, Richard K. *Hunters of the Northern Ice*. Chicago: University of Chicago Press, 1969. 429 pp. $8.50.

2192. * Nettl, Bruno. *Folk and Traditional Music of the Western Continents*. New York: Prentice-Hall, 1965. $5.95. In paper: $2.95.

2193. * ——. *Introduction to Folk Music in the United States*. 2nd ed. Detroit: Wayne State University Press, 1962. $4.50.In paper: $2.50.

2194. ——. *Music in Primitive Culture*. Cambridge: Harvard University Press, 1956. $6.50.

2195. * ——. *North American Indian Musical Styles.* Memoirs of the American Folklore Series, Vol. 45. Austin: University of Texas Press, 1954. $2.50.

2196. ——. *Theory and Method in Ethnomusicology.* New York: Free Press, 1964. $7.50.

2197. Newberry Library. *Narratives of Captivity Among the Indians of North America.* A List of Books and Manuscripts on the Subject in the Edward E. Ayer Collection of the Newberry Library. With Supplement. 1938; rpt. Highland Park, New Jersey: Gryphon Press, 1970. $10.00. Also: New York: Burt Franklin Pub., 1970. $15.00.

2198. Newcomb, C. G. *The Smoke Hole.* San Antonio, Texas: Naylor Company, 1968. (Grades 6 up) 198 pp. $6.95.

2199. * Newcomb, Franc Johnson. *Hosteen Klah: Navajo Medicine Man and Sand Painter.* Civilization of the American Indian Series, No. 73. Norman: University of Oklahoma Press, 1964; rpt. 1971. 227 pp. $6.95. In paper: 1972. $2.50.

2200. ——. *Navaho Neighbors.* Norman: University of Oklahoma Press, 1966. 236 pp. $5.95.

2201. * ——. *A Study of Navajo Symbolism.* 3 Parts in 1. Part I: *Navajo Symbols in Sand Paintings and Ritual Objects.* By Franc J. Newcomb. Part II: *Navajo Picture Writing.* By S. A. Fishler. Part III: *Notes on Corresponding Symbols in Various Parts of the World.* By Mary C. Wheelwright. 1956; rpt. New York: Kraus Reprint Co., 1970. $9.50.

2202. * Newcomb, W. W., Jr. *The Indians of Texas From Prehistoric to Modern Times.* Austin: University of Texas Press, 1961; rpt. 1969. 404 pp. $7.50. In paper: Texas History Paperbacks, 4. 1969. $2.95.

2203. * Newell, H. Perry, and Alex D. Krieger. *The George C. Davis Site, Cherokee County, Texas.* 1949; rpt. New York: Kraus Reprint Co., 1971. $20.00.

2204. Newell, William B. *Crime and Justice Among the Iroquois.* Montreal: Caughnawaga Historical Society, 1965. 92 pp. Author is Mohawk.

2205. Newman, Stanley. *A Practical Zuni Orthography.* See Smith, W., No. 2614.

2206. ——. *Yokuts Language of California.* 1944; rpt. New York: Johnson Reprint Corp., 1970. $10.00.

2207. * ——. *Zuni Grammar.* Anthropology Series, No. 14. Albuquerque: University of New Mexico Press, 1965. 77 pp. $2.00.

2208. Newman, Tillie K. *Black Dog Trail.* North Quincy, Mass.: Christopher Publishing House, 1957. $3.00.

2209. Niblack, Albert P. *The Coast Indians of Southern Alaska and Northern British Columbia.* 1890; rpt. New York: Johnson Reprint Corp., 1971. $15.00.

2210. Nichols, Claude A. *Moral Education Among the North American Indians.* 1930; rpt. New York: AMS Press, 1972. $10.00.

2211. Nichols, Roger L. *General Henry Atkinson, a Western Military Career.* Norman: University of Oklahoma Press, 1965. $7.95.

2212. * Nichols, Roger L., and George R. Adams, eds. *The American Indian: Past and Present.* Xerox College, 1971. $3.95.

2213. Nicholson, John D. *The White Buffalo.* Bronx, New York: Platt and Munk Company, 1965. (Grades 2-5) $1.50.

2214. * Nimuendaju, Curt. *Apinqye.* Trans. Robert H. Lowie. New York: Humanities Press, 1968. $7.25. See also Nos. 4041 and 4045.

2215. * ——. *Tukuna.* Ed. Robert H. Lowie. 1952; rpt. New York: Kraus Reprint Co., 1970. $20.00.

2216. * Nitz, Henry C. *Trophies of Grace.* Milwaukee: Northwestern Publishing House, 1962. $1.25. On missionaries to Indians.

2217. * Nomland, Gladys A. See No. 4035 and 4036.

2218. * Noon, John A. *The Law and Government of the Grand River Iroquois.* 1949; rpt. New York: Johnson Reprint Corp., 1970. $10.00.

2219. * Norbeck, Oscar E. *Indian Crafts for Campers.* New York: Association Press, 1967. (Grades 9 up) $1.75.

2220. North, Luther. *Man of the Plains: Recollections of Luther North, 1856-1882.* Ed. Donald F. Danker. Lincoln: University of Nebraska Press, 1961. $4.75.

2221. Northey, Sue. *The American Indian.* Rev. ed. San Antonio, Texas: The Naylor Company, 1964. 228 pp. (Grades 4-9) $4.95.

2222. * Novack, George. *Genocides Against the Indians.* New York: Pathfinder Press, Inc., 1971. $ .50.

2223. * Nowell, Charles J. *Smoke From Their Fires. The Life of a Kwakiutl Chief.* Ed. Chellan S. Ford. New Haven, Connecticut: Yale University Press, 1940. Author is a Kwakiutl Indian. In paper: Rpt. Hamden, Connecticut: Archon Press, 1968. 284 pp.

2224. Nurge, Ethel, ed. *The Modern Sioux. Social Systems and Reservation Culture.* Lincoln: University of Nebraska Press, 1970. 352 pp. $12.50.

2225. * *Nursing Careers in the Indian Health Service.* Rev. ed. Washington, D.C.: Government Printing Office, 1971. 11 pp. $ .30.

2226. Nuttall, Thomas. *A Journal of Travels into the Arkansas Territory. During the Year 1819.* 1821; rpt. March of America Series. Ann Arbor, Michigan: University Microfilms, 1966. $7.75.

2227. Nye, Wilbur S. *Carbine and Lance: The Story of Old Fort Sill.* Norman: University of Oklahoma Press, 1967. $6.50.

2228. Nye, Wilbur S. *Plains Indian Raiders: The Final Phases of Warfare from the Arkansas to the Red River.* Norman: University of Oklahoma Press, 1968. 418 pp. $9.50.

2229. * *Ocmulgee National Monument, Georgia.* 1956; rpt. Washington, D.C.: Government Printing Office, 1961. 58 pp. $ .40.

2230. O'Connor, Richard. *Sitting Bull: War Chief of the Sioux.* New York: McGraw-Hill, 1970. $3.95.

2231. * O'Daffer, Floyd C. *American Indian Wars Sixteen Twenty One-Eighteen Ninety.* New York: Carlton Press, 1970. $7.50.

2232. O'Dell, Scott. *Sing Down the Moon: A Story of the Navajo.* Boston: Houghton Mifflin Co., 1970. (Grades 5 up) 137 pp. $3.75.

2233. Ogden, Peter S. *Traits of American Indian Life and Character.* 2nd edition. 1933; rpt. New York: AMS Press, 1970. $15.00.

2234. * Ogle, Ralph H. *Federal Control of the Western Apaches, 1848-1886.* Rev. Ed. Albuquerque: University of New Mexico Press, 1969. 289 pp. $6.95. In paper: $3.95.

2235. Oglesby, Catharine. *Modern Primitive Art of Mexico, Guatamala, and the Southwest.* 1939; rpt. Essay Index Reprint Series. Freeport, New York: Books for Libraries, Inc., 1970. $8.50.

2236. O'Kane, Walter C. *The Hopis: Portrait of a Desert People.* Civilization of the American Indian Series, No. 35. Norman: University of Oklahoma Press, 1953; rpt. 1969. 267 pp. $8.95.

2237. ——. *The Intimate Desert.* Tucson: University of Arizona Press, 1969. $2.95.

2238. ——. *Sun in the Sky.* Civilization of the American Indian Series, No. 30. Norman: University of Oklahoma Press, 1970. 261 pp. $7.50.

2239. Olden, Sarah Emilia. *The People of Tipi Sapa.* Milwaukee, Wisconsin: Morehouse Publishing Company, 1918. (Tipi Sapa is Rev. Philip Joseph Deloria, father of Vine Deloria.) This is, in part, Deloria's story told by himself.

2240. Oliva, Leo E. *Soldiers on the Sante Fe Trail.* Norman: University of Oklahoma Press, 1970. $6.95.

2241. * Oliver, Symmes Co., See No. 4048.

2242. Olson, James C. *Red Cloud and the Sioux Problem.* Lincoln: University of Nebraska Press, 1965. 375 pp. $5.95.

2243. Olson, Ronald L. *The Quinault Indians, and Adze, Canoe, and House Types of the Northwest Coast.* 1927; rpt. together. Seattle: University of Washington Press, 1955 and 1967. 194 pp. / 38 pp. $6.95. See also Nos. 4028 and 4033.

2244. O'Meara, Walter. *Daughters of the Country: The Women of the Fur Traders and Mountain Men.* New York: Harcourt Brace Jovanovich, 1968. $6.95.

2245. ———. *The Sioux Are Coming.* Boston: Houghton Mifflin Co., 1971. 105 pp. $3.95.

2246. * O'Neale, Lila M. See Nos. 4028, 4032, 4039, and 4040.

2247. Opler, Morris E. *An Apache Life-Way, the Economic, Social, and Religious Institutions of the Chiricahua Indians.* University of Chicago Publications in Anthropology. Ethnological Series. Chicago: University of Chicago Press, 1941; rpt. New York: Cooper Square Publishers, Inc., 1970. 500 pp. $10.00.

2248. Orcutt, Samuel. *A History of the Indians of Western Connecticut.* Stratford, Conn.: J. E. Edwards, 1972. $10.00.

2249. Orrmont, Arthur. *Diplomat in Warpaint: Chief Alexander Magillivray of the Creeks.* New York: Abelard-Schuman, Ltd., 1967. (Grades 7 up) $4.75.

2250. Ortiz, Alfonso. *Project Head Start in an Indian Community.* Chicago: University of Chicago Press, 1965. 70 pp. Author is San Juan Pueblo.

2251. ———. *The Tewa World.* Chicago: University of Chicago Press, 1969. 197 pp. $8.00.

2252. ———, ed. *New Perspectives on the Pueblos.* Albuquerque: University of New Mexico Press, 1971. Outgrowth of a seminar held in 1969 at the School of American Research in Sante Fe. Includes essays on many aspects of Pueblo culture. 320 pp. $10.95.

2253. Osborne, Chester G. *The First Bow and Arrow.* Illustrations by Richard N. Osborne. Chicago: Wilcox and Follett Company, 1951. (Grades 3-5) $3.48.

2254. ———. *The First Lake Dwellers.* Chicago: Wilcox and Follett Company, 1956. (Grades 3-5) $3.48.

2255. * Osgood, Cornelius. *Contributions to the Ethnography of the Kutchin.* Yale University Publications in Anthropology, No. 14. New Haven: Yale University Press, 1936. 189 pp. $5.50.

2256. * ———. *Ethnography of the Tanaina.* Rpt. New York: Human Relations Area File Press, 1966. $7.50.

2257. * ———. *Ingalik Mental Culture.* Yale University Publications in Anthropology, No. 56. New Haven: Department of Anthropology, 1959. New York: Human Relations Area File Press, 1970. 195 pp. $2.50.

2258. Oskison, John M. *Brothers Three*. New York: Macmillan, 1935. 448 pp. Author is Cherokee.

2259. ———. *Tecumseh and His Times: The Story of a Great Indian*. New York: G. P. Putnam's Sons, 1938. 244 pp.

2260. ———. *A Texas Titan: The Story of Sam Houston*. Garden City, New York: Doubleday, Doran and Company, Inc., 1929. 311 pp.

2261. * Oswalt, Wendell H. *The Alaskan Eskimos*. Trenton, New Jersey: Chandler-Davis Publishing Company, 1971. $7.50. In paper: $4.25.

2262. * ———. *Napaskiak: An Alaskan Eskimo Community*. Tucson: University of Arizona Press, 1963. $3.50.

2263. ———. *This Land Was Theirs*. New York: John Wiley and Sons, 1966. $11.95.

2264. Otis, D. S. *The Dawes Act and the Allotment of Indian Land*. Ed. Francis P. Prucha. Civilization of the American Indian Series, No. 123. Norman: University of Oklahoma Press, 1972. 215 pp. $6.95.

2265. Overton, Gwendolen. *The Heritage of Unrest*. 1901; rpt. Upper Saddle River, New Jersey: Literature House / The Gregg Press, 1969. $12.00.

2266. Overton, Jacqueline M. *Indian Life on Long Island*. Empire State Historical Publications Series, No. 23. Port Washington, New York: Ira J. Friedman, Inc., 1963. $6.00.

2267. Owen, Roger C. *Morabavi: A Study of an Assimilated Group in Northern Sonora*. Tucson: University of Arizona Press, 1963. $1.50.

2268. Paige, Harry W. *Songs of the Seton Sioux*. Great West and Indian Series, Vol. 39. Los Angeles: Western Lore Press, 1969. $7.50.

2269. * Palladino, Lawrence. *Coeur D'Alene Reservation and Our Friends the Coeur D'Alene Indians*. 1967; rpt. Fairfield, Washington: Ye Galleon Press, 1970. $3.00.

2270. Parish, Peggy. *Good Hunting Little Indian*. New York: William R. Scott, Inc., 1962. (Grades 1-3) $3.50.

2271. ———. *Granny and the Indians*. New York: Macmillan, 1969. (Grades 1-3) $3.95.

2272. ———. *Let's Be Indians*. New York: Harcourt Brace and Row, 1962. (Grade 1-5) 95 pp. $3.95.

2273. ———. *The Little Indian*. New York: Simon and Shuster, 1968. (Grades K-3) $3.95.

2274. ———. *Ootah, Little Hunter*. New York: Harper Row, 1970. (Grades K-3) $2.50.

2275. ———. *Ootah's Lucky Day*. I Can Read Books. New York: Harper Row, 1970. (Grades K-3) $2.50.

2276. Parker, Arthur C. *The Code of Handsome Lake, the Seneca Prophet.* New York State Museum, Bulletin No. 162 (November, 1912), 5-148. 144 pp. Author was Seneca.

2277. ———. *A History of the Seneca Indians.* Empire State Historical Publications. No. 43. 1926; rpt. Port Washington, New York: Friedman, 1967. 162 pp.

2278. ———. *The Indian How Book.* Garden City, New York: Doubleday, Doran and Company, 1937. 355 pp.

2279. ———. *The Life of General Ely S. Parker: Last Grand Sachem of the Iroquois and General Grant's Military Secretary.* Buffalo Historical Society Publications. Vol. 23. Buffalo, New York: Buffalo Historical Society, 1919. 346 pp.

2280. ———. *A Manual for History Museums.* 1935; rpt. New York: AMS Press, 1970. $8.00.

2281. ———. *Red Jacket: Last of the Senecas.* New York: McGraw-Hill, 1952. 288 pp.

2282. * Parker, Horace. *The Early Indians of Temecula.* Balboa Island, California: Paisano Press, Inc., 1965. $1.00.

2283. * ———, ed. *Thriving, Tempting Temecula of 1909.* Balboa Island, California: Paisano Press, 1967. $1.00.

2284. * ———. *The Treaty of Temecula.* Balboa Island, California: Paisano Press, 1967. $1.00.

2285. Parker, Mack. *The Amazing Red Man.* San Antonio, Texas: Naylor Company, 1960. (Grades 6 up) 66 pp. $3.95.

2286. Parker, Samuel. *Journal of Exploring Tour, Etc.* Minneapolis: Ross and Haines, Inc., 1970. $10.00.

2287. Parker, Watson. *Gold in the Black Hills.* Norman: University of Oklahoma Press, 1970. $6.95.

2288. Parkhill, Forbes. *The Last of the Indian Wars.* New York: Crowell-Collier Press, 1962. 127 pp.

2289. Parkman, Francis. *The Conspiracy of Pontiac and the Indian War after the Conquest of Canada.* 2 vols. Boston: Little, Brown, and Company, 1933; rpt. 1962. 381 pp. / 484 pp. In paper: Collier Books. New York: Macmillan Company, 1962. $1.50.

2290. ———. *The Oregon Trail.* Ed. E. N. Feltskog. Madison: University of Wisconsin Press, 1969. $15.00. Numerous other editions exist.

2291. ———. *Vassall Morton.* 1956; rpt. Upper Saddle River, New Jersey: Literature House / The Gregg Press, 1971. $15.50.

2292. * Parks, Jack. *Who Killed Custer.* New York: Tower Publications, Inc., 1971. 154 pp. $ .95.

2293. Parmee, Edward A. *Formal Education and Culture Change: A Modern Apache Indian Community and Government Education Program.* Tucson: University of Arizona Press, 1968. 123 pp. $5.00.

2294. Parry, William E. *Journal of a Second Voyage for the Discovery of a Northwest Passage from the Atlantic to the Pacific.* 1824; rpt. Westport, Connecticut: Greenwood Press, Inc., 1971. $29.50.

2295. Parsons, Elsie C. *Isleta Paintings.* Ed. Ester S. Goldrank. Bureau of American Ethnology Bulletin 181. Washington, D.C.: Smithsonian Institution, 1970. (Distributed by Random House) $13.95. See also No. 4017.

2296. *——. *A Pueblo Indian Journal.* 1925; rpt. New York: Kraus Reprint Co., 1970. $5.00.

2297. *——. *The Social Organization of the Tewa of New Mexico.* 1929; rpt. New York: Kraus Reprint Co., 1970. $15.00.

2298. *——, ed. *American Indian Life.* Illustrated by C. Grant LaFarge. 1922; rpt. Bison Book. Lincoln: University of Nebraska Press, 1967. 419 pp. $2.95. Also: Gloucester, Mass.: Peter Smith, Inc., 1971. $5.00.

2299. *Parsons, F. W. *Notes on the Caddo.* 1941; rpt. New York: Kraus Reprint Co., 1970. $4.00.

2300. *Patten, Lewis B. *Apache Hostage.* Signet Book. New York: New American Library, 1970. $ .60.

2301. Patten, Lewis B., and Wayne D. Overholser. *The Meeker Massacre.* New York: Cowles Book Corp., Inc., 1969. (Grades 5-9) $3.50.

2302. Paul, Frances. *Spruce Root Basketry of the Alaska Tlingit.* Lawrence, Kansas: Haskell Press, 1960. 80 pp. $ .55.

2303. Payne, Doris P. *Captain Jack, Modoc Renegade.* Portland, Oregon: Binfords and Mort, Pub., 1938. $5.50.

2304. *Payne, Elizabeth. *Meet the North American Indians.* Step-Up Book. New York: Random House, 1965. (Grades 2-6) 84 pp. $3.37. In paper: $1.95.

2305. Payne, Mildred Y., and Harry H. Kroll. *Mounds in the Mist.* Cranbury, New Jersey: A. S. Barnes and Company, 1969. $7.50.

2306. *Peabody, C. *Exploration of Mounds, Coahoma County, Mississippi.* 1904; rpt. New York: Kraus Reprint Co., 1971. $2.50.

2307. *Pearce, Roy H. *The Savages of America.* Rev. Ed. Baltimore: Johns Hopkins University Press, 1965. Reissued as *Savagism and Civilization,* 1967. 260 pp. In paper: Baltimore: Johns Hopkins University Press, 1970. $2.45.

2308. Peckham, Howard, ed. *The Attitudes of the Colonial Powers Toward the American Indians.* Salt Lake City: University of Utah Press, 1969. $6.00.

2309. ——. *Pontiac and the Indian Uprising.* Princeton: Princeton University Press, 1947; rpt. New York: Russell and Russell, 1970. $13.50.

2310. ——. *Pontiac: Young Ottawa Leader.* Indianapolis: Bobbs-Merrill Company, 1963. (Grades 3-7) $2.75.

2311. Peirce, Parker L. *Antelope Bill.* Limited Edition. Minneapolis: Ross and Haines, Inc., 1970 $12.50.

2312. Peithmann, Irvin M. *Broken Peace Pipes: A Four-Hundred-Year History of the American Indian.* Springfield, Illinois: Charles C. Thomas, publisher, 1964. 298 pp. $7.50.

2313. ——. *The Indians of Southern Illinois.* Springfield, Illinois: Charles C. Thomas, Inc., 1964. 125 pp. $6.50.

2314. ——. *Red Man on Fire.* A History of the Cherokee Indians. Springfield, Illinois: Charles C. Thomas, Inc., 1964. 165 pp. $6.50.

2315. *Penney, Grace J. *Moki.* Camelot Books. New York: Avon Books, 1970. 146 pp. Also: Boston: Houghton Mifflin Company, 1960. $2.75.

2316. Pennhallow, S. *The History of the Wars of New England with the Eastern Indians.* 1859; rpt. New York: Kraus Reprint Co., 1970. $10.00.

2317. *Pepper, G. H., and G. L. Wilson. *Hidatsa Shrine and the Beliefs Respecting It.* 1915; rpt. New York: Kraus Reprint Co., 1970. $3.50.

2318. Perceval, Don, and Clay Lockett. *Navajo Sketch Book.* 2nd ed. Flagstaff, Arizona: Northland Press, 1968. $14.50.

2319. Perez De Luxan, Diego. *An Expedition into New Mexico Made by Antonio De Espejo, 1582-1883.* Ed. George P. Hammond. 1929; rpt. Quivira Society Publications, Vol. I. New York: Arno Press, 1967. $12.00.

2320. Perkins, James H. *Annals of the West.* Rev. Ed. 1850; rpt. J. M. Peck, ed. New York: Augustus M. Kelley Pub., 1970. $22.50.

2321. Perkins, Lucy F. *Eskimo Twins.* Twins Series. Ed. Beth Walker and Rosemary Jones. New York: Walker and Company, 1969. (Grades 4-5).

2322. ——. *Indian Twins.* New York: Walker and Company, 1969. $3.95.

2323. Perrot, Nicholas. *Memoire Sur les Moeurs, Coustumes et Religion Des Sauvages De l'Amerique Septentrionale.* 1864; rpt. New York: Johnson Reprint Corp., 1970. $13.50.

2324. Peter, R. *Sketch of the Cheyenne Grammar.* See Mooney, James, No. 2124.

2325. Peters, Joseph P., compiler. *Indian Battles and Skirmishes on the American Frontier 1790-1898.* New York: Arno Press, 1966. $27.50.

2326. Petersen, Karen D. *Plains Indian Art from Fort Marion.* Civilization of the American Indian Series, Vol. 101. Norman: University of Oklahoma Press, 1971. 340 pp. $9.95.

2327. * Peterson, Harold C. *American Indian Tomahawks*. Rev. ed. New York: Museum of the American Indian, Heye Foundation, 1970. 142 pp. $10.00.

2328. * Pettitt, George A. See No. 4043.

2329. Phebus, George E. *Alaskan Eskimo Life in the 1890s as Sketched by Native Artists*. Washington, D.C.: Smithsonian Institution, 1972. 168 pp. $15.00.

2330. Phelps, Thomas. *Reminiscences of Seattle, Washington Territory and the United States Sloop-Of-War Decatur During the Indian War of 1855-1856*. Rpt. Fairfield, Washington: Ye Galleon Press, 1971. $3.50.

2331. * Phillips, P. et al. *Archaeological Survey in the Lower Mississippi Alluvial Valley, 1940-1947*. 1951; rpt. New York: Kraus Reprint Co., 1970. $42.00.

2332. Phillips, Paul C., and J. W. Smurr. *The Fur Trade*. Norman: University of Oklahoma Press, 1968. $25.00.

2333. * *Photographs and Poems by Sioux Children*. From the Porcupine Day School, Pine Ridge Indian Reservation, South Dakota. Selected by Myles Libhart and Arthur Amiotte. With an essay by Arthur Amiotte. Rapid City, South Dakota: Tipi Shop, Inc., 1971. 77 pp.

2334. Piere, George. *The American Indian Crisis*. San Antonio, Texas: Naylor Company, 1971. $8.95.

2335. ———. *Autumn's Bounty*. San Antonio, Texas: Naylor Company, 1972. $7.95. Author is a Colville Indian.

2336. * Pietroforte, Alfred. *Songs of the Yokuts and Paiutes of California and Nevada*. Healdsburg, California: Naturegraph Pub., 1965. (Grades 4 up) $3.50. In paper: $1.50.

2337. Pine, Tillie S., and Joseph Levine. *The Eskimos Knew*. New York: McGraw Hill, 1962. (Grades 1-4) $3.95.

2338. ———. *The Indians Knew*. New York: McGraw Hill, 1957. (Grades 1-4) $3.95.

2339. * Pistorius, Anna. *What Indian Is It?* Rev. ed. Chicago: Follett Publishing Company, 1968. (Grades K-3) $1.95.

2340. * Pitt-Rivers, Julian. *People of the Sierra*. 2nd ed. rev. Chicago: University of Chicago Press, 1970. In paper: University of Chicago Press, 1961. $1.95.

2341. Place, Marian T. *Buckskins and Buffalo: The Story of the Yellowstone River*. New York: Holt, Rinehart and Winston, 1964. (Grades 4-6) $3.50.

2342. ———. *The Comanches and Other Indians of Texas*. A Curriculum Related Book. New York: Harcourt Brace Jovanovich, 1970. (Grades 7 up) 131 pp. $4.25.

2343. ———. *Rifles and War Bonnets*. New York: Washburn Ives, Inc., 1968. (Grades 6-8) $3.95.

2344. Poe, Charlsie. *Angel to the Papagos.* San Antonio, Texas: Naylor Company, 1964. (Grades 7 up) $4.95.

2345. Point, Nicholas, S. J. *Wilderness Kingdom: Indian Life in the Rocky Mountains: 1840-1847.* Trans. and Ed. Joseph P. Donnelly, S. J. New York: Holt, Rinehart and Winston, 1967. 274 pp. $17.95.

2346. Polingaysi Qoyawayma, See White, Elizabeth, No. 202.

2347. Pollock, Dean. *Joseph, Chief of the Nez Perce.* Portland, Oregon: Binfords and Mort, 1950. (Grades 7-9) $3.00.

2348. Pope, Saxton T. See No. 4013.

2349. Porter, C. Fayne. *Our Indian Heritage.* Profiles of 12 Great Leaders. Philadelphia: Chilton Books, 1964. (Grades 9 up) 228 pp. $4.95.

2350. Potomac Corral of the Westerners. See *Great Western Indian Fights,* No. 1399.

2351. Potter, Woodburne. *The War in Florida.* 1836; rpt. March of America Series. Ann Arbor, Michigan: University Microfilms, 1966. $6.75.

2352. Pouchot, M. *Memoir Upon the Late War in North America, Between the French and English, 1755-1760.* 2 vols. 1866; rpt. Ed. Franklin B. Hough. St. Clair Shores, Michigan: Scholarly Press, 1970. $21.00.

2353. Pound, Arthur, and Richard F. Day. *Johnson of the Mohawks.* 1930; rpt. Select Bibliographies Reprint Series. Facsimile ed. New York: Books for Libraries, 1972. $27.50.

2354. Pound, Merritt B. *Benjamin Hawkins: Indian Agent.* Athens: University of Georgia Press, 1951. 270 pp. $5.00.

2355. *Powell, John W., and Lollie W. Campbell. *The Hopi Villages.* Wild and Woolly West Series, No. 21. Palmer Lake, Colorado: Filter Press, 1972. $3.50. In paper: $1.00.

2356. Powers, William. *Here is Your Hobby: Indian Dancing and Costumes.* New York: G. P. Putnam's Sons, 1966. (Grades 5-8) 125 pp. $3.86.

2357. ——. *The Indians of the Northern Plains.* New York: G. P. Putnam's Sons, 1969. (Grades 8 up) $4.50.

2358. ——. *The Indians of the Southern Plains.* Indians Then and Now Series. New York: G. P. Putnam's Sons, 1971. (Grades 7 up) $4.50.

2359. Prassel, Frank R. *The Western Peace Officer: A Legacy of Law and Order.* Norman: University of Oklahoma Press, 1972.

2360. Pratson, Frederick J. *The Land of the Four Directions.* Old Greenwich, Connecticut: Chatham Press, Inc., 1970. $7.95.

2361. Praus, Alexis. *The Sioux, 1798-1922.* A Dakota Winter Count. Cranbrook Institute of Science. Bulletin No. 44. Bloomfield Hills, Michigan: Cranbrook Press, 1962. 31 pp.

2362. Prescott, Philander. *The Recollections of Philander Prescott: Frontiersman of the Old Northwest, 1819-1862.* Ed. Donald D. Parker. Lincoln: University of Nebraska Press, 1966. $5.95.

2363. Prettyman, W. S. *Indian Territory: A Frontier Photographic Record.* Ed. Robert E. Cunningham. Norman: University of Oklahoma Press, 1957. $7.50.

2364. Price, Archibald G. *White Settlers and Native Peoples.* 1949; rpt. Westport, Connecticut: Greenwood Press, Inc., 1970. $11.50.

2365. Priest, Loring B. *Uncle Sam's Stepchildren: The Reformation of United States Indian Policy, 1865-1887.* 1942; rpt. New York: Octagon Books, 1969. $9.00.

2366. Proper, Churchill. *Indian Crafts.* New ed. Handicraft Series, No. 4. Samhar Press, 1971. (Grades 7-12) $1.98. In paper: $ .95.

2367. * Prucha, Francis P. *American Indian Policy in the Formative Years: The Indian Trade and Intercourse Acts 1790-1834.* Cambridge: Harvard University Press, 1962. 303 pp. In paper: Lincoln: University of Nebraska Press, 1970. 303 pp. $2.25.

2368. * ——. *Broadax and Bayonet: The Role of the United States Army in the Development of the Northwest, 1815-1860.* Lincoln: University of Nebraska Press, 1967. $1.95.

2369. * ——. *The Indian in American History.* New York: Holt, Rinehart and Winston, 1970. $12.45.

2370. ——. *Indian Peace Medals in American History.* Madison, Wisconsin: Society Press, 1971. $15.00.

2371. * ——. *Lewis Cass and American Indian Policy.* Detroit: Wayne State University Press, 1967. $1.50.

2372. * Prudden, P. M. *Further Study of Prehistoric Small House-Ruins in the San Juan Watershed.* 1918; rpt. New York: Kraus Reprint Co., 1970. $3.50.

2373. Prufer, Olaf H., and Douglas H. McKenzie. *Studies in Ohio Archaeology.* Cleveland: Press of Case Western Reserve University, 1967. $11.00.

2374. Prufer, Olaf H., and Orrin C. Shane. *Blain Village and the Fort Ancient Tradition in Ohio.* Kent: Kent State University Press, 1970. 280 pp. $10.00.

2375. * Quimby, George I. *Indian Culture and European Trade Goods.* Madison: University of Wisconsin Press, 1966. 217 pp. In paper: 1970. 217 pp. $2.95.

2376. * ——. *Indian Life in the Upper Great Lakes: 11,000 B.C. to A.D.1800.* Chicago: University of Chicago Press, 1960; rpt. 1971. 182 pp. In paper: $2.45.

2377. Rabin, David, et al. *Health Problems and Disease of the United States and North American Indian Populations.* New York: Mss Information Corp., 1972. $15.00.

2378. Rachlis, Eugene, and J. C. Ewers. *The Indians of the Plains.* The American Heritage Junior Library. New York: Harcourt Brace Row, 1960. (Grades 5 up) 153 pp. $5.95.

2379. Radin, Paul. See Crashing Thunder. See also Nos. 4014, 4016, 4017, 4027, and 4031.

2380. ———. *The Grammar of the Wappo Language.* 1929; rpt. New York: Kraus Reprint Co., 1971. $25.00.

2381. * ———. *The Method and Theory of Ethnology.* Rpt. New York: Basic Books, Inc., 1963. $7.50. In paper: $3.45.

2382. * ———. *Primitive Man as Philosopher.* 1927; rpt. New York: Dover Publications, 1970. $3.00.

2383. * ———. *Primitive Religion: Its Nature and Origin.* 1937; rpt. New York: Dover Publications, 1970. $3.00.

2384. ———. *The Road of Life and Death.* Bollingen Series, Vol. 5. Princeton: Princeton University Press, 1945. $6.50.

2385. ———. *The Story of the American Indian.* Rev. ed. New York: Liveright, 1944. 391 pp. $6.95.

2386. * ———. *The Winnebago Tribe.* 1915; rpt. Lincoln: University of Nebraska Press, 1970. (Reprinted from original Thirty-Seventh Annual Report of the Bureau of American Ethnology, Smithsonian Institution, Washington, D.C., 1923.) 511 pp. $3.50. Also: 1915; rpt. New York: Johnson Reprint Corp., 1971. $27.50. Also: Rpt. Gloucester, Mass.: Peter Smith, 1970. $6.00.

2387. Rahti, Tom. *Southwestern Indian Arts and Crafts.* Flagstaff, Arizona: KC Publications, 1970.

2388. Rand, Silas T. *Dictionary of the Languages of the Micmac Indians, Who Reside in Nova Scotia, New Brunswick, Prince Edward Island, Cape Breton, and Newfoundland.* 1888; rpt. New York: Johnson Reprint Corp., 1970. $17.50.

2389. * Randall, Florence. *The American Indians.* Rev. ed. Highlights Handbooks Series. Columbus, Ohio: Highlights for Children, Inc., 1972. (Grades 2-5) $1.00.

2390. Randolph, J. Ralph. *British Travelers Among the Southern Indians, 1660-1763.* American Exploration and Travel Series, Vol. 62. Norman: University of Oklahoma Press, 1972. 200 pp. $8.95.

2391. Raphael, Ralph B. *The Book of American Indians.* New York: Arco Publishing Company, Inc., 1959. (Grades 5 up) $3.50.

2392. * Rapoport, Robert N. *Changing Navaho Religious Values: A Study of Christian Missions to the Rimrock Navahos.* 1954; rpt. New York: Kraus Reprint Co., 1971. $13.00.

2393. Rasmussen, Knud J. *Across Arctic America, Narrative of the Fifth Thule Expedition.* Westport, Connecticut: Greenwood Press, Inc., 1968. $24.50.

2394. ——. *The Intellectual Culture of the Iglulik Eskimos.* Copenhagen: Glydendalske Boghandel, 1929.

2395. ——. *Observations on the Intellectual Culture of the Caribou Eskimos.* Copenhagen, 1930.

2396. Ray and Murdock. *Vocabulary of the Eskimos of Point Barrow.* 1885; rpt. Facsimile ed. Seattle: Shorey Publications, 1968. $1.25.

2397. Ray, Dorothy J. *Artists of the Tundra and the Sea.* Seattle: University of Washington Press, 1961. 170 pp. $6.50.

2398. ——. *Eskimo Masks: Art and Ceremony.* Seattle: University of Washington Press, 1967. 246 pp. $12.50.

2399. *——, ed. *The Eskimo of St. Michael and Vicinity as Related by H. M. W. Edmonds.* Anthropological Papers of the University of Alaska, Vol. 13, No. 2. College, Alaska: University of Alaska Press, 1966. 143 pp.

2400. Ray, Verne F. *Primitive Pragmatists; the Modoc Indians of Northern California.* Seattle: University of Washington Press, 1963. $6.50.

2401. Reading, Robert S. *Arrows Over Texas.* San Antonio, Texas: Naylor Company, 1960. (Grades 7 up) 269 pp. $5.95.

2402. ——. *Indian Civilizations.* San Antonio, Texas: Naylor Company, 1970. (Grades 7 up) 200 pp. $4.95.

2403. Recinos, Adrian, and Delia Goetz, trans. *The Annals of the Cakchiquels,* Including *The Journal of Captain Robert Cholmley's Batman: The Journal of a British Officer, Halkett's Orderly Book.* Civilization of American Indian Series, No. 37. 1953; rpt. Norman: University of Oklahoma Press, 1957. $6.95.

2404. *Red Horse Owner's Winter Count: The Oglala Sioux 1786-1968.* Ed. Joseph S. Karol. Martin, S.D.: The Booster Publishing Co., 1969. 68 pp.

2405. *The Red Man in the United States: An Intimate Study,* etc. See Lindquist, G. E. E., No. 1898.

2406. Reichard, Gladys A. *Dezba, Woman of the Desert: Life Among the Navajo Indians.* Glorieta, New Mexico: Rio Grande Press, 1971. See also No. 4022.

2407. ——. *Navajo Medicine Man.* New York: J. J. Augustin, 1939.

2408. ——. *Navaho Religion: A Study of Symbolism.* 2nd ed. 2 vols. Princeton: Princeton University Press, 1964. 800 pp. $7.50.

2409. ——. *Navajo Shepherd and Weaver.* 2nd ed. Rio Grande Classics Series. 1936; rpt. Glorieta, New Mexico: Rio Grande Press, Inc., 1968. 222 pp. $8.00.

2410. ——. *Prayer: The Compulsive Word.* American Ethnological Society Monographs. Seattle: University of Washington Press, 1966. $5.00.

2411. ——. *The Social Life of the Navajo Indians.* Columbia University Contributions to Anthropology Series, Vol. 7. 1928; rpt. New York: AMS Press, 1969. 239 pp. $27.50.

2412. ——. *Spider Woman: A Story of Navajo Weavers and Chanters.* 2nd ed. Rio Grande Classics Series. 1934; rpt. Glorieta, New Mexico: Rio Grande Press, Inc., 1968. 287 pp. $8.00.

2413. Reid, John P. *A Law of Blood: The Primitive Law of the Cherokee Nation.* New York: New York University Press, 1970. 336 pp. $10.00.

2414. Reid, William, and Adelaide De Menil. *Out of the Silence.* New York: Harper and Row, 1972. $4.95.

2415. Reit, Seymour. *Child of the Navajos.* New York: Dodd, Mead and Company, 1971. (Grades 6-9) 64 pp. $3.95.

2416. *Relation of Maryland, Together with a Map of the Country, the Conditions of Plantation, His Majesties Charter to Lord Baltimore.* 1635; rpt. March of America Series. Ann Arbor, Michigan: University Microfilms, 1966. $4.55.

2417. Remington, Frederic. *Artist Wanderings Among the Cheyennes.* 1889; rpt. Seattle: Shorey Publications, 1970. $1.50.

2418. ——. *Pony Tracks.* Rpt. Columbus, Ohio: Long's College Book Company, 1951. $5.00. Also: Western Frontier Library, No. 19. Rpt. Norman: University of Oklahoma Press, 1969. $2.95.

2419. ——. *Remington's Frontier Sketches.* 1898; rpt. Research and Source Work Series, No. 398. New York: Burt Franklin Pub., 1970. $19.50.

2420. ——. *The Way of an Indian.* 1906; rpt. Upper Saddle River, New Jersey: Literature House / McGregg Press, 1971. $11.00.

2421. * *Report on the Transitional Housing Experiment, Rosebud Indian Reservation.* Washington, D.C.: Government Printing Office, 1969. 43 pp. $ .50.

2422. Reynolds, Charles R. *American Indian Portraits.* Brattleboro, Vermont: Stephen Greene Press, 1971. $12.50.

2423. * Rich, John M. *Chief Seattle's Unanswered Challenge.* Fairfield, Washington: Ye Galleon Press, 1970. $2.50.

2424. Richardson, Jane. *Law and Status Among the Kiowa Indians.* American Ethnological Society Monographs. Seattle: University of Washington Press, 1940. $5.00.

2425. Richardson, Rupert N. *The Comanche Barrier to South Plains Settlement.* 1933; rpt. New York: Kraus Reprint Co., 1971. $18.00.

2426. Rickey, Don. *Forty Miles a Day on Beans and Hay: The Enlisted Soldier Fighting the Indain Wars.* 1963; rpt. Norman: University of Oklahoma Press, 1966. $6.95.

2427. Ridge, John Rollin (Yellow Bird). *The Life and Adventures of Joaquin Murietta, the Celebrated California Bandit.* Norman: University of Oklahoma Press, 1962. 159 pp. Author is Cherokee.

2428. ———. *Poems.* San Francisco, California: Henry Payot and Company, 1968. 137 pp.

2429. Riggs, Sidney N. *Arrows and Snakeskin.* Philadelphia: J. B. Lippincott Company, 1962. (Grades 7-9) $3.25.

2430. Riggs, Stephen R. *Dakota Sioux-English Dictionary.* Rpt. Facsimile ed. Minneapolis: Ross and Haines, 1968. $17.50.

2431. ———. *Mary and I: Forty Years with the Sioux.* Boston: Congregational House, 1887; rpt. Corner Hse, 1971. 437 pp. $12.00. Also: Minneapolis: Ross and Haines, Inc., 1971. $12.50.

2432. ———. *Tah-Koo Wah-Kan; or, the Gospel Among the Dakotas.* 1869; rpt. Religion in America Series, No. 2. New York: Arno Press, 1972. $24.00.

2433. Rights, Douglas L. *The American Indian in North Carolina.* 2nd ed. Winston-Salem, N.C.: Blair, 1972. $10.00.

2434. Ritchie, William A. *Archaeology of New York State.* Rev. ed. Garden City, New York: Natural History Press, 1969. $15.00.

2435. *Ritzenthaler, Robert E., and Pat Ritzenthaler. *The Woodland Indians of the Western Great Lakes.* American Museum Science Book. Garden City, New York: The Natural History Press, 1970. 178 pp. $1.95.

2436. *Roberts, John M. *Three Navaho Households: A Comparative Study in Small Group Culture.* 1951; rpt. New York: Kraus Reprint Co., 1971. $9.00.

2437. *Robertson, Donald. *Pre-Columbian Architecture.* Great Ages of the World Architecture Series. New York: George Braziller, Inc., 1963. $5.93. In paper: $2.95.

2438. Robertson, Wyndam. *Pocahontas, Alias Matooka, and Her Descendants.* 1887; rpt. Baltimore: Genealogical Publishing Company, 1971. $7.50.

2439. Robinson, Doane. *A History of the Dakota or Sioux Indians.* 1904; rpt. Minneapolis: Ross and Haines, Inc., 1967. 523 pp. $10.00.

2440. Robinson, Dorothy F. *The Navajo Indians Today.* Rev. ed. Enlarged. San Antonio, Texas: Naylor Company, 1969. (Grades 7-12) 80 pp. $3.95.

2441. Roe, Frank Gilbert. *The Indian and the Horse.* Civilization of the American Indian Series, No. 41. 1955; rpt. Norman: University of Oklahoma Press, 1968. 434 pp. $7.95.

2442. ———. *The North American Buffalo; A Critical Study of the Species in its Wild State.* 2nd ed. Toronto: University of Toronto Press, 1970. $35.00.

2443. Roehm, Marjorie C., ed. *The Letters of George Catlin and His Family: A Chronicle of the American West.* Berkeley: University of California Press, 1966. $10.00.

2444. Roessel, Robert A. *Indian Communities in Action.* Tempe: Arizona State University, 1967. 225 pp.

2445. Rogers, Edward. *The Indians of Canada.* Canadian Jackdaw, No. C Sixteen. New York: Grossman Publishers, Inc., 1969. $3.95.

2446. Rogers, George W. *Alaska in Transition.* Baltimore: John Hopkins University Press, 1960. $12.00.

2447. ——. *The Future of Alaska.* Baltimore: Johns Hopkins University, 1962. $8.50.

2448. ——, ed. *Change in Alaska: People, Politics, and Petroleum.* Seattle: University of Washington Press, 1970. $7.95.

2449. Rogers, Robert. *Concise Account of North America.* 1765; rpt. New York: Johnson Reprint Corp., 1967. $9.50.

2450. ——. *Ponteach, Or: The Savages of America: A Tragedy.* 1914; rpt. New York: Burt Franklin, Pub., 1969. $16.50.

2451. *Rohner, Ronald P., and E. C. Rohner. *The Kwakiutl: Indians of British Columbia.* New York: Holt, Rinehard and Winston, 1970. $2.35.

2452. ——, eds. *The Ethnography of Franz Boas.* Trans. H. Parker. Chicago: University of Chicago Press, 1969. $12.50.

2453. Roland, Albert. *Great Indian Chiefs.* New York: Macmillan, 1966. (Grades 7-9) $4.50.

2454. Romans, Bernard. *The Concise Natural History of East and West Florida.* 1775; rpt. Gretna, Louisiana: Pelican Publishing House, 1970. $12.50.

2455. Ronan, Peter. *A Historical Sketch of the Flathead Nation.* 1890; rpt. Minneapolis: Ross and Haines, Inc., 1970. $4.95.

2456. *Roseman, Bernard. *The Peyote Story.* North Hollywood, California: Wilshire Book Company, 1968. 96 pp. $1.00.

2457. Ross, Alexander. *The Adventures of the First Settlers on the Oregon or Columbia River.* 1849; rpt. March of America Series. Ann Arbor, Michigan: University Microfilms, 1966. $7.75.

2458. ——. *The Fur Hunters of the Far West.* Ed. Kenneth A. Spaulding. 1956; rpt. American Exploration and Travel Series, No. 20. Norman: University of Oklahoma Press, 1967. $7.95.

2459. Ross, Eric. *Beyond the River and the Bay: Some Observations on the State of the Canadian Northwest in 1811 with a View to Providing the Intending Settler with an Intimate Knowledge of that Country.* Rpt. Toronto: University of Toronto Press, 1970. $8.50.

2460. Ross, Marvin E. ed. *George Catlin: Episodes From Life Among the Indians and Last Rambles.* Norman: University of Oklahoma Press, 1959. 354 pp. $12.50.

2461. Royce, Charles C., ed. *Indian Land Cessions in the United States.* 1899; rpt. New York: AMS Press, 1971. $37.50. Also: New York: Arno Press, 1971. $32.00.

2462. Rudy, Sara Sue. See Jennings, Jesse D., No. 1683.

2463. Ruby, Robert H. *The Oglala Sioux: Warrior in Transition.* New York: Vantage Press, 1955. 115 pp.

2464. Ruby, Robert H., and John A. Brown. *The Cayuse Indians.* Civilization of the American Indians Series, No. 120. Norman: University of Oklahoma Press, 1972. 349 pp. $8.95.

2465. Ruby, Robert H., and John A. Brown. *Half-Sun on the Columbia: A Biography of Chief Moses.* Civilization of the American Indian Series, No. 80. Norman: University of Oklahoma Press, 1965. 377 pp. $ .95.

2466. ——. *The Spokane Indians.* Civilization of the American Indian Series, No. 104. Norman: University of Oklahoma Press, 1970. 346 pp.

2467. * Rudman, Jack. *Civil Service Examination Passbook: Indian Education-Elementary Teacher.* Brooklyn: National Learning Corp., 1971. $8.00. In paper: $5.00.

2468. * ——. *Civil Service Examination Passbook: Indian Education-Guidance Counselor.* Brooklyn: National Learning Corp., 1971. $8.00. In paper: $5.00.

2469. * ——. *Civil Service Examination Passbook: Indian Education-Secondary Teacher.* Brooklyn: National Learning Corp., 1971. $8.00. In paper: $5.00.

2470. * *Rural Indian Americans in Poverty.* Washington, D.C.: Government Printing Office, 1969. 27 pp. $ .25.

2471. Russell, Don. *The Lives and Legends of Buffalo Bill.* Norman: University of Oklahoma Press, 1970. $7.95.

2472. Russell, Frank. *The Pima Indians.* 26th Annual Report of the Bureau of American Ethnology. Washington, D.C., 1908; rpt. Tucson: University of Arizona Press, 1971.

2473. Russell, Solveig. *Indian Big and Indian Little.* Indianapolis: Bobbs Merrill, 1964. (Grades K-3) $2.95.

2474. ——. *Navaholand.* Chicago: Melmont Publishers, Inc., 1961. (Grades 2-5) $2.75.

2475. Russell, Virgil T. *Indian Artifacts.* Boulder, Colorado: Johnson Publishing Company, 1970. $4.00.

2476. Ruth, Kent. *Great Day in the West: Forts, Posts, and Rendezvous Beyond the Mississippi.* Norman: University of Oklahoma Press, 1970. $12.50.

2477. Rutsch, Edward S. *The Smoking Technology of the Aborigines of the Iroquois Area of New York State.* Rutherford, New Jersey: Fairleigh Dickinson University Press, 1970. $12.00.

2478. Ruttan, Robert A. *Adventures of Oolakuk.* New York: Prentice-Hall, Inc., 1969. (Grades 3-6) 95 pp. $4.50.

2479. Ruttenber, Edward M. *The History of the Indian Tribes of Hudson's River.* 1872; rpt. Empire State Historical Publications Series. Port Washington, New York: Kennikat Press, Inc., 1971. $14.50. Also: St. Clair Shores, Michigan: Scholarly Press, 1971. $16.50.

2480. Ruxton, George F. *The Mountain Men.* Ed. Glen Rounds. New York: Holiday House, Inc., 1966. (Grades 6-10) $3.95.

2481. Ryan, J. C., ed. *Custer Fell First: The Adventures of John C. Lockwood.* San Antonio, Texas: Naylor Company, 1970. (Grades 6-8) $3.95.

2482. ———. *Revolt Along the Rio Grande.* San Antonio, Texas: Naylor Company, 1970. (Grades 7 up) $4.95.

2483. Rydjord, John. *Indian Place-Names.* Their Origin, Evolution, and Meanings, Collected in Kansas from the Siouan, Algonquian, Shoshonean, Caddoan, Iroquoian, and Other Tongues. Norman: University of Oklahoma Press, 1968. 380 pp. $7.95.

2484. Sagard-Theodat, Gebriel. *The Long Journey to the Country of the Hurons.* Ed. George W. Wrong. Trans. H. H. Langton. 1939; rpt. Westport, Connecticut: Greenwood Publishing Company, 1968. $25.75.

2485. Salisbury, O. M. *Quoth the Raven.* Seattle, Washington: Superior Publishing Company, 1962. 275 pp. $5.95.

2486. Salomon, Julian H. *The Book of Indian Crafts and Indian Lore.* New York: Harper and Row, 1928. Reprinted 1970. 418 pp. $7.95.

2487. Salsbury, Clarence G., and Paul Hughes. *The Salsbury Story: A Medical Missionary's Lifetime of Public Service.* Tucson: University of Arizona Press, 1969. $7.50.

2488. * Sanders, William T., and Joseph Marino. *New World Prehistory: Archaeology of the American Indian.* Foundations of Modern Anthropology Series. Englewood Cliffs, New Jersey: Prentice-Hall, Inc., 1970. 120 pp. $4.95. In paper: $1.95.

2489. * Sando, Joe S. *The Pueblo Indians.* San Francisco: American Indian Historical Society, 1972. $10.00. Author is Jemez Pueblo. In paper: $6.00.

2490. * Sandoz, Mari. *The Battle of the Little Bighorn.* New York: Modern Literary Editions Publishing Company, 1966. 238 pp. $1.25.

2491. ———. *Buffalo Hunters.* Rpt. American Procession Series. New York: Hastings House Publishers, Inc., 1971.

2492. *——. *Cheyenne Autumn.* New York: Avon Books, 1964. 336 pp. $1.25.

2493. *——. *Crazy Horse.* 1942; rpt. Lincoln: University of Nebraska Press, 1961. 428 pp. $1.75.

2494. *——. *These Were the Sioux.* 1961; rpt. A Yearling Book. New York: Dell Publishing Company, 1971. 118 pp. $ .75.

2495. *Sandpaintings of the Navaho Shootingway and the Walcott Collection.* Smithsonian Institution Contributions to Anthropology, Vol. 13. Washington, D.C.: Government Printing Office, 1970. 102 pp. $3.75.

2496. Sanford, George B. *Fighting Rebels and Redskins: Experiences in Army Life of Colonel George B. Sanford, 1861-1892.* Ed. E. R. Hagemann. Norman: University of Oklahoma Press, 1968. $7.95.

2497. Sanford, Paul. *Sioux Arrows and Bullets.* San Antonio, Texas: Naylor Company, 1969. (Grades 7 up) $5.95.

2498. ——. *Where the Old West Never Died.* San Antonio, Texas: Naylor Company, 1968. (Grades 7 up) $4.95.

2499. *Santee, Ross. *Apache Land.* 1947; rpt. Lincoln: University of Nebraska Press, 1971. 216 pp. $2.25.

2500. *Sapir, Edward. *Culture, Language and Personality: Selected Essays.* Ed. David G. Mandelbaum. Berkeley: University of California Press, 1929. $1.95. See also Nos. 4009, 4013, and 4020.

2501. ——. *Selected Writings of Edward Sapir in Language, Culture, and Personality.* Ed. David Mandelbaum. Berkeley: University of California Press, 1949. $11.50.

2502. *——. *Time Perspective in Aboriginal American Culture, a Study in Method.* Rpt. Landmarks in Anthropology Series. New York: Johnson Reprint Corp., 1968. $4.00.

2503. *Sapir, Edward, and Harry Hoijer. *Phonology and Morphology of the Navaho Language.* University of California Publications in Linguistics Series, Vol. 50. Berkeley: University of California Press, 1967. $3.50.

2504. Sasaki, Tom T. *Fruitland, New Mexico: A Navaho Community in Transition.* Ithaca: Cornell University Press, 1960. 217 pp.

2505. *Saucier, Roger T. *Recent Geomorphic History of the Pontchartrain Basin.* Baton Rouge: Louisiana State University Press, 1964. $3.00.

2506. *Saum, Lewis O. *The Fur Trader and the Indian.* Seattle: University of Washington Press, 1965. 324 pp. In paper: 1966. $3.45.

2507. *Sawyer, Jesse, ed. *Studies in American Indian Language.* University of California Publications in Linguistics Series, Vol. 65. Berkeley: University of California Press, 1970. $4.50.

2508. *Saxton, Dean, and Lucille Saxton. *Papago and Pima to English and English to Papago and Pima.* Tucson: University of Arizona Press, 1969. 191 pp. $2.50.

2509. Scheele, William E. *Cave Hunters.* New York: World Publishers, 1959. (Grades 4-6) $3.75.

2510. ——. *The Earliest Americans.* Cleveland, Ohio: World Publishing Company, 1963. 59 pp.

2511. ——. *The Mound Builders.* Cleveland, Ohio: World Publishing Company, 1960. 61 pp. $3.75.

2512. *Schell, Rolfe F. *De Soto Didn't Land at Tampa.* Rev. ed. Fort Myers Beach, Florida: Island Press, 1967. $2.95.

2513. ——. *One Thousand Years on Mound Key.* Rev. ed. Fort Myers Beach, Florida: Island Press, 1968. $1.50.

2514. *Schellie, Don. *A Vast Domain of Blood.* New York: Tower Publications, Inc., 1970. $.95. Also: Great West and Indian Series, Vol. 37. Los Angeles: Westernlore Press, 1968. 268 pp. $7.50.

2515. *Schenck, William E. See Nos. 4023, 4025, and 4029.

2516. Schiel, Jacob H. *Journey Through the Rocky Mountains and the Humboldt Mountains to the Pacific Ocean.* Ed. Thomas N. Bonner. Norman: University of Oklahoma Press, 1967. $5.95.

2517. Schmeckebier, Laurence F. *The Office of Indian Affairs, Its History, Activities and Organizations.* 1927; rpt. New York: AMS Press, 1970. 591 pp. $19.50.

2518. Schmitt, Martin F., and Dee Brown. *Fighting Indians of the West.* New York: Scribners, 1948; rpt. New York: Bonanza, 1969. 362 pp. Also: Scribner's, 1972. $15.00.

2519. Schoolcraft, Henry R. *The American Indians: Their History, Condition, and Prospects.* Rochester, New York: Wanzer, Foot and Company, 1851.

2520. ——. *A Narrative Journal of Travels Through the Northwestern Regions of the United States in the Year 1820.* March of America Series. 1821; rpt. Ann Arbor, Michigan: University Microfilms, 1966. $8.95.

2521. ——. *Narrative Journals of Travels from Detroit Northwest Through the Great Chain of American Lakes to the Sources of the Mississippi River in the Year 1820.* Rpt. American Environmental Studies. New York: Arno Press, 1970. $16.00.

2522. ——. *Notes on the Iroquois* . . . 1846; rpt. New York: Kraus Reprint Co., 1971. $16.50.

2523. ——. *Schoolcraft: Literary Voyager.* Ed. Philip Mason. East Lansing: Michigan State University Press, 1962. $5.00.

2524. ———. *Schoolcraft's Expedition to Lake Itasca: The Discovery of the Source of the Mississippi.* Ed. Philip P. Mason. East Lansing: Michigan State University Press, 1958. $7.50.

2525. Schroeder, Albert H. *Archaeological Excavations at Willow Beach, Arizona.* 1950; rpt. Salt Lake City: University of Utah Press, 1961. $3.25.

2526. * ———. *Archaeology of Zion Park.* 1955; rpt. New York: Johnson Reprint Corp., 1970. $12.00.

2527. Schroeder, Albert H., and Dan S. Matson, eds. *Colony on the Move: Gaspor Castano De Sosa's Journal, 1590-1591.* School of American Research Series. Albuquerque: University of New Mexico Press, 1965. $6.50.

2528. Schultz, George A. *An Indian Canaan: Isaac McCoy, Missionary and Reformer.* Civilization of the American Indian Series, No. 121. Norman: University of Oklahoma Press, 1972.

2529. Schultz, James. *Blackfeet and Buffalo.* Memories of Life Among the Indians. Ed. Keith C. Seele. Norman: University of Oklahoma Press, 1968. 384 pp. $5.95.

2530. * Schultz, James W. *My Life as an Indian.* 1907; rpt. Adapted by Robert E. Gard. New York: Duell, Sloan and Pearce, 1957. 151 pp. (Grades 7-10) Also: New York: Hawthorn Books, Inc., 1957. $3.00. In paper: Premier Books. New York: Fawcett World Library, 1968. $ .75.

2531. ———. *The Quest of the Fish-Dog Skin.* Rpt. Boston: Houghton Mifflin, 1960. $3.25.

2532. ———. *Trail of the Spanish Horse.* Rpt. Boston: Houghton Mifflin, 1960. (Grades 6-8) $3.25.

2533. ———. *With the Indians in the Rockies.* Rpt. Boston: Houghton Mifflin, 1960. (Grades 6-10) $3.25.

2534. Schultz, James W., and Jessie L. Donaldson. *The Sun God's Children* (Blackfeet). Boston: Houghton Mifflin, 1930.

2535. * Schusky, Ernest L. *A Manual for Kinship Analysis: A Study in Anthropological Method.* Studies in Anthropological Method. New York: Holt, Rinehart and Winston, 1965. $1.95.

2536. * ———. *The Right to Be Indian.* Vermillion, South Dakota: Board of Missions of the United Presbyterian Church and Institute of Indian Studies, 1965. Pamphlet of 92 pp.

2537. Schwartz, Douglas W. *Conceptions of Kentucky Prehistory: A Case Study in the History of Archaeology.* Lexington: University Press of Kentucky, 1967. $6.00.

2538. Scrivner, Fulsom C. *Mohave People.* San Antonio, Texas: Naylor Company, 1970. (Grades 8 up) 144 pp. $6.95.

2539. Scull, Florence D. *Bear Teeth for Courage.* New York: Van Nostrand Reinhold Company, 1964. (Grades 4-6) $3.75.

2540. Scull, Gideon D.,ed. *Voyages of Peter Esprit Radisson*. Being An Account of his Travels and Experiences Among the North American Indians from 1652 to 1684. 1885; rpt. New York: Burt Franklin, Publisher, 1970. $20.00.

2541. Seaman, Norma G. *Indian Relics of the Pacific Northwest*. 3rd ed. Portland, Oregon: Binfords and Mort, Publishers, 1966. $4.95.

2542. * Sears, William H. *Excavations at Kolomoki: Final Report*. University of Georgia Series in Anthropology, No. 5. Athens: University of Georgia Press, 1956. $4.50.

2543. Seaver, James E. *The Narrative of the Life of Mrs. Mary Jemison*. Gloucester, Mass.: Peter Smith, 1971. $3.50. Jemison was an Indian captive.

2544. Secoy, Frank R. *Changing Military Patterns on the Great Plains: (17th Century through Early 19th Century)*. Monographs of the American Ethnological Society, XXI. Locust Valley, New York: J. J. Augustin Publisher, 1953. 112 pp. Also: Seattle: University of Washington Press, 1953. $5.00.

2545. Seger, John H. *Early Days Among the Cheyenne and Arapahoe Indians*. Ed. Stanley Vestal. Norman: University of Oklahoma Press, 1956. 143 pp. $3.50.

2546. Seibert, Jerry. *Sacajawea, Guide to Lewis and Clark*. Boston: Houghton Mifflin Company, 1971. $2.20.

2547. * Seig, Louis. *Tobacco, Peacepipes and Indians*. Wild and Woolly West Series, No. 15. Palmer Lake, Colorado: Filter Press, 1970. $3.50. In paper: $1.00.

2548. Sellards, Elias H. *Early Man in America: A Study in Prehistory*. 1952; rpt. New York: Greenwood Publishers, 1969. 211 pp. $10.00.

2549. * Seltzer, Carl C. *Racial Prehistory in the Southwest and the Hawikuh Zunis*. 1944; rpt. New York: Kraus Reprint Co., 1970. $3.00.

2550. * Seton, Ernest Thompson and Julia M. Seton. *The Gospel of the Redman: A Way of Life*. 1937; rpt. Sante Fe, New Mexico: Seton Village, 1966. A compilation of material by and about Indians taken from many sources. 109 pp. $2.00.

2551. Seton, Julia M. *American Indian Arts: A Way of Life*. New York: Ronald Press, 1962. (Grades 9 up) $6.00. Also: Sante Fe, New Mexico: Seton Village, 1970. 246 pp. $6.00.

2552. Sevareid, Eric. *Canoeing With the Cree*. 1930; rpt. St. Paul: Minnesota Historical Society, 1968. 206 pp. $4.50.

2553. Seymour, Flora W. *Indian Agents of the Old Frontier*. New York: D. Appleton-Century Company, 1941.

2554. ——. *Pocahontas: Brave Girl*. Rpt. Indianapolis: Bobbs-Merrill, 1970. (Grades 3-7) $2.75.

2555. ——. *Sacagawea: Bird Girl.* Rpt. Indianapolis: Bobbs-Merrill, 1970. (Grades 3-7) $2.75.

2556. ——. *The Story of the Red Man.* New York: Longmans, Green and Company, 1925; rpt. Facsimile Ed. Select Bibliographies Reprint Series. Freeport, New York: Books for Libraries, 1970. $16.50.

2557. Shannon, Terry. *Dog Team for Ongluk.* Chicago: Melmont Publishers, Inc., 1962. (Grades K-3) $2.75.

2558. ——. *Stones, Bones and Arrowheads.* Racine, Wisconsin: Whitman Publishing Company, 1970. (Grades 4-7) $3.00.

2559. ——. *Wakappo and the Flying Arrows.* Chicago: Albert Whitman and Company, 1963. (Grades 3-5) $2.75.

2560. Shapp, Charles, and Martha Shapp. *Let's Find Out About Indians.* New York: Franklin Watts, Inc., 1962. $3.75.

2561. Sharp, Edith L. *Nkwala.* Boston: Little, Brown and Company, 1958. (Grades 3-7) $3.95.

2562. * Shay, C. Thomas. *The Itasca Bison Kill Site: An Ecological Analysis.* St. Paul: Minnesota Historical Society, 1971. 133 pp. $5.50.

2563. Shea, John G. *A French-Onondaga Dictionary, From a Manuscript of the Seventeenth Century.* 1860; rpt. New York: AMS Press, 1970. $12.50.

2564. ——. *The History of the Catholic Missions Among the Indian Tribes of the United States, 1529-1854.* 1857; rpt. Religion in America Series. New York: Arno Press, 1969. $17.50. Also: New York: AMS Press, 1970. $17.50.

2565. ——. *The Perils of the Ocean and Wilderness; Or, Narratives of Shipwreck and Indian Captivity.* 1856; rpt. Dubuque, Iowa: William C. Brown Company, 1970. $7.00.

2566. ——, ed. *Library of American Linguistics.* 13 vols. 1860-1864; rpt. New York: AMS Press, Inc., 1970. $175.00.

2567. Sheehan, Bernard W. *Seeds of Extinction: Jeffersonian Philanthropy and the American Indian.* Chapel Hill: University of North Carolina Press, 1972.

2568. Shelling, William J. *Tales of the Northwest.* Minneapolis: Ross and Haines, 1972. $10.00.

2569. Shepard, Betty, ed. *Mountain Man, Indian Chief: The Life and Adventures of Jim Beckwourth.* New York: Harcourt Brace Jovanovich, 1968. (Grades 7 up) $3.95.

2570. * Shepardson, Mary. *Navajo Ways in Government. A Study in Political Process.* 1963; rpt. New York: Kraus Reprint Co., 1971. $8.00.

2571. Shepardson, Mary, and Blodwen Hammond. *A Navajo Mountain Community: Social Organization and Kinship Terminology.* Berkeley: University of California Press, 1970. 278 pp. $9.50.

2572. Sheridan, Lt. Gen. P. H. *Record of Engagements with Hostile Indians within the Military Division of the Missouri, from 1868 to 1882.* Washington, D.C.: Government Printing Office, 1969. 112 pp.

2573. Sherin, Erek, and Erik Sherin. *America Needs Indians.* New York: Doubleday and Company, 1973. $6.95.

2574. Shetrone, Henry Clyde. *The Mound Builders.* New York: D. Appleton-Century, 1936.

2575. Shippen, Katherine B. *Lightfoot.* New York: Viking Press, Inc., 1950. (Grades 4-6) $3.37.

2576. Shorris, Earl. *The Death of the Great Spirit: An Elegy for the American Indian.* New York: Simon and Shuster, 1971. 253 pp.

2577. Showers, Paul. *Indian Festivals.* A Crowell Holiday Book. New York: T. Y. Crowell Company, 1969. (Grades K-3) 40 pp. $3.50.

2578. * Sides, Dorothy S. *Decorative Art of the Southwestern Indians.* 1936; rpt. New York: Dover Publications, 1961. $1.50. Also: Gloucester, Mass.: Peter Smith, 1971. $3.50.

2579. Siebert, Erna, and Werner Forman. *North American Indian Art.* New York: Tudor Publishing Company, 1967. $12.50.

2580. Siegal, Beatrice. *Indians of the Woodland Before and After the Pilgrims.* New York: Walker and Company, 1972. $4.50.

2581. * Silverberg, Robert. *Home of the Red Man: Indian North America Before Columbus.* Greenwich, Connecticut: New York Graphic Society, 1963. (Grades 7-11) 252 pp. $4.95. In paper: New York: Washington Square Press, 1971. $ .75.

2582. ——. *Mound Builders.* Greenwich, Connecticut: New York Graphic Society, Ltd., 1970. (Grades 9 up) $5.95.

2583. ——. *Mound Builders of Ancient America: The Archaeology of a Myth.* Greenwich, Connecticut: New York Graphic Society, 1968. $10.00.

2584. ——. *Old Ones: Indians of the American Southwest.* Greenwich, Connecticut: New York Graphic Society, Ltd., 1965. 269 pp. $5.50.

2585. ——. *Pueblo Revolt. New York: Weybright and Talley,* Inc., 1970. $6.95.

2586. Simmons, Leo W. *The Role of the Aged in Primitive Society.* Rpt. Hamden, Connecticut: Shoe String Press, 1970. $10.00.

2587. ——, ed. *The Social Systems of American Ethnic Groups.* Rpt. New Haven: Yale University Press, 1970. $7.50.

2588. ——, ed. *Sun Chief.* See Talayesva, Don C., Nos. 198.

2589. Simmons, William S. *Cautantowwit's House: An Indian Burial Ground on the Island of Conanicut in Narragansett Bay.* Providence, Rhode Island: Brown University Press, 1970. 198 pp. $8.50.

2590. Simms, William Gilmore. *Mellichampe: A Legend of the Santee.* Rpt. New York: AMS Press, 1970. $10.00.

2591. ——. *The Wigwam and the Cabin.* Rpt. New York: AMS Press, 1970. $10.00. Also: Americans in Fiction Series. Upper Saddle River, New Jersey: Gregg Press, Inc., 1968. $8.00.

2592. *——. *The Yemassee.* 1835; rpt. Ed. Alexander Cowie. Hafner Library of Classics, No. 26. Darien, Connecticut: Hafner Publishing Company, Inc., 1962. $3.50. Also: Ed. Joseph J. Ridgely. Masterworks of Literature Series. New Haven: College and University Press, 1964. $8.95. This same edition in Paper: $3.95. Also: Ed. Hugh C. Holman. New York: Houghton Mifflin Company, 1971. $1.45.

2593. Simonin, Louis L. *The Rocky Mountain West in 1867.* Trans. W. Clough. Rpt. Lincoln: University of Nebraska Press, 1966. $5.50.

2594. Simpson, Lieutenant James H. *A Navaho Expedition: The Journal of a Military Reconnaissance from Sante Fe, New Mexico, to the Navaho Country, Made in 1849.* Rpt. Ed. Frank McNitt. American Exploration and Travel Series, No. 43. Norman: University of Oklahoma Press, 1964. $7.50.

2595. * Sinclair, William. See Nos. 4002 and 4007.

2596. Sipe, C. Hale. *The Indian Chiefs of Pennsylvania: Or, a Story of the Part Played by the American Indian in the History of Pennsylvania. Based Primarily on the Pennsylvania Archives and Colonial Records, and Built Around the Outstanding Chiefs.* 1927; rpt. New York: Arno Press, 1971. $23.00.

2597. ——. *The Indian Wars of Pennsylvania: An Account of the Indian Events, in Pennsylvania, of the French and Indian War, Pontiac's War, Lord Dunmore's War, the Revolutionary War and the Indian Uprising from 1789 to 1795.* 1929; rpt. New York: Arno Press, 1971. $36.00.

2598. Skinner, Alanson B. *The Indians of Greater New York.* 1915; rpt. Ann Arbor, Mich.: Finch Press, 1972. $12.00.

2599. ——. *Mascoutens of the Prairie Patawatomi Indians.* 1924; rpt. Westport, Connecticut: Greenwood Press, Inc., 1970. $13.25.

2600. ——. *Observations on the Ethnology of the Sauk Indians.* 1923-1925; rpt. Westport, Connecticut: Greenwood Press, 1970. 181 pp. $11.00.

2601. Skinner, Constance L. *Becky Landers, Frontier Warrior.* 1927; rpt. New York: Macmillan Company, 1970. (Grades 4-6) $3.95. In paper: Acorn Books. New York: Macmillan, 1970. $ .90.

2602. ——. *Pioneers of the Old Southwest: A Chronicle of the Dark and Bloody Ground.* 1921; rpt. Yale Chronicles of America Series, Vol. 18. New York: United States Publishers Assoc., Inc., 1970. $3.95. Also: New York: Reprint House International, 1970. $13.50.

2603. Sloan, John, and Oliver LaFarge. *Introduction to American Indian Art.* Sante Fe, New Mexico: William Gannon, 1931. $15.00.

2604. * Slocum, Robert, and Kenneth Matsen. *Shoto Clay.* Portland, Oregon: Binfords and Mort, 1968. $1.50.

2605. Slotkin, James S. *The Peyote Religion: A Study in Indian-White Relations.* Glencoe, Illinois: The Free Press, 1956. 195 pp.

2606. ——, ed. *Readings in Early Anthropology.* New York: Aldine Press, 1970. $12.50.

2607. Smith, Huron H. *The Ethnobotany of the Menomini Indians.* 1923; rpt. Westport, Connecticut: Greenwood Publishing Corp., 1970. $11.50.

2608. Smith, James F. *Cherokee Land Lottery: Of Georgia.* 1838; rpt. Rev. ed. Baltimore, Maryland: Geneological Publishing Company, Ltd., 1968. $15.00.

2609. Smith, John. *The Generall Historie of Virginia, New-England, and the Summer Isles.* 1624; rpt. March of America Series. Ann Arbor, Michigan: University Mcrofilms, 1966. $8.95.

2610. * Smith, Marian W. *Archaeology of the Columbia-Frazer Region.* 1950; rpt. New York: Kraus Reprint Co., 1971. $3.50.

2611. ——. *Indians of the Urban Northwest.* New York: Columbia University Press, 1949; rpt. University Contributions to Anthropology Series, Vol. 36. New York: AMS Press, 1969. $17.50.

2612. ——. *The Pyallup-Nisqually.* 1940; rpt. New York: Columbia University Press, 1970; rpt. New York: AMS Press, 1969. 336 pp. $19.50.

2613. * Smith, W. *Kiva Mural Decorations at Awatovi and Kawaika-a: With a Survey of Other Wall Paintings in the Pueblo Southwest.* 1952; rpt. New York: Kraus Reprint Co., 1971. $15.00.

2614. * Smith, W. and J. Roberts. *Zuni Law: A Field of Values.* With an Appendix: *A Practical Zuni Orthography.* By Stanley Newman. 1954; rpt. New York: Kraus Reprint Co., 1971. $14.00.

2615. Smith, William. *Historical Account of the Expedition Against the Ohio Indians.* 1765; rpt. March of America Series. Ann Arbor, Michigan: University Microfilms, Xerox Company, 1972.

2616. ———. *The Saint Clair Papers: The Life and Public Services of Arthur St. Clair, with his Correspondence and Other Papers.* 2 vols. 1881; rpt. Facsimile Ed. Select Bibliographies Reprint Series. Freeport, New York: Books for Libraries, Inc., 1970. $38.50. Also: 1882; rpt. 2 vols. New York: Plenum Publishing Company, 1970. $47.50. each.

2617. Smithson, Carma L. *The Havasupai Woman.* 1959; rpt. New York: Johnson Reprint Corp., 1972. $12.00.

2618. Sneve, Virginia Driving Hawk. *High Elk's Treasure.* New York: Holiday House, 1972. $4.95.

2619. ———. *Jimmy Yellow Hawk.* New York: Holiday House, 1972. 76 pp. $4.50. Author is Sioux.

2620. Socolofsky, Homer, and Huber Self. *Historical Atlas of Kansas.* Norman: University of Oklahoma Press, 1972.

2621. Solomon, Glenn. *The Odyssey of Montezuma.* San Francisco: Indian Historian Press, 1971. $10.00.

2622. *Son of Former Many Beads. *The Ramah Navajos.* Ed. Robert W. Young and William Morgan. Lawrence, Kansas: Haskell Press, 1967. 17 pp. $ .10.

2623. Sonne, Conway, B. *The World of Wakara.* San Antonio, Texas: Naylor Company, 1962. (Grades 9 up) $4.95.

2624. Sonnichsen, Charles L. *The Mescalero Apaches.* Civilization of the American Indian Series, No. 51. Norman: University of Oklahoma Press, 1958; rpt. 1970. 299 pp. $6.95. Rev. ed., 1972. $8.95.

2625. ———. *Pass of the North: Four Centuries on the Rio Grande.* El Paso, Texas: Texas Western Press, 1968. $10.00.

2626. ———. *The Southwest in Life and Literature.* Old Greenwich, Connecticut: Devin-Adair Company, Inc., 1962. $7.50.

2627. Sorkin, Alan L. *American Indians and Federal Aid.* Washington, D.C.: The Brookings Institution, 1971. 231 pp. $7.50.

2628. *Sosin, Jack M. *Revolutionary Frontier, 1763-1783.* Histories of the American Frontier. New York: Holt, Rinehart and Winston, 1970. $7.95. In paper: $3.25.

2629. ———. *Whitehall and the Wilderness: The Middle West in British Colonial Policy, 1760-1775.* Lincoln: University of Nebraska Press, 1961. $6.50.

2630. ———, ed. *The Opening of the West.* Documentary History of the United States Series. Columbia: University of South Carolina Press, 1970. $7.95.

2631. *South, Stanley A. *The Indians in North Carolina.* 1965; rpt. Raleigh: North Carolina State Department of Archives and History, 1971. $. 25.

2632. Sowell, Andrew J. *Early Settlers and Indian Fighters of Southwest Texas.* 2 vols. 1900; rpt. New York: Argosy-Antiquarian, Ltd., 1970. $27.50 boxed.

2633. * Sparkman, Philip. See No. 4008.

2634. * Speck, Frank G. *The Creek Indians of Taskigi Town.* 1908; rpt. New York: Kraus Reprint Co., 1970. $3.50.

2635. ——. *The Ethnology of the Yucki Indians.* New York: Humanities Press, Inc., 1972. $8.50.

2636. * ——. *The Functions of Wampum Among the Eastern Algonkian.* 1919; rpt. New York: Kraus Reprint Co., 1970. $5.00.

2637. ——. *Penobscot Man: The Life History of a Forest Tribe in Maine.* Rpt. New York: Octagon Books, 1970. $11.50.

2638. * ——. *Penobscot Shamanism.* 1919; rpt. New York: Kraus Reprint Co., 1970. $3.50.

2639. Speck, Frank G. *A Study of the Delaware Indian Big House Ceremony.* Publications of the Pennsylvania Historical Commission. Vol. 2. Harrisburg, 1931.

2640. * Spence, Lewis. *The North American Indians.* Rpt. Blauvelt, New York: Rudolph Steiner, 1972. $2.45.

2641. Spencer, Oliver M. *Indian Captivity.* 1835; rpt. March of America Series. Ann Arbor: University Microfilms, 1966. $5.75.

2642. Spencer, Robert F. *The North Alaskan Eskimo: A Study in Ecology and Society.* Bureau of American Ethnology Bulletin, No. 171. Washington, D.C.: Smithsonian Institution, 1969. 477 pp. $15.00.

2643. * ——, ed. *Forms of Symbolic Action.* American Ethnological Society Proceeding. 1969. Seattle: University of Washington Press, 1970. $4.50.

2644. ——, ed. *Method and Perspective in Anthropology: Papers in Honor of Wilson D. Wallis.* Minneapolis: University of Minnesota Press, 1954. $4.50.

2645. Spencer, Robert F., Jesse D. Jennings, and others. *The Native Americans.* Prehistory and Ethnology of the North American Indians. New York: Harper and Row, 1965. 539 pp. $13.95.

2646. * Spicer, Edward H. *Cycles of Conquest: The Impact of Spain, Mexico, and the United States on the Indians of the Southwest, 1533-1960.* Tucson: University of Arizona Press, 1962. $5.95.

2647. ——. *Pascua, A Yaqui Village in Arizona.* Chicago: University of Chicago Press, 1940. 319 pp.

2648. * ——. *A Short History of the Indians of the United States.* An Anvil Original. New York: Van Nostrand Reinhold Company, 1969. 319 pp. $2.95.

2649. ——, ed. *Perspectives in American Indian Culture Change.* Chicago: University of Chicago Press, 1961. 544 pp. $10.00.

2650. * Spicer, Edward H., and Louis P. Caywood. *Two Pueblo Ruins in West Central Arizona.* University of Arizona Social Science Bulletin, No. 10. Tucson: University of Arizona Press, 1936. $1.00.

2651. * Spier, Leslie. *Klamath Ethnography.* 1930; rpt. New York: Kraus Reprint Co., 1971. $25.00. See also Nos. 4020 and 4030.

2652. ——. *The Prophet Dance of the Northwest and its Derivatives: The Source of the Ghost Dance.* General Series in Anthropology. Vol. Part I. Menasha, Wisconsin, 1935.

2653. ——. *Southern Diegueno Customs.* University of California Publications in American Archaeology and Ethnology, Vol. 20. Berkeley: University of California Press, 1923.

2654. ——. *Yuman Tribes of the Gila River.* Chicago: University of Chicago Press, 1933; rpt. New York: Cooper Square Pubs., 1970. $12.50.

2655. Spier, Leslie, and Edward Sapir. *Wishram Ethnography.* University of Washington Publications in Anthropology. Vol. 3. Seattle: University of Washington Press, 1930.

2656. Spier, Leslie, A. Irving Hallowell, and Stanley S. Newman, eds. *Language Culture, and Personality: Essays in Memory of Edward Sapir.* Menasha, Wisconsin: Sapir Memorial Publication Fund, 1941. 298 pp. Also: Salt Lake City: University of Utah Press, 1960.

2657. * Spinden, Herbert J. *The Nez Perce Indians.* Memoirs of the American Anthropological Society. Vol. II, Part 3. Lancaster, Pennslyvania: New Era Printing Company, 1908; rpt. New York: Kraus Reprint Corp., 1970. $6.00.

2658. * Spindler, Will H. *Tragedy Strikes at Wounded Knee.* And Other Essays on Indian Life in South Dakota and Nebraska. Vermillion, S.D.: Dakota Press, 1972. 138 pp. $2.00.

2659. * Spoehr, Alexander. *Camp, Clan, and Kin, Among the Cow Creek Seminole of Florida.* 1941; rpt. New York: Kraus Reprint Corp., 1970. $8.00.

2660. Sprague, John T. *The Origin, Progress, and Conclusion of the Florida War.* 1848; rpt. Foridiana Facsimile and Reprint Series. Ed. John K. Mahon. Gainesville: University of Florida Press, 1964. $12.50.

2661. Sprague, Marshall. *Massacre: The Tragedy at White River.* New York: Little, Brown and Company, 1957. $6.75.

2662. * Spring, Agnes W. *Caspar Collins: The Life and Exploits of an Indian Fighter of the Sixties.* 1927; rpt. New York: AMS Press, 1969. $7.50. In paper: Lincoln: University of Nebraska Press, 1969. 188 pp. $1.80.

2663. Spring, John A. *John Spring's Arizona*. Ed. A. M. Gustafson. Tucson: University of Arizona Press, 1966. $7.50.

2664. Springer, Charles. *Soldiering in Sioux Country*. 1865; rpt. Ed. Benjamin F. Cooling. Los Angeles: Nash Publishing Company, 1971. $7.50.

2665. Squires, John L., and Robert E. McLean. *American Indian Dances: Steps, Rhythms, Costumes, and Interpretation*. New York: The Ronald Press, 1963. 132 pp. $5.50.

2666. Stafford, Harry E. *The Early Inhabitants of the Americas*. New York: Vantage Press, 1959. 492 pp.

2667. Starkey, Marion I. *The Cherokee Nation*. New York: Alfred A. Knopf, 1946. Rpt. New York: Russell and Russell, 1972. $20.00.

2668. Starr, Emmet. *History of the Cherokee Indians and Their Legends and Folk Lore*. 1921; rpt. New York: Kraus Reprint Co., 1969. 680 pp. $25.00.

2669. Starr, Frederick. *American Indians*. Ethno-Geographic Reader, No. 2. Boston: D. C. Heath, 1898; rpt. 1926. 243 pp.

2670. Stearn, Esther W., and Allen E. Stearn. *Effects of Smallpox on the Destiny of the Amerindian*. Deer Park, New York: Brown Book Company, 1970. $2.50.

2671. Steckmesser, Kent L. *The Western Hero in History and Legend*. Norman: University of Oklahoma Press, 1967. $6.95.

2672. Steele, William O. *Westward Adventure: The True Stories of Six Pioneers*. New York: Harcourt Brace and Row, 1962. (Grades 4-6) $4.50.

2673. Steele, Zadock. *The Indian Captive; Or, a Narrative of the Captivity and Sufferings of Zadock Steele*. Rpt. Bronx, New York: Benjamin Blom, 1972. $13.50.

2674. Stefansson, Evelyn. *Here Is Alaska*. Rev. ed. New York: Charles Scribner, Sons, 1959. (Grades 7 up) $4.95.

2675. *Stefansson, Vilhjalmur. *My Life with the Eskimo*. New York: Macmillan Company, 1962. $1.50.

2676. Steiner, Stan. *George Washington: The Indian Influence*. American Hero Biographies Series. New York: G. P. Putnam's Sons, 1970. $3.29.

2677. * ——. *The New Indians*. New York: Harper and Row, 1968. 348 pp. $7.95. In paper: New York: Dell Publishing Company, 1969. $2.45.

2678. ——. *The Tiguas: The Last Tribe of City Indians*. New York: Macmillan, 1972. (Grades 5 up) $4.95.

2679. Stember, Sol. *Heroes of American Indians*. M. C. Goodman, ed. New York: Fleet Press Corp., 1970. (Grades 10-12) $5.00.

2680. Stephen, Alexander M. *Hopi Journal*. Ed. Elsie C. Parsons. 2 vols. Columbia University Contributions in Anthropology Series, Vol. 23. 1936; rpt. New York: AMS Press, 1969. $84.50 / $45.00 ea.

2681. Stern, Bernhard J. *The Lummi Indians of Northwest Washington*. Columbia University Contributions to Anthropology Series, Vol. 17. 1934; rpt. New York: AMS Press, 1969. $8.50.

2682. Stern, Theodore. *The Klamath Tribe: A People and Their Reservation*. American Ethnological Society Monographs. Seattle: University of Washington Press, 1965. 356 pp. $7.50.

2683. * Stevens, Isaac I. *The Treaty Between the United States and the Dwamish, Suquamish, and Other Allied and Subordinate Tribes of Indians in Washington Territory*. 1855; rpt. Facsimile Ed. Seattle: Shorey Publications, 1971. $2.00.

2684 * ——. *The Treaty Between the United States and the Makah Tribe*. 1855; rpt. Facsimile Ed. Seattle: Shorey Publications, 1971. $2.00.

2685. Stevenson, Augusta. *Sitting Bull: Dakota Boy*. Indianapolis: Bobbs-Merrill Co., 1970. $2.75.

2686. ——. *Squanto: Young Indian Hunter*. Indianapolis: Bobbs-Merrill Company, 1971. $2.75.

2687. ——. *Tecumseh: Shawnee Boy*. Indianapolis: Bobbs-Merrill Company, 1955. (Grades 3-7) $2.75.

2688. Stevenson, Mathilde C. *The Religious Life of the Zuni Child*. 5th Annual Report of the Bureau of American Ethnology. Washington, 1887.

2689. ——. *The Zuni Indians: Their Mythology, Esoteric Fraternities and Ceremonies*. U. S. Bureau of American Ethnology, 23rd Annaul Report. 1901, 1902, 1904; rpt. Glorietta, New Mexico: Rio Grande Press, Inc., 1970. 634 pp. $25.00. Also: New York: Johnson Reprint Corp., 1970. $45.00.

2690. Steward, Julian H. *Basin-Plateau Aboriginal Sociopolitical Groups*. Rpt. Salt Lake City: University of Utah Press, 1971. $5.00. See also Nos. 4024, 4029, 4033, and 4034.

2691. Stewart, Edgar I. *Custer's Luck*. 1955; rpt. Norman: University of Oklahoma Press, 1967. $8.95.

2692. ——. *Penny-an-Acre Empire in the West*. Norman: University of Oklahoma Press, 1965. $6.95.

2693. * Stewart, O. C. *Ute Peyotism: A Study of a Cultural Complex*. 1948; rpt. New York: Kraus Reprint Corp., 1970. $4.00. See also No. 4040.

2694. * Stone, Eric. *Clio Medica: Medicine Among the American Indians*. 1932; rpt. New York: Hafner Publishing Company, Inc., 1962. 139 pp. $4.95.

2695. Stone, William L. *The Life and Times of Red Jacket or Sa-Go-Ye-Wat-Ha.* American Indian History Series. St. Clair Shores, Michigan: Scholarly Press, 1970. $15.00.

2696. ———. *Life of Joseph Brant—Thayendanegea, Including the Indian Wars of the American Revolution.* 2 vols. 1838; rpt. New York: Kraus Reprint Co., 1969. 425 pp. II, 537 pp. $39.00. Also: St. Clair Shores, Michigan: Scholarly Press, 1970. $21.00.

2697. Story, G. L. *A Morphological Study of Tlingit.* Janua Linguarum, Series Practica, No. 118. The Hague: Mouton Publishers, 1972. $14.80.

2698. Stoutenburgh, John. *Dictionary of the American Indian.* New York: Philosophical Library, 1955. 459 pp. $6.00.

2699. Strange, James. *James Stange's Journal and Narrative of the Commercial Expedition from Bombay to the Northwest Coast of America.* 1928; rpt. Facsimile ed. Seattle, Washington: Shorey Publications, 1970. $5.00.

2700. Stratton, Royal B. *Captivity of the Oatman Girls.* 1857; rpt. Upper Saddle River, New Jersey: Literature House / The Gregg Press, 1971. $11.50.

2701. * Streiff, Jan E. *Roster of Excavated Prehistoric Sites in Minnesota to 1972.* St. Paul: Minnesota Historical Society, 1972. 38 pp. $2.50.

2702. Stricklen, Edward G. *Notes on Eight Papago Songs.* See No. 4020.

2703. Strong, Emory. *The Stone Age in the Great Basin.* Portland, Oregon: Binfords and Mort, 1970. $5.95.

2704. ———. *The Stone Age on the Columbia River.* 2nd ed. Portland, Oregon: Binfords and Mort, Pubs., 1960. $4.95.

2705. ———, ed. *Wakemap Mound.* Portland, Oregon: Binfords and Mort, Publishers, 1959. $1.50.

2706. Strong, Thomas N. *Cathlamet on the Columbia.* New ed. Portland, Oregon: Binfords and Mort, Pubs., 1954. $3.50.

2707. * Strong, William D. *Aboriginal Society in Southern California.* 1922; rpt. New York: Kraus Reprint Co., 1971. $25.00. See also Nos. 4021, 4026, and 4029.

2708. Stroud, Harry A. *The Conquest of the Prairies.* Waco, Texas: Texian Press, 1970. 281 pp. $9.50.

2709. * Stuart, Collin. *Shoot an Arrow Into the Wind.* New York: Popular Library, 1970. 285 pp. $ .95.

2710. Stuart, John. *A Memoir of Indian Wars and Other Occurrences by the Late Colonel Stuart of Greenbrier.* Ed. Charles A. Stuart. 1833; rpt. Eyewitness Accounts of the American Revolution Series, No. 3. New York: Arno Press, 1970. $6.00. Also: Parsons, West Virginia: McClain Printing Company, 1972. $4.00.

2711. * Stubbs, Stanley A., and W. S. Stallings, Jr. *The Excavations of Pindi Pueblo, New Mexico.* School of American Research Publications No. 18. Albuquerque: University of New Mexico Press, 1953. 165 pp. $6.00.

2712. Stutler, Boyd B. *The Kinnan Massacre.* Parsons, West Virginia: McClain Printing Company, 1969. $2.00.

2713. Subcommittee on Economy in Government. See *American Indians, Facts and Future,* No. 532.

2714. Suggs, Robert C. *Archaeology of New York.* New York: T. Y. Crowell Publishing Company, 1966. (Grades 7 up) $3.50.

2715. ———. *Archaeology of San Francisco.* New York: T. Y. Crowell Publishing Company, 1965. $3.50.

2716. * *Suicide Among the American Indians.* Washington, D.C.: Government Printing Office, 1969. 37 pp. $ .50.

2717. Sunder, John E. *Fur Trade on the Upper Missouri, 1840-1865.* Norman: University of Oklahoma Press, 1965. $6.95.

2718. ———. *Joshua Pilcher: Fur Trader and Indian Agent.* Lincoln: University of Nebraska Press, 1968. $5.95.

2719. * Sunset Editors. *Alaska.* Rev. ed. Menlo Park, California: Lane Magazine and Book Company, 1966. $1.95.

2720. * ———. *Southwest Indian Country.* Menlo Park, California: Lane Magazine and Book Company, 1970. $1.95.

2721. Sutton, Felix. *Indian Chiefs of the West.* New York: Julian Messner, Inc., 1970. (Grades 3-6) $3.95.

2722. Swan, James G. *The Haidah Indians of Queen Charlotte's Island.* 1874; rpt. Facsimile ed. Seattle, Washington: Shorey Publications, 1970. $5.00.

2723. ———. *The Indians of Cape Flattery.* 1868; rpt. Facsimile ed. Seattle, Washington: Shorey Publications, 1970. $7.50.

2724. ———. *The Northwest Coast.* Rpt. New York: Harper Row, 1970. $25.00.

2725. * Swanton, John R. *An Early Account of the Choctaw Indians.* 1918; rpt. New York: Kraus Reprint Co., 1970. $3.50.

2726. ———. *An Early History of the Creek Indians and Their Neighbors.* 1922; rpt. New York: Johnson Reprint Corp., 1971. $25.00.

2727. ———. *The Haida Indian Language.* 1911; rpt. Seattle: Shorey Publications, 1970. $5.00.

2728. ———. *The Indians of the Southeastern United States.* 1946; rpt. St. Clair Shores, Michigan: Scholarly Press, 1968. $12.00. Also: Westport, Connecticut: Greenwood Press, Inc., 1971. $46.25.

2729. Swanton, John R. *The Indian Tribes of Alaska and Canada.* Rpt. Facsimile ed. Extracts. Seattle: Shorey Publications, 1952. $4.00.

2730. ———. *The Indian Tribes of the American Southwest.* Rpt. Facsimile ed. Extracts. Seattle: Shorey Publications, 1952. $6.00.

2731. ———. *The Indian Tribes of the Lower Mississippi Valley and the Adjacent Coast of the Gulf of Mexico.* U. S. Bureau of American Ethnology Bulletin 43. 1911; rpt. New York: Johnson Reprint Corp., 1970. $17.50.

2732. ———. *Indian Tribes of North America.* Bureau of American Ethnology Bulletin No. 45. 1952; rpt. Washington, D.C.: Smithsonian Institution Press, 1969. $15.00. Also: St. Clair Shores, Michigan: Scholarly Press, 1968. $15.00.

2733. ———. *The Indian Tribes of the Pacific Northwest.* Rpt. Facsimile ed. Extracts. Seattle, Washington: Shorey Publications, 1952. $6.00.

2734. ———, ed. *Indian Tribes of the Southeast.* 1925; rpt. Nashville, Tennessee: The Blue and Gray Press, 1971. 132 pp. $10.00.

2735. ———. *Indian Tribes of Washington, Oregon, and Idaho.* Fairfield, Washington: Ye Galleon Press, 1968. $3.50.

2736. ———. *Religious Beliefs and Medical Practices of the Creek Indians.* 42nd Annual Report of the Bureau of American Ethnology. Washington, D.C., 1928, pp. 473-672.

2737. ———. *The Social Conditions, Beliefs and Linguistic Relationship of the Tlingit Indians.* U. S. Bureau of American Ethnology Twenty Sixth Annual Report, 1904-1905. 1908; rpt. New York: Johnson Reprint Corp., 1970. $10.00.

2738. ———. *The Social Organization and the Social Usages of the Indians of the Creek Confederacy.* U. S. Bureau of American Ethnology, Forty Second Annual Report, 1924-1925. 1928; rpt. New York: Johnson Reprint Corp., 1970. $20.00.

2739. ———. *The Tlingit Indian Language.* 1911; rpt. Seattle: Shorey Publications, 1970. $3.00.

2740. ———, et al. *Anthropology in North America.* 1915; rpt. New York: Kraus Reprint Co., 1971. $17.00.

2741. Swinton, George. *Eskimo Sculpture.* Chester Springs, Pa.: Dufour Editions Inc., 1965. $12.50.

2742. ———. *Sculpture of the Eskimo.* Greenwich, Connecticut: New York Graphic Society, 1972. $18.50.

2743. Sylvester, Herbert M. *Indian Wars of New England.* 3 vols. Boston: W. B. Clarke Company, 1910.

2744. Tabeau, Pierre-Antoine. *Tabeau's Narrative of Loisel's Expedition to the Upper Missouri.* 1939; rpt. American Exploration and Travel Series, No. 3 Norman: University of Oklahoma Press, 1968. $7.95.

2745. Tache, Alexandre A. *Vingt Annees De Missions Dans le Nordouest De l'Amerique.* 1866; rpt. Canadiana Before 1867 Series. New York: Johnson Reprint, 1969. $9.50.

2746. Tanner, Clara L. *Southwest Indian Craft Arts.* Tucson: University of Arizona Press, 1968. 206 pp. $15.00.

2747. ———. *Southwest Indian Painting.* Rev. ed. Tucson: University of Arizona Press, 1972. $35.00.

2748. * Tantaquidgeon, Gladys. *Folk Medicine of the Delaware and Related Algonkian Indians.* Anthropological Series, No. 3. Harrisburg: Historical Society of Pennsylvania, 1972. $4.00. In paper: $2.50.

2749. Tarbox, Increase N. *Sir Walter Raleigh and His Colony in America.* New York: Burt Franklin, Inc., 1966. $17.50.

2750. * Tatum, Lawrie. *Our Red Brothers and the Peace Policy of President Ulysses S. Grant.* 1899; rpt. Lincoln: University of Nebraska Press, 1970. 366 pp. $5.50. In paper: 366 pp. $1.95.

2751. Tax, Sol. *Acculturation in the Americas.* 1952; rpt. New York: Cooper Square Publishers, Inc., 1966. $12.50.

2752. ———. *Indian Tribes of Aboriginal America.* 1952; rpt. New York: Cooper Square Publishers, Inc., 1966. $15.00.

2753. Taxay, Don. *Money of the American Indians and Other Primitive Currencies of the Americas.* New York: Nummus Press, 1970. 158 pp. Also: New York: Arco Publishing Company, 1972. $5.95.

2754. * Taylor, Theodore W. *The States and Their Indian Citizens.* Washington, D. C. Government Printing Office, 1972. 307 pp. $2.25.

2755. * Tebbel, John. *The Compact History of the Indian Wars.* New York: Hawthorn Books, Inc., 1966. 334 pp. $7.95. Author is Ojibwa Indian. In paper: New York: Tower Books, 1970. 318 pp. $1.25.

2756. * Teicher, Morton I. *Windigo Psychosis: A Study of a Relationship Between Belief and Behavior Among the Indians of Northeastern Canada.* Ed. Verne F. Ray. American Ethnological Society Proceedings. Seattle: University of Washington Press, 1960. $3.50.

2757. Teichmann, Emil. *Journey to Alaska in 1868.* 1925; rpt. New York: Argosy-Antiquarian, 1963. $15.00.

2758. Teit, James A. *The Tatooing and Face and Body Painting of the Thompson Indians of British Columbia.* Seattle: Shorey Publications, 1971. $4.50.

2759. ———. *Traditions of the Thompson River Indians of British Columbia.* 1898; rpt. New York: Kraus Reprint Co., 1970. $7.50.

2760. Terrell, John U. *American Indian Almanac.* New York: World Publishing Company, 1971. $12.50.

2761. ———. *Apache Chronicle.* New York: World Publishing Company, 1972. $12.50.

2762. *———. *The Navajos: The Past and Present of a Great People.* New York: Weybright and Talley, Inc., 1970. $7.95. In paper: New York: Harper Row, 1972. $1.50.

2763. ———. *The War for the Colorado River.* 2 vols. Glendale, California: Arthur H. Clark, 1966. $17.50.

2764. Terrell, John U., and G. Walton. *Faint the Trumpet Sounds: The Life and Trial of Major Reno.* New York: David McKay Company, 1966. $6.95.

2765. Thalbitzer, William. *The Amassalik Eskimo.* Copenhagen, 1923.

2766. ———. *The Eskimo Language.* 1911; rpt. Seattle: Shorey Publications, 1970. $6.50.

2767. Thatcher, Benjamin B. *Indian Biography: Famous American Indians.* 2 vols. 1848; rpt. Detroit, Michigan: Gale Research Corp., 1970.

2768. Thomas, Alfred B. *After Coronado, Spanish Exploration Northeast of New Mexico, 1696-1727.* Civilization of the American Indian Series, No. 9. 1935; rpt. Norman: University of Oklahoma Press, 1969. $5.95.

2769. ———, ed. *Forgotten Frontiers: A Study of the Spanish Indian Policy of Don Juan Bautista De Anza, Governor of New Mexico, 1777-1787.* Civilization of the American Indian Series, No. 1. 1932; rpt. Norman: University of Oklahoma Press, 1969. $8.50.

2770. ———, ed. *Teodoro De Croix and the Northern Frontier of New Spain 1776-1783.* 1941; rpt. Norman: University of Oklahoma Press, 1967. $8.95.

2771. Thompson, Hildegard. *Getting to Know American Indians Today.* New York: Coward-McCann, Inc., 1965. (Grades 3-5) 64 pp. $3.29.

2772. Thompson, Laura. *Culture in a Crisis: A Study of the Hopi Indians.* New York: Octagon Books, 1972. $10.50.

2773. Thompson, Laura, and Alice Joseph. *The Hopi Way.* 1944; rpt. New York: Russell and Russell, 1965. 151 pp. $8.50.

2774. Thomson, Charles. *An Enquiry into the Causes of the Alienation of the Delaware and the Shawanee Indians from British Interests.* 1759; rpt. St. Clair Shores, Michigan: Scholarly Press, 1970. $11.00.

2775. Thrapp, Dan L. *Al Sieber, Chief of Scouts.* Norman: University of Oklahoma Press, 1964. $8.95.

2776. ———. *The Conquest of Apacheria.* Norman: University of Oklahoma Press, 1967. 405 pp. $8.95.

2777. ———. *General Crook and the Sierra Madre Adventure.* Norman: University of Oklahoma Press, 1970. $7.95.

2778. Thwaites, Reuben G., ed. *Jesuit Relations and Allied Documents: The Travels and Explorations of the Jesuit Missionaries in New France, 1610-1791.* Rpt. 73 vols. in 36. New York: Rowman and Littlefield, Inc., 1971. $400.00.

2779. Tibbles, Thomas H. See *Buckskin and Blanket Days*, No. 799.

2780. Timberlake, Henry. *The Memoirs of Lieutenant Henry Timberlake.* 1765; rpt. First American Frontier Series. New York: Arno Press, 1971. $9.00.

2781. * Titiev, Mischa. *The Hopi Indians of Old Oraibi: Change and Continuity.* Rpt. Ann Arbor: University of Michigan Press, 1971. $12.50. In paper: 1944; rpt. New York: Kraus Reprint, 1971. $18.00.

2782. Tixier, Victor. See McDermott, John F. *Tixier's Travels*, No. 2032.

2783. * *To the First Americans, the 4th Annual Report on the Indian Health Program of the U.S. Public Health Service.* Rev. ed. Washington, D.C.: Government Printing Office, 1970. 16 pp. $ .30.

2784. Tolbloom, Wanda. *People of the Snow: The Challenge of Eskimo Canada.* New York: Coward, McCann, Inc., 1957. (Grades 6-8) $3.40.

2785. * Tomkins, William. *Indian Sign Language.* New York: Dover Publications, Inc., 1969. 107 pp. Unabridged and corrected republication of the 1931 fifth ed. of the *Universal Indian Sign Language of the Plains Indians of North America.* $1.25.

2786. * ——. *Universal Indian Sign Language of the Plains Indians of North America,* etc. Eighteenth Ed. San Diego, California: Neyenesch Printers, 1970. 106 pp. $1.50.

2787. Tooker, Elisabeth. *The Iroquois Ceremonial of Midwinter.* New York State Studies Series. Syracuse: Syracuse University Press, 1970. 189 pp. $7.50.

2788. Toponce, Alexander. *Reminiscences of Alexander Toponce.* Ed. Robert A. Griffen. Norman: University of Oklahoma Press, 1970. He was an Indian fighter. $4.95.

2789. *Touch the Earth. A Self-Portrait of Indian Existence.* Compiled by T. C. McLuhan. New York: Outerbridge and Dienstfrey, 1971. 185 pp. $6.95.

2790. Townsend, E. D. *Bird Stones of the American Indian.* New York: William S. Heinman, 1959. $50.00.

2791. Travers, Milton A. *The Last of the Great Wampanoag Indian Sachems.* North Quincy, Mass.: Christopher Publishing House, 1963. $2.75.

2792. ——. *The Wampanoag Indian Federation.* Rev. ed. North Quincy, Mass.: Christopher Publishing House, 1961. $4.50.

2793. Trelease, Allen W. *Indian Affairs in Colonial New York.* Rpt. Port Washington, New York: Kennikat Press, Inc., 1971. $12.00.

2794. Trenholm, Virginia C. *The Arapahoes, Our People.* Civilization of the American Indian Series, No. 105. Norman: University of Oklahoma Press, 1970. 367 pp.

2795. Trenholm, Virginia C., and Maurine Carley. *The Shoshonis: Sentinels of the Rockies.* Civilization of the American Indian Series, No. 74. Norman: University of Oklahoma Press, 1964. 363 pp. $8.95.

2796. Trent, William. *The Journel of Captain William Trent From Logstown to Pickawillany, A.D. 1752.* 1871; rpt. First American Frontier Series. New York: Arno Press, 1971. $6.00.

2797. * Tribbles, Thomas H. *The Ponca Chiefs; An Account of the Trial of Standing Bear.* Ed. Kay Graber. Lincoln: University of Nebraska Press, 1972. $5.50. In paper: $2.25.

2798. * Trigger, Bruce G. *The Huron: Farmers of the North.* New York: Holt, Rinehart and Winston, 1969. 130 pp. In paper: $2.65.

2799. Trotter, George A. *From Feather, Blanket and Tepee: The Indian's Fight for Equality.* Deer Park, New York: Brown Book Company, 1970. $3.50.

2800. Tschopik, Harry. *Navaho Pottery Making.* 1941; rpt. New York: Kraus Reprint Co., 1970. 116 pp. $6.00.

2801. Tuck, James A. *Onondaga Iroquois Prehistory: A Study in Settlement Archaeology.* Syracuse: Syracuse University Press, 1971. 255 pp. $13.50.

2802. Tucker, Glenn. *Tecumseh: Vision of Glory.* Indianapolis: Bobbs-Merrill Company, 1956. 399 pp.

2803. Tunis, Edwin. *Indians.* New York: World Publishing Company, 1965. (Grades 6 up) 157 pp. $6.95.

2804. Turner, Frederick, J. *The Character and Influence of the Indian Trade in Wisconsin.* 1891; rpt. New York: Burt Franklin, Inc., 1970. $7.50.

2805. Turner, Henry S. *The Original Journals of Henry Smith Turner . . . 1846-1847.* Ed. Dwight L. Clarke. Norman: University of Oklahoma Press, 1970. $5.95.

2806. Turner, Katherine C. *Red Men Calling on the Great White Father.* Civilization of the American Indian Series, No. 32. Norman: University of Oklahoma Press, 1951. 235 pp. $6.95.

2807. * Turney-High, Harry H. *The Ethnography of the Kutenai.* 1941; rpt. New York: Kraus Reprint Co., 1970. $10.00.

2808. * ——. *The Flathead Indian of Montana.* 1937; rpt. New York: Kraus Reprint Co., 1970. $6.00.

172

2809. Udall, Louise. *Me and Mine.* See Sekaquaptewa, Helen. No. 188.

2810. * Udell, I. L. *In the Dust of the Valley.* South Dakota Review, 7, No. I (Spring, 1969). 120 pp. $3.00.

2811. * Uhle, Max. See Nos. 4007 and 4021.

2812. Underhill, Ruth M. *Ceremonial Patterns in the Greater Southwest.* Rpt. Seattle: University of Washington Press, 1966. 110 pp. $5.00.

2813. ———. *First Came the Family.* New York: William Morrow and Company, 1958. (Grades 7 up) $4.25.

2814. * ———. *Here Come the Navaho!* History of the Largest Indian Tribe in the United States. Lawrence, Kansas: Haskell Institute, 1953. 285 pp. $1.50.

2815. ———. *Indians of the Pacific Northwest.* Lawrence, Kansas: Haskell Institute, 1950. 232 pp. $1.50.

2816. * ———. *The Indians of Southern California.* Lawrence, Kansas: Haskell Institute, 1953. $ .55.

2817. ———. *The Navajos.* Rev. ed. Civilization of the American Indian Series, No. 43. Norman: University of Oklahoma Press, 1967; rpt. 1971. 292 pp. $6.95.

2818. * ———. *The Northern Paiute Indians.* Lawrence, Kansas: Haskell Institute, 1953. 71 pp. $ .60.

2819. ———. *The Papago Indian Religion.* Columbia University Contributions to Anthropology Series, Vol. 33. 1946; rpt. New York: AMS Press, 1969. 259 pp. $17.50.

2820. * ———. *The Papago Indians of Arizona and Their Relatives the Pima.* Lawrence, Kansas: Haskell Institute, 1950. 68 pp. $ .55.

2821. * ———. *People of the Crimson Evening.* Lawrence, Kansas: Haskell Institute, 1950. 127 pp. $1.00.

2822. * ———. *Pueblo Crafts.* Lawrence, Kansas: Haskell Press, 1960. $ .75.

2823. ———. *Red Man's America: A History of the Indians in the United States.* Chicago: University of Chicago Press, 1953; rpt. 1970. 400 pp. $7.95.

2824. ———. *Red Man's Religion: Beliefs and Practices of the Indians North of Mexico.* Chicago: University of Chicago Press, 1965. 301 pp. A companion to *Red Man's America.*

2825. ———. *Singing for Power: The Song Magic of the Papago Indians of Southern Arizona.* Berkeley: University of California Press, 1938; rpt. 1969 158 pp. $5.75.

2826. ———. *The Social Organization of the Papago Indians.* Columbia University Contributions in Anthropology. Vol. XXX. 1939; rpt. New York: AMS Press, 1969. 280 pp. $14.50.

2827. * ———. *Workaday Life of the Pueblos.* Lawrence, Kansas: Haskell Institute, 1950. 174 pp. $1.00.

2828. United States Bureau of Census. *Indian Population in the United States and Canada.* 13th Census. 1910; rpt. New York: Kraus Reprint Co., 1971. $35.00.

2829. United States Bureau of Census. *Indian Populations in the United States and Canada.* 15th Census. 1930; rpt. New York: Kraus Reprint Co., 1971. $14.50.

2830. United States Bureau of Education. *Indian Education and Civilization.* Rpt. New York: Kraus Reprint Co., 1971. $25.00.

2831. United States Department of the Interior. The Office of Indian Affairs. *Biographical and Historical Index of American Indians and Persons Involved in Indian Affairs.* 8 vols. Boston: G. K. Hall Co., 1965. $705.00.

2832. United States Office of Indian Affairs. *Reports of the Commissioners of Indian Affairs, 1835-1870.* 36 vols. Rpt. New York: AMS Press, 1970. $575.00 / $16.00 each.

2833. United States Solicitor for the Department of the Interior. *Federal Indian Law.* Dobbs Ferry, New York: Oceana Publications, Inc., 1958. $38.00.

2834. United States Twenty-First Congress, 1st Session, 1829-30. *Speeches on the Passage of the Bill for the Removal of the Indians.* 1830; rpt. New York: Kraus Reprint Co., 1971. $15.00.

2835. Unrau, William E. *The Kansa Indians: A History of the Wind People, 1673-1873.* Civilization of the American Indian Series, No. 114. Norman: University of Oklahoma Press, 1971. 244 pp. $8.95.

2836. Urlsperger, Samuel. *Detailed Report on the Salzburger Emigrants Who Settled in America, 1734-1735.* Ed. George F. Jones. Trans. Herman J. Lacher. Vol. 2. Wormsloe Foundations Publications, No. 10. Athens: University of Georgia Press, 1969. $ .75.

2837. * Urquhart, Lena M. *Colorow, the Angry Chieftain.* Denver: Golden Bell Press, 1968. $1.25.

2838. Utley, Robert M. *Custer and the Great Controversy.* Los Angeles: Westernlore Press, 1970. $6.75.

2839. ——. *Frontiersmen in Blue: The United States Army and the Indian, 1848-1865.* New York: Macmillan, 1967. $9.95.

2840. * ——. *The Last Days of the Sioux Nation.* New Haven: Yale University Press, 1963. Approx. 340 pp. $8.50. In paper: Yale University Press, 1963. $2.75.

2841. * Valentine, Victor F., and Frank G. Vallee, eds. *Eskimo of the Canadian Arctic.* Princeton, New Jersey: D. Van Nostrand Company, Inc., 1968. 241 pp. $2.75.

2842. Van Der Donck, Adriaen. *A Description of the New Netherlands.* Ed. Thomas F. O'Donnell. Rpt. New York State Books Series. Syracuse: Syracuse University Press, 1968. $5.50.

2843. Vanderwerth, W. C., ed. *Indian Oratory: Famous Speeches by Noted Indian Chieftains.* Civilization of the American Indian Series, No. 110. Norman: University of Oklahoma Press, 1971. 292 pp.

2844. * Van Every, Dale. *The Art of Empire: The American Frontier 1784-1803.* New York: William Morrow and Company, 1963. $6.95. In paper: New York: New American Library, 1971. $ .75.

2845. * ———. *The Company of Heroes: The First American Frontier, 1775-1783.* New York: William Morrow and Company, 1962. $6.00. In paper: New American Library, 1970. $ .75.

2846. * ———. *Disinherited: The Lost Birthright of the American Indians.* New York: William Morrow and Company, 1966. 279 pp. $8.50. In paper: Avon Book. New York: Avon Books, 1970. 302 pp. $1.25.

2874. ———. *Final Challenge: The American Frontier, 1804-1845.* New York: William Morrow and Company, 1964. $6.00.

2848. * ———. *Forth to the Wilderness.* New York: William Morrow and Company, 1961. In paper: New York: New American Library, 1971. $ .75.

2849. Van Stone, James W. *Eskimos of the Nushagak River: An Ethnographic History.* Seattle: University of Washington Press, 1967. $6.95.

2850. ———. *Point Hope: An Eskimo Village in Transition.* Seattle: University of Washington Press, 1962. 177 pp. $5.95.

2851. * Vaughan, Alden T. *New England Frontier: Indians and Puritans, 1620-1675.* New York: Little Brown, and Company, 1965. $7.50. In paper: $2.95.

2852. Vaughan, Jesse W. *The Battle of Platte Bridge.* Norman: University of Oklahoma Press, 1963. $5.95.

2853. * ———. *Indian Fights: New Facts on Seven Encounters.* Norman: University of Oklahoma Press, 1966. 250 pp. $6.95.

2854. * ———. *The Reynolds Campaign on Powder River.* Norman: University of Oklahoma Press, 1961. 239 pp. $7.95. In paper: 1972. $2.50.

2855. ———. *With Crook at the Rosebud.* Harrisburg, Pennsylvania: Stackpole Books, 1956. $5.00.

2856. Venables, Robert W. *The Crowded Wilderness: The Indian in American History.* New York: Scribner's, 1970. $9.95.

2857. Verrill, A. Hyatt. *The American Indian: North, South and Central America.* 1927; rpt. New York: The New Home Library, 1943. 485 pp.

2858. * Verrill, A. Hyatt, and Ruth Verrill. *America's Ancient Civilizations.* Capricorn Books. New York: G. P. Putnam, 1967. $1.95.

2859. Verwyst, F. Chrysostom. *Chippewa Exercises*. Minneapolis: Ross and Haines, 1972. $12.50.

2860. * Vestal, Paul A. *Ethnobotany of the Ramah Navaho*. 1952; rpt. New York: Kraus Reprint Co., 1971. 98 pp. $8.00.

2861. Vestal, Stanley. *New Sources of Indian History 1850-1891*. Norman: University of Oklahoma Press, 1934; rpt. New York: Burt Franklin, Publisher, 1971. 351 pp. $17.50.

2862. Vestal, Stanley. *Sitting Bull Champion of the Sioux*. A Biography. Boston: Houghton-Mifflin Company, 1932. 380 pp. Also: Civilization of the American Indian Series, No. 46. Rev. ed. 1957; rpt. Norman: University of Oklahoma Press, 1969. $6.95.

2863. ——. *Warpath: The True Story of the Fighting Sioux Told in a Biography of Chief White Bull*. Boston: Houghton-Mifflin, 1934. 291 pp.

2864. ——. *Warpath and Council Fire: The Plains Indians' Struggle for Survival in War and in Diplomacy 1851-1891*. New York: Random House, 1948. 338 pp.

2865. Viereck, Philip. *Eskimo Island: A Story of the Bering Sea Hunters*. New York: John Day Company, Inc., 1962 (Grades 4-9) $3.96.

2866. * Villasenor, David. *Tapestries in Sand: The Spirit of Indian Sandpainting*. Rev. ed. Healdsburg, California: Naturegraph Publishers, 1969. 112 pp. $4.95. Author is Otomi Indian. In paper: $2.95.

2867. * Vivian, Gordon. *The Three-C Site: An Early Pueblo II Ruin in Chaco Canyon, New Mexico*. Anthropology Series, No. 13. Albuquerque: University of New Mexico Press, 1965. 48 pp. $2.00.

2868. * Vivian, Gordon, and Paul Reiter. *The Great Kivas of Chaco Canyon and Their Relationships*. School of American Research Publications No. 22. Albuquerque: University of New Mexico Press, 1960. 119 pp. $3.00.

2869. * Vivian, Gordon, et al. *Kin Kletso, A Pueblo Three Community in Chaco Canyon, New Mexico, and Tree-Ring Dating of the Archaeological Sites in the Chaco Canyon Region, New Mexico*. Vol. 6. Parts I and 2. Globe, Arizona: South-Western Publishing Company, 1965. $5.00.

2870. Vizenor, Carl. *The Everlasting Sky: New Voices from the People Called the Chippewa*. New York: Macmillan, 1972. 140 pp. $4.95. Author is Chippewa.

2871. * Vlahos, Olivia. *New World Beginnings: Indian Cultures in the Americas*. A Viking Compass Book. New York: The Viking Press, 1971. 320 pp. $6.50. In paper: $2.75. Also: New York: Fawcett World Library, 1972. $ .95.

2872. Voegelin, C. F., and F. M. Voegelin. *Map of North American Indian Languages.* Rev. ed. American Ethnological Society Publications. Seattle: University of Washington Press, 1967. $3.00. See also No. 4034.

2873. Vogel, Virgil J. *American Indian Medicine.* Civilization of the American Indian Series, Vol. 95. Norman: University of Oklahoma Press, 1970. 578 pp. $10.00.

2874. *———. *The Indian in American History.* Chicago: Integrated Education Associates, 1968. $ .50.

2875. *———. *This Country Was Ours: A Documentary History of the American Indian.* New York: Harper Row, 1972. $1.95.

2876. *Vogt, Evon Z. *Navaho Veterans: A Study of Changing Values.* 1951; rpt. New York: Kraus Reprint Co., 1971. $18.00.

2877. Voight, Virginia F. *Massasoit: Friend of the Pilgrims.* Indian Series. Champaign, Illinois: Garrard Publishing Company, 1971. (Grade 3) $2.59.

2878. ———. *A Mohegan Chief: The Story of Harold Tantaquidgeon.* New York: Funk and Wagnalls Company, 1971. (Grades 7-11) $3.95.

2879. ———. *Sacajawea.* See and Read Beginning to Read Biography. New York: G. P. Putnam's Sons, 1967. (Grades 3-6) $2.68.

2880. ———. *Uncas: Sachem of the Wolf People.* New York: Funk and Wagnalls, 1970. (Grades 7-10) 209 pp. $3.50.

2881. Volney, Constan F. *A View of the Soil and Climate of the United States of America.* 1804; rpt. Trans. C. B. Brown. Contributions to the History of Geology. Darien, Connecticut: Hafner Publishing Company, 1968. $20.00. Also: New York: Augustus M. Kelley, 1969. $18.50.

2882. Volwiler, Albert T. *George Croghan and The Westward Movement Seventeen Forty-One to Seventeen Eighty-Two.* 1926; rpt. New York: AMS Press, 1970. $11.50. Also: New York: Reprint House International, 1970. $15.50.

2883. Von Mittenwailner, Grith. *Chaul: Eine Unerforschte Stadt an der Weskueste Indiens. Wehr Sakralorchitektur, Profanarchitektur.* New York: De Gruyter, Inc., 1964. $17.50.

2884. *Voth, H. R. *Oraibu Marau Ceremony.* Chicago Field Museum of Natural History Fieldiana Anthropology Series. 1912; rpt. New York: Kraus Reprint Co., 1971. $3.25. See also: Dorsey, George A., and H. R. Voth, No. 1107.

2885. ———. *The Traditions of the Hopi.* Chicago Field Museum of Natural History Fieldiana Anthropology Series. 1905; rpt. New York: Kraus Reprint Co., 1970. $4.50.

2886. *Waddell, Jack O. *The Papago Indians at Work.* Anthropological Papers, No. 12. Tucson: University of Arizona Press, 1969. 159 pp. $5.00.

2887. * Waddell, Jack O., and O. M. Watson. *The American Indian in Urban Society.* Boston: Little, Brown and Company, 1971. $5.95.

2888. Wadsworth, Beula. *Design Motifs of the Pueblo Indians.* San Antonio, Texas: Naylor Company, 1957. (Grades 7 up) $5.95.

2889. Walker, Deward E., Jr. *Conflict and Schism in Nez Perce Acculturation.* A Study of Religion and Politics. Pullman: Washington State University Press, 1971. 171 pp.

2890. ——, ed. *The Emergent Native Americans: A Reader in Culture Contact.* Boston: Little, Brown and Company, 1972. $12.50.

2891. * Walker, George. *Miracle in Moccasins.* My 40 Years as a Missionary to the Indians of the Southwest. Phoenix, Arizona: Phoenician Books, Inc., 1969. 137 pp. $1.50.

2892. Walker, Henry P. *The Wagonmasters: High Plains Freighting From the Earliest Days of the Santa Fe Trail to 1880.* Norman: University of Oklahoma Press, 1970. $8.95.

2893. Walker, Judson E. *The Campaigns of General Custer in the Northwest and the Final Surrender of Sitting Bull.* 1881; rpt. Ann Arbor, Michigan: University Microfilms, 1966. $10.00.

2894. Walker, Robert S. *Torchlights to the Cherokees: The Brainerd Mission.* New York: Macmillan, 1931. 339 pp.

2895. * Wallace, Anthony F. C. *The Death and Rebirth of the Seneca.* With the Assistance of Sheila C. Steen. New York: Alfred A. Knopf, 1970. 384 pp. $8.95. Also: New York: Random House, 1972. $2.45.

2896. ——. *King of the Delawares: Teedyuscung, 1700-1763.* Philadelphia: University of Pennsylvania Press, 1949; rpt. Facsimile ed. Select Bibliographies Reprint Series. New York: Books for Libraries, Inc., 1972. $12.50.

2897. Wallace, Ernest. *Texas in Turmoil: Eighteen Forty-Nine to Eighteen Seventy-Five.* Austin, Texas: Steck-Vaughn Company, 1965. (Grades 9 up) $3.95.

2898. Wallace, Ernest, and E. Adamson Hoebel. *The Comanches; Lords of the Southern Plains.* Civilization of the American Indian Series, No. 34. Norman: University of Oklahoma Press, 1952; rpt. 1969. 381 pp. $7.50.

2899. Wallace, Ernest, and David M. Vigness, eds. *Documents of Texas History.* Austin, Texas: Steck-Vaughn Company, 1963. $5.95.

2900. Wallace Paul. A. *Conrad Weiser, 1696-1760: Friend of Colonist and Mohawk.* 1945; rpt. New York: Russell and Russell, 1972. $27.50.

2901. ——. *Indian Paths of Pennsylvania.* Philadelphia: Pennsylvania Historical and Museum Commission, 1965. $6.00.

2902. * ——. *Indians in Pennsylvania.* Philadelphia: Pennsylvania Historical and Museum Commission, 1964. $2.50.

2903. ——. *White Roots of Peace.* Empire State Historical Publications Series, No. 54. 1946; rpt. Port Washington, New York: Ira J. Friedman, Inc., 1968. $5.00.

2904. Wallower, Lucille. *Hippity Hopper.* New York: David McKay Company, 1957. (Grades 2-4) $2.50.

2905. * Walton, Clyde C., ed. *The Indian War of 1864.* By Captain Eugene F. Ware, 1911. Rpt. New York: St. Martin's Press, 1960. 483 pp. In paper: Lincoln: University of Nebraska Press, 1963. $2.45.

2906. Walton, Joseph S. *Conrad Weiser and the Indian Policy of Colonial Pennsylvania.* 1900; rpt. First America Frontier Series. New York: Arno Press, 1971. $19.00.

2907. Waltrip, Lela, and Rufus Waltrip. *Indian Woman.* New York: David McKay Company, 1964. (Grades 5-9) 169 pp. $3.75.

2908. Ward, Edmund. *Boston in Sixteen Eighty-Two and Sixteen Ninety-Nine: A Trip to New England.* 1905; rpt. Research and Source Works Series, no. 312. New York: Burt Franklin Pub., 1969. $16.50.

2909. Ware, Eugene F. See Walton, Clyde C., No. 2905.

2910. * Waring, Antonio J., ed. *The Laws of the Creek Nation.* University of Georgia Libraries Publications, No. 1. Athens: University of Georgia Press, 1960. $1.50.

2911. ——. *The Waring Papers: Collected Works.* Ed. Stephen Williams. Athens: University of Georgia Press, 1968. $12.50.

2912. Warren, William W. *History of the Ojibway Nation.* 1850; rpt. Minneapolis: Ross and Haines, 1957. 527 pp. $10.00.

2913. Washburn, Cephas. *Reminiscences of the Indians.* 1869; rpt. New York: Johnson Reprint Corp., 1971. $12.50.

2914. Washburn, Wilcomb E. *Red Man's Land, White Man's Law.* New York: Scribner's, 1970. $7.95.

2915. * ——, ed. *The Indian and the White Man.* Documents in American Civilization Series. Garden City, New York: Doubleday and Company, Inc., 1964. 480 pp. $2.95.

2916. * Waterman, T. T. *The Whaling Equipment of the Makah Indians.* University of Washington Publications in Anthropology, Vol. 1, No. 1. Seattle: University of Washington Press, 1967. $2.00. See also Nos. 4008, 4010, 4011, 4013, 4016, 4020, and 4035.

2917. * Waters, Frank. *The Man Who Killed the Deer.* 1942; rpt. Chicago: Swallow Press, Western Sage Paperbook, [1969]. 311 pp. $2.50.

2918. * ——. *People of the Valley.* 1941; rpt. Chicago: The Swallow Press, Inc., 1971. 201 pp. $2.50.

2919. * ——. *Pumpkin Seed Point.* Chicago: Sage Books, 1969. 175 pp. $6.00.

2920. ——. *The Woman at Otowi Crossing.* Chicago: Chicago Press, 1966. $4.95.

2921. * Watson, James B. *Cayuga Culture Change: A Study in Acculuration and Methodology.* 1952; rpt. New York: Kraus Reprint Co., 1971. $8.00.

2922. Wauchope, Robert. *Lost Tribes and Sunken Continents: Myth Method in the Study of the American Indians.* Chicago: University of Chicago Press, 1962. $5.95.

2923. Wax, Murray L. *Indian-Americans: Unity and Diversity.* New York: Prentice Hall, 1970. $5.95. In paper: New York: Prentice-Hall, 1970. $2.95.

2924. Weathers, Winston. *Indian and White: Sixteen Eclogues.* Lincoln: University of Nebraska Press, 1970. $3.95.

2925. Weaver, Thomas, ed. *The Arizona Indian People.* Tucson: University of Arizona Press, 1972.

2926. * Webb, Clarence H. *The Belcher Mound: A Stratified Caddoan Site in Caddo Parish, Louisiana.* 1959; rpt. New York: Kraus Reprint Co., 1971. $18.00.

2927. Webb, Nancy M. *Aguk of Alaska.* Englewood Cliffs, New Jersey: Prentice-Hall, Inc., 1963. (Grades 3-6) $4.50.

2928. Weber, David J. *The Taos Trappers: The Fur Trade in the Far Southwest.* Norman: University of Oklahoma Press, 1971. $8.95.

2929. Wedel, Waldo R. *An Introduction to Pawnee Archaeology.* 1936; rpt. Nashville, Tennessee: The Blue and Gray Press, 1971. 122 pp. $10.00.

2930. ——. *Prehistoric Man on the Great Plains.* Norman: University of Oklahoma Press, 1961; rpt. 1970. 355 pp. $6.95.

2931. Weed, Alberta L. *Grandma Goes to the Arctic.* 4th ed. Philadelphia: Dorrance and Company, Inc. 1957. $3.50.

2932. * Weiner, Michael. *Earth Medicine—Earth Foods: Plant Remedies, Drugs and Natural Foods of the North American Indians.* New York: Macmillan, 1972. $8.95. In paper: $3.95.

2933. Welch, James. *Riding the Earthboy 40.* New York: World Publishing Co., 1971. 55 pp. $6.95. Author is Blackfeet.

2934. Wellman, Paul I. *Indian Wars and Warriors.* North Star Books. Riverside Editions. Boston: Houghton Mifflin Company, 1959. (Grades 7-11) 184 pp. $2.95.

2935. * ——. *The Indian Wars of the West.* New York: Modern Library Editions Publishing Company, [1971]. Originally published as *Death on Horseback.*, 1934. 479 pp. $1.25.

2936. Welsh, Herbert. *Four Weeks Among Some of the Sioux Tribes of Dakota and Nebraska, Together with a Brief Consideration of the Indian Problem.* Philadelphia: Horace F. McCann, 1882. 31 pp.

2937. * Weltfish, Gene. *The Lost Universe: The Way of Life of the Pawnee.* New York: Basic Books, Inc., 1965. 506 pp. $12.50. In paper: Walden Editions. New York: Ballantine Books, 1971. 617 pp. $1.65.

2938. Weslager, Clinton A. *The Delaware Indians: A History.* New Brunswick: Rutgers University Press, 1972. $17.50.

2939. ———. *Delaware's Buried Past: A Story of Archaeological Adventure.* 1944; rpt. New Brunswick: Rutgers University Press, 1968. $6.00. In paper: $2.75.

2940. West, George A. *Copper: Its Mining and Use by the Oborigines of the Lake Superior Region.* 1929; rpt. Westport, Connecticut: Greenwood Press, Inc., 1970. $11.50.

2941. ———. *Tabacco, Pipes and the Smoking Customs of the American Indians.* 1934; rpt. Westport, Connecticut: Greenwood Press, Inc., 1970. $49.50.

2942. West, John. *The Substance of a Journal During a Residence at the Red Colony, British North America.* 1824; rpt. New York: Johnson Reprint Corp., 1970. $9.00.

2943. Weyer, Edward M. *Eskimos: Their Environment and Folkways.* Archon Books. Hamden, Connecticut: Shoe String Press, 1969. $12.50.

2944. Weyer, Montana H. *Trailing the Teepees.* New York: Vantage Press, 1968. $3.75.

2945. * Wheat, Joe B. *Crooked Ridge Village.* University of Arizona Social Science Bulletin No. 24. Tucson: University of Arizona Press, 1954. $1.00.

2946. * ———. *Mogollon Culture Prior to A.D. 1000.* 1955; rpt. New York: Kraus Reprint Co., 1971.

2947. Wheat, Margaret M. *The Survival Arts of the Primitive Paiutes.* Reno: University of Nevada Press, 1967. 117 pp. $10.00.

2948. Wheelwright, Mary C. *Notes on Corresponding Symbols* [of the Navaho] *in Various Parts of the World.* See Newcomb, Franc J. *A Study of Navajo Symbolism,* No. 2201.

2949. Wherry, Joseph H. *Red Blueprint for the Conquest of America.* San Antonio, Texas: Naylor Company, 1970. $4.95.

2950. ———. *Totem Pole Indians.* New York: Funk and Wagnalls, 1970. 152 pp. $6.50.

2951. * White, E. E. *Experiences of a Special Indian Agent.* Rev. ed. 1893; rpt. Norman: University of Oklahoma Press, 1965. A Western Frontier Library Book. 336 pp. $2.95.

2952. White, George. *The Historical Collections of Georgia.* 1855; rpt. Baltimore: Genealogical Publishing Company, 1968. $17.50.

2953. White, Leslie A. *The Acoma Indians.* 47th Annual Report of the Bureau of American Ethnology. Washington, D.C., 1930.

2954. ——, ed. *Lewis Henry Morgan: The Indian Journals 1859-62.* Ann Arbor: University of Michigan Press, 1959. 232 pp.

2955. * ——. *The Pueblo of San Felipe, New Mexico.* The American Anthropological Association. Memoirs, Vol. 38. Washington, D.C., 1932; rpt. New York: Kraus Reprint Co., 1970. $5.00.

2956. * ——. *The Pueblo of Santa Ana, New Mexico.* 1942; rpt. New York: Kraus Reprint Co., 1970. $15.00.

2957. * ——. *The Pueblo of Santo Domingo, New Mexico.* The American Anthropological Association Memoirs, Vol. 43. Washington, D.C., 1935; rpt. New York: Kraus Reprint Co., 1970. $10.00.

2958. * White, Mary. *How to do Bead Work.* 1904. Abridged. New York: Dover Publications, 1972. 142 pp. $1.75.

2959. * White, Raymond C. See No. 4048.

2960. Whiteford, Andrew H. *North American Indian Arts.* New York: Western Publishing Company, 1970. 160 pp. $1.25. Also entitled *Indians: Their Arts and Crafts.*

2961. * Whiting, Alfred F. *The Ethnobotany of the Hopi.* Rpt. Flagstaff, Arizona: Northland Press, 1966. $2.25.

2962. * Whiting, Beatrice B. *Paiute Sorcery.* 1950; rpt. New York: Johnson Reprint Corp., 1963.

2963. Whitman, Alberry A. *Twasinta's Seminoles, or the Rape of Florida.* 1886; rpt. New York: AMS Press, 1970. $5.00.

2964. Whitman, William. *Oto.* Columbia University Contributions to Anthropology Series, Vol. 28. 1937; rpt. New York: AMS Press, 1969. $8.50.

2965. ——. *The Pueblo Indians of San Ildefonso.* A Changing Culture. Columbia University Contributions to Anthropology Series, Vol. 34. 1947; rpt. New York: AMS Press, 1969. 164 pp. $12.50.

2966. Wiesenthal, Eleanor, and Ted Wiesenthal. *Let's Find Out About Eskimos.* New York: Franklin Watts, Inc., 1969. (Grades K-3) 46 pp. $3.75.

2967. Wilcox, Frank N. *Ohio Indian Trails.* Ed. William McGill. 1933; rpt. Kent: Kent State University Press, 1970. 184 pp. $15.00.

2968. *Wild Life on the Plains and Horros of Indian Warfare.* 1891; rpt. St. Louis Missouri: Continental Publishing Company, [1971]. 592 pp. $20.50.

2969. * Wilder, Mitchell A. *Quiet Triumph: Forty Years with the Indian Arts Fund, Santa Fe.* Amon Carter Museum of Western Art Publications. Austin: University of Texas Press, 1971. $2.00.

2970. *Wilderness Kingdom: Indian Life in the Rocky Mountains: 1840-1847.* The Journals and Paintings of Nicolas Point, S.D. Trans. and Introduction by Joseph P. Donnelly, S.J. New York: Holt, Rinehart and Winston, 1967. 274 pp. $17.95.

2971. * Wilford, Lloyd A., et al. *Burial Mounds of Central Minnesota: Excavation Reports.* Prehistoric Archaeology Series. St. Paul: Minnesota Historical Society, 1969. 72 pp. $3.25.

2972. * ——. *Burial Mounds of the Red River Headwaters.* Prehistoric Archaeology Series. St. Paul: Minnesota Historical Society, 1970. 36 pp. $2.00.

2973. * ——. *Late Prehistoric Burial Mounds of the Red River Valley.* Prehistoric Archaeology Series. St. Paul: Minnesota Historical Society, 1970. $2.00.

2974. Wilkins, Thurman. *Cherokee Tragedy: The Story of the Ridge Family and the Decimation of a People.* New York: Macmillan, 1970. 398 pp. $10.00.

2975. ——. *Trail of Tears: The Forced Exodus of an Indian Nation from Appalachia to the West.* New York: Macmillan Company, 1970. $10.00.

2976. * Will, George F., and George E. Hyde. *Corn Among the Indians of the Upper Missouri.* 1917; rpt. Lincoln: University of Nebraska Press, 1960. 323 pp. Also: Gloucester, Mass.: Peter Smith, 1971. $3.75.

2977. * Will, George F., and H. J. Spinden. *The Mandans, A Study of Their Culture, Archaeology and Language.* 1906; rpt. New York: Kraus Reprint Co., 1967. 138 pp. $7.00.

2978. * Willey, Gordon R., ed. *Prehistoric Settlement Patterns in the New World.* 1956; rpt. New York: Johnson Reprint, 1963. $10.00.

2979. Williams, Jean. *Trails of Tears.* New York: G. P. Putnam's Sons, 1972. $4.29.

2980. * Williams, Lewis R. *The Chinook by the Sea.* 1924; rpt. Facsimile ed. Seattle, Washington: Shorey Publications, 1970. $7.50.

2981. Williams, Roger. *A Key into the Language of America.* 5th ed.; rpt. Highland Park, New Jersey: Gryphon Press, 1971. $12.50.

2982. Williams, Stephen W. *The Redeemed Captive Returning to Zion; Or, A Faithful History of Remarkable Occurrences in the Captivity and Deliverance of Mr. John Williams.* 1853; rpt. Select Bibliographies Reprint Series. Freeport, New York: Books for Libraries Inc., 1970. $9.50. Also: 1908; ed.; rpt. New York: Kraus Reprint Co., 1970. $12.00. Also: 1795 ed.; rpt. Ann Arbor, Michigan: University Microfilms, 1966. $5.75.

2983. Williamson, George H. *Road in the Sky.* Hackensack, New Jersey: Wehman Brothers, 1971. $4.50.

2984. * Willoughby, C. C. *Indian Burial Place at Winthrop, Massachusetts.* 1924; rpt. New York: Kraus Reprint Co., 1971. $1.75.

2985. * ——. *Prehistoric Burial Places in Maine.* 1898; rpt. New York: Kraus Reprint Co., 1971. $1.75.

2986. * Willoya, William, and Vinson Brown. *Warriors of the Rainbow: Strange and Prophetic Dreams of the Indians.* Healdsburg, California: Naturegraph, Company, 1962. 94 pp. $4.25.

2987. Wilmsen, Edwin N. *Lithic Analysis and Cultural Inference: A Paleo-Indian Cave.* Anthropological Papers Series. Tucson: University of Arizona Press, 1970. $6.00.

2988. Wilson, Blanche N. *Minnetonka Story.* Minneapolis: Ross and Haines, 1972. $ .95.

2989. * Wilson, Edmund. *Apologies to the Iroquois.* With a study of the Mohawks in High Steel by Joseph Mitchell. New York: Farrar, Straus and Cudahy, 1959. 310 pp. In paper: New York: Random House, 1971. $1.95.

2990. ——. *Red, Black, Blond and Olive.* Fairlawn, New Jersey: Oxford University Press, 1956. $8.50.

2991. Wilson, Elijah N. *Among the Shoshones.* 1910; rpt. Medford, Oregon: Pine Cone Publishers, 1971. 222 pp.

2992. Wilson, Elinor. *Jim Beckwourth: Black Mountain Man and War Chief of the Crows.* Norman: University of Oklahoma Press, 1972. 280 pp. $8.95.

2993. Wilson, George L. *The Hidatsa Indians.* Washington, D.C.: Bureau of American Ethnology, 1924.

2994. Wilson, Gilbert L. *The Horse and the Dog in Hidatsa Culture.* Anthropological Papers of the American Museum of Natural History, Vol. XV, Part II. New York: American Museum Press, 1924; pp. 127-311.

2995. Winslow, Ola Elizabeth. *John Eliot: "Apostle to the Indians."* Boston: Houghton, Mifflin, 1968. 225 pp. $5.95.

2996. Wise, Jennings, C. *Ye Kingdom of Accumacke or the Eastern Shore of Virginia, in the Seventeenth Century.* Baltimore: Regional Publishing Company, 1967. $10.00. Also: See Deloria, Vine, Jr., No. 1042.

2997. Wislizenus, Frederick A. *A Journey to the Rocky Mountains, 1839.* 2nd ed. 1912; rpt. Glorieta, New Mexico: Rio Grande Press, Inc., 1969. $10.00.

2998. Wissler, Clark. *The American Indian, An Introduction to the Anthropology of the New World.* 3rd ed. New York: Oxford University Press, 1938. Also: Gloucester, Mass.: Peter Smith Publisher, Inc., 1971. $5.95.

2999. ——. *Ceremonial Bundles of the Blackfoot Indians.* Papers of the American Museum of Natural History. Vol. 7. Washington, D.C., 1912.

3000. ——. *Indian Costumes in the United States.* A Guide to the Study of the Collections in the Museum. New York: The American Museum of Natural History, 1931. Guide Leaflet, No. 63. 31 pp.

3001. * ——. *Indians of the United States.* Rev. ed. by Lucy W. Kluckhohn. Anchor Book. Garden City, New York: Doubleday and Company, Inc., 1966. 381 pp. $1.95. Also: New York: Doubleday and Company, 1966. $5.95.

3002. ——. *Man and Culture.* 1923; rpt. New York: Johnson Reprint Corp., 1970. $12.50.

3003. ——. *North American Indians of the Plains.* 1920; rpt. New York: Burt Franklin, Pub., 1970. $13.00.

3004. * ——. *Red Man Reservations.* 1938; rpt. Collier Books Edition. New York: Macmillan Company, 1971. 297 pp. $1.95.

3005. ——. *Relations of Nature to Man in Aboriginal America.* 1926; rpt. New York: AMS Press, 1970. $8.50.

3006. ——, et al. *Adventures in the Wilderness.* Yale Pageant of America Series, Vol. 1. Rpt. New York: United States Publishers Association, 1970. $10.75.

3007. Withers, Alexander S. *Chronicles of Border Warfare.* 1831; rpt. Parsons, West Virginia: McClain Printing Company, 1970. $9.00.

3008. Witt, Shirley H. *The Tuscaroras.* New York: Macmillan, 1972. (Grades 5 up) $4.95.

3009. * Witthoft, John. *The American Indian as Hunter.* Rev. ed. Philadelphia: Pennsylvania Historical and Museum Commission, 1967. $ .50.

3010. * ——. *Indian Prehistory of Pennsylvania.* Harrisburg: Pennsylvania Historical and Museum Commission, 1965. $ .50.

3011. * Witthoft, John, and Fred W. Kinsey, eds. *Susquehannock Miscellany.* Harrisburg: Pennsylvania Historical and Museum Commission, 1969. $1.50.

3012. * Wolcott, Harry F. *A Kwakiutl Village and School.* Studies in Education and Culture Series. New York: Holt, Rinehart, and Winston, 1967. 132 pp. $3.25. In paper: 1971. $2.65.

3013. Wolf Eric. *Sons of the Shaking Earth.* Chicago: University of Chicago Press, 1959. $5.50. In paper: $1.95.

3014. Wolfe, Ellen, and Howard Rock. *William E. Beltz (The Story of an American Eskimo).* Minneapolis: Dillon Press, Inc., 1971. $3.95.

3015. Woloshuk, Nicholas, ed. *Edward Borein.* Indians Series, Vol. I. Flagstaff, Arizona: Northland Press, 1968. $12.00.

3016. * Woodbury, Richard B. *Prehistoric Agriculture at Point of Pines, Arizona.* 1961; rpt. New York: Kraus Reprint Co., 1971. $3.50.

3017. * ———. *Prehistoric Stone Implements of Northeastern Arizona.* 1954; rpt. New York: Kraus Reprint Co., 1972. $14.50.

3018. * Woodward, Arthur. *Indian Trade Goods.* Ed. Emory Strong. Portland, Oregon: Binfords and Mort, Publishers, 1967. $1.50.

3019. Woodward, Grace. *The Cherokees.* Civilization of the American Indian Series, No. 65. Norman: University of Oklahoma Press, 1965. 355 pp. $5.95.

3020. ———. *Pocahontas.* Civilization of the American Indian Series, Vol. 93. Norman: University of Oklahoma Press, 1969. 227 pp. $6.95.

3021. * Woodward, Thomas S. *Woodward's Reminiscences of the Creek or Muscogee Indians.* Rev. ed. 1859; rpt. Birmingham, Alabama: Southern University Press, 1969. $7.95. In paper: $3.95.

3022. Woodyard, Darrel. *Dakota Indian Lore.* San Antonio: Naylor Company 1968. (Grades 6-9) $3.95.

3023. Work, John. *The Snake Country Expedition of 1930-31: John Work's Field Journal.* Ed. Francis D. Haines. Norman: University of Oklahoma Press, 1970. $7.95.

3024. * Wright, Barton, and Evelyn Roat. *This is a Hopi Kachina.* Flagstaff, Arizona: Northland Press, 1965. $1.00.

3025. Wright, J. Leitch, Jr. *William Augustus Bowles Director General of the Creek Nation.* Athens: University of Georgia Press, 1967. 211 pp. $6.95.

3026. Wright, Muriel H. *A Guide to the Indian Tribes of Oklahoma.* Civilization of the American Indian Series, No. 33. Rpt. University of Oklahoma Press, 1968. 300 pp. $5.95. Author is Choctaw.

3027. ——. *Springplace: Morawian Mission and the Ward Family of the Cherokee Nation.* Guthrie, Oklahoma: Co-operative Publishing Co., 1940. 93 pp.

3028. Wright, Muriel H., and Joseph B. Thoburn. *Oklahoma: A History of the State and its People.* 4 vols. New York: Lewis Historical Co., 1929.

3029. Wyatt, Edgar. *Cochise: Apache Warrior and Statesman.* Young Pioneer Books. New York: McGraw-Hill, 1953. (Grades 5-8) $3.95.

3030. ——. *Geronimo: Last Apache War Chief.* Young Pioneer Books. New York: McGraw-Hill, 1952. (Grades 5-8) $1.25.

3031. Wyman, Leland C. *Blessingway.* Trans. Father B. Haile. Tucson: University of Arizona Press, 1969. 660 pp. $19.50.

3032. Wyman, Leland, C., ed. *Beautyway: A Navaho Ceremonial.* Bollingen Series, Vol. 58. Princeton: Princeton University Press, 1957. $10.00.

3033. Wyman, Leland C., and Flora L. Bailey. *Navaho Indian Ethnoentomology.* Anthropology Series, No. 12. Albuquerque: University of New Mexico Press, 1964. 158 pp. $3.00.

3034. * Wyman, Leland C., and Clyde Kluckhohn. *Navaho Classification of Their Song Ceremonials.* 1938; rpt. New York: Kraus Reprint Co., 1971. 38 pp. $3.00.

3035. Wyss, Thelma H. *Star Girl.* New York: Viking Press, 1967. (Grades 4-7) $3.95.

3036. Yakima Indians. *An Agreement with the Yakima Nation of Indians and a Draft of a Bill to Ratify Same.* 1894; rpt. Seattle: Shorey Publications, 1972. $4.00.

3037. Young, Mary Elizabeth. *Redskins, Ruffleshirts, and Rednecks.* Indian Allotments in Alabama and Mississippi 1830-1860. Civilization of the American Indian Series, No. 61. Norman: University of Oklahoma Press, 1961. 213 pp.

3038. * Zuni People. *The Zunis: Self Portrayals.* Albuquerque: University of New Mexico Press, 1972. $7.95. In paper: $3.95.

ADDENDA

3041. *American Indian Civil Rights Handbook, See No. 3059.

3042. * Contributions and Accomplishments of the American Indian. San Francisco: The Indian Historian Press, 1972. Nine handbooks are planned for publication in 1972. $2.00 each.

3043. Coombs, L. Madison. The Educational Disadvantage of the American Indian Student. Albuquerque: New Mexico State University Press, 1970. 156 pp.

3044. Fay, George E., ed. Charters, Constitutions and By-Laws of Indian Tribes of North America. Colorado State Occasional Publications in Anthropology. Ethnology Series, No. 1. Greeley: Colorado State College Press, 1967. 120 pp.

3045. ———. Treaties and Land Cessions Between the Bands of the Sioux and the United States of America. Colorado State College Occasional Publications in Anthropology. Ethnology Series, No. 1. Greeley: Colorado State College Press, 1972. 139 pp.

3046. Gray, Andrew B. A. B. Gray Report. Ed. L. R. Bailey. Great West and Indian Series. Vol. 24; rpt. Los Angeles: Westernlore Press, 1971. $7.95.

3047. * Haslam, Gerald W. Forgotten Pages of American Literature. Boston: Houghton Mifflin Co., 1970. 398 pp. (77 pp. on the American Indian)

3048. * Index to Literature on the American Indian: 1970. San Francisco: The Indian Historian Press, 1972. $12.00. In paper $7.00.

3049. * Index to Literature on the American Indian: 1971. San Francisco: The Indian Historian Press, 1972. $10.00. In paper $7.00.

3050. * Indian Voices: The First Convocation of American Indian Scholars. San Francisco: The Indian Historian Press, 1970. $8.00.

3051. Kelley, William F. Pine Ridge 1890. Ed. Alexander Kelley and Pierre Bovis. San Francisco: Pierre Bovis, 1971. 267 pp.

3052. Mooney, James. The Siouan Tribes of the East. Smithsonian Institution Bureau of Ethnology. Bulletin No. 22. Rpt. New York: Johnson Reprint Corp., 1970. 100 pp.

3053. Native Americans Today: Issues and Answers. San Francisco: The Indian Historian Press, 1972. $10.00. The report on the second convocation of American Indian Scholars.

3054. Rinehart, Frank A. *The Faces of Courage: The Indian Photographs of Frank A. Rinehart.* Fort Collins, Colorado: Old Army Press, 1972. 106 pp.

3055. Sanders, Thomas E., and Walter W. Peek, eds. *Literature of the American Indian.* New York: Glencoe Press, 1973. 534 pp. Sanders is Nippawanock-Cherokee. Peek is Metacomet-Narragansett-Wampanoag.

3056. Scneider, Mary J. *Contemporary Indian Crafts.* University of Missouri Museum of Anthropology. Columbia: University of Missouri Press, 1972. 51 pp.

3057. Shames, Deborah, eds. *Freedom with Reservation: The Menominee Struggle to Save Their Land and People.* Madison, Wisconsin: National Committee to Save the Menominee People and Forests, 1972. 116 pp.

3058. Turner, William W. *The Literature of American Aboriginal Languages.* Ed. Nicholas Turner. 1858; rpt. New York: Kraus Reprint Co., 1971. $13.00.

3059. * United States Commission on Civil Rights. *American Indian Civil Rights Handbook.* Washington, D.C.: Government Printing Office, 1972. 96 pp. $ .55.

3060. Winther, Oscar O. *A Classified Bibliography of the Periodical Literature of the Trans-Mississippi West, 1811-1957.* Bloomington: Indiana University Press, 1961. 626 pp.

3061. Winther, Oscar O., and Richard Van Orman. *A Classified Bibliography of the Periodical Literature of the Trans-Mississippi West: A Supplement, 1957-67.* Bloomington: Indiana University Press, 1970. 340 pp.

3062. * Wright, Kathleen. *The Other Americans: Minorities in American History.* Ed. Bernadette Giles. Greenwich, Conn.: Fawcett Publications, Inc., 1971. 256 pp. $ .95.

REPRINTS IN AMERICAN ARCHAEOLOGY
AND ETHNOLOGY

New York: Kraus Reprint Co., 1971

4001. Volume I, 1903-1904. Paperbound $25.00. (See also No. 4003.)

    1. Goddard, Pliny E. *Life and Culture of the Hupa.* 1903.
    2. Goddard, Pliny E. *Hupa Texts.* 1904.

4002. Volume 2, 1904-1907. Paperbound $25.00.

    1. Sinclair, William J. *The Exploration of the Potter Creek Cave* (California) 1904.
    2. Kroeber, Alfred L. *The Languages of the Coast of California South of San Francisco.* 1904.
    3. Kroeber, Alfred L. *Types of Indian Culture in California.* 1904.
    4. Kroeber, Alfred L. *Basket Designs of the Indians of Northwestern California.* 1905.
    5. Kroeber, Alfred L. *The Yokuts Language of South Central California.* 1907.

4003. Volume 3, 1905. Paperbound $25.00

    1. Goddard, Pliny E. *The Morphology of the Hupa Language.* 1905.

4004. Volume 4, 1906-1907. Paperbound $25.00

    1. Nutail, Zelia. *The Earliest Historical Relations between Mexico and Japan.* (From original documents preserved in Spain and Japan.) 1906.
    2. Hrdlicka, Ales. *Contribution to the Physical Anthropology of California.* 1906.
    3. Kroeber, Alfred L. *Shoshonean Dialects of California.* 1907.
    4. Kroeber, Alfred L. *Indian Myths of South Central California.* 1907.
    5. Kroeber, Alfred L. *The Washo Language of East Central California and Nevada.* 1907.
    6. Kroeber, Alfred L. *The Religion of the Indians of California.* 1907.

4005. Volume 5, 1907-1910. Paperbound $25.00

    1. Goddard, Pliny E. *The Phonology of the Hupa Language: Part I. The Individual Sounds.* 1907.

    2. Matthews, Washington (P. E. Goddard, ed.). *Navaho Myths, Prayers and Songs, with Texts and Translations.* 1907.

    3. Goddard, Pliny E. *Kato Texts.* 1909.

    4. Barrett, Samuel A. *The Material Culture of the Klamath Lake and Modoc Indians of Northeastern California and Southern Oregon.* 1910.

    5. Dixon, Roland B. *The Chimariko Indians and Language.* 1910.

4006. Volume 6, 1906. Paperbound $25.00

    1. Barrett, Samuel A. *The Ethno-Geography of the Pomo and Neighboring Indians.* 1908.

    2. Barrett, Samuel A. *The Geography and Dialects of the Miwok Indians.*

    3. Kroeber, Alfred L. *On the Evidences of the Occupation of Certain Regions by the Miwok Indians.* 1908.

4007. Volume 7, 1907-1910. Paperbound $25.00

    1. Uhle, Max. *The Emeryville (California) Shellmound.* 1907.

    2. Sinclair, William J. *Recent Investigations Bearing on the Question of the Occurrence of Neocene Man in the Auriferous Gravels of the Sierra Nevada.* 1908.

    3. Barrett, Samuel A. *Pomo Indian Basketry.* 1908.

    4. Nelson, Nels C. *Shellmounds of the San Francisco Bay Region (California).* 1909.

    5. Nelson, Nels C. *The Ellis Landing (California) Shellmound.* 1910.

4008. Volume 8, 1908-1910. Paperbound $25.00

    1. Kroeber, Alfred L. *A Mission Record of the California Indians.* (From a manuscript in the Bancroft Library.) 1908.

    2. Kroeber, Alfred L. *Ethnography of the Cahuilla Indians.* 1908.

    3. Du Bois, Constance G. *The Religion of the Luiseno Indians of Southern California.* 1908.

    4. Sparkman, Philip S. *The Culture of the Luiseno Indians.* 1908.

    5. Kroeber, Alfred L. *Notes on Shoshonean Dialects of Southern California.* 1909.

    6. Waterman, Thomas T. *The Religious Practices of the Diegueno Indians.* 1910.

4009. Volume 9, 1910-1911. Paperbound $25.00

    1. Sapir, Edward. *Yana Texts.* (Together with Yana myths collected by R. B. Dixon). 1910.

    2. Kroeber, Alfred L. *The Chumash and Costanoan Languages.* 1910.

    3. Kroeber, Alfred L. *The Languages of the Coast of California North of San Francisco.* 1911.

4010. Volume 10, 1911-1914. Paperbound $25.00

    1. Kroeber, Alfred L. *Phonetic Constituents of the Native Languages of California.* 1911.

    2. Waterman, Thomas T. *The Phonetic Elements of the Northern Paiute Language.* 1911.

    3. Kroeber, Alfred L. *Phonetic Elements of the Mohave Language.* 1911.

    4. Mason, John A. *The Ethnology of the Salinan Indians.* 1912.

    5. Dolores, Juan. *Papago Verb Stems.* 1913.

    6. Goddard, Pliny E. *Notes on the Chilula Indians of Northwestern California.* 1914.

    7. Goddard, Pliny E. *Chilula Texts.* 1914.

4011. Volume 11, 1912-1916. Paperbound $25.00

    1. Goddard, Pliny E. *Elements of the Kato Language.* 1912.

    2. Kroeber, Alfred L. and J. P. Harrington. *Phonetic Elements of the Diegueno Language.* 1914.

    3. Goddard, Pliny E. *Sarsi Texts.* 1915.

    4. Kroeber, Alfred L. *Serian, Tequistlatecan and Hokan.* 1915.

    5. Gifford, Edward W. *Dichotomous Social Organization in South Central California.* 1916.

    6. Waterman, Thomas T. *The Delineation of the Day-Signs in the Aztec Manuscripts.* 1916.

    7. Mason, John A. *The Mutsun Dialect of Costanoan, Based on the Vocabulary of De la Cuesta.* 1916.

4012. Volume 12, 1916-1917. Paperbound $25.00

    1. Gifford, Edward. *Composition of California Shellmounds.* 1916.

    2. Kroeber, Alfred L. *California Place Names of Indian Origin.* 1916.

    3. Kroeber, Alfred L. *Arapaho Dialects.* 1916.

    4. Gifford, Edward W. *Miwok Moieties.* 1916.

    5. Bradley, Cornelius B. *On Plotting the Inflections of the Voice.* 1916.

6. Gifford, Edward W. *Tubatulabal and Kawaiisu Kinship Terms.* 1917.
7. Waterman, Thomas T. *Bandelier's Contribution to the Study of Ancient Mexican Social Organization.* 1917.
8. Gifford, Edward W. *Miwok Myths.* 1917.
9. Kroeber, Alfred L. *California Kinship Systems.* 1917.
10. Barrett, Samuel A. *Ceremonies of the Pomo Indians.* 1917.
11. Barrett, Samuel A. *Pomo Bear Doctors.* 1917.

4013. Volume 13, 1917-1923. Paperbound $25.00

1. Sapir, Edward. *The Position of Yana in the Hokan Stock.* 1917.
2. Waterman, Thomas T. *The Yana Indians.* 1918.
3. Pope, Saxton T. *Yahi Archery.* 1918.
4. Sapir, Edward. *Yana Terms of Relationship.* 1918.
5. Pope, Saxton T. *The Medical History of Ishi.* 1920.
6. Sapir, Edward. *The Fundamental Elements of Northern Yana.* 1922.
7. McKern, Will C. *Functional Families of the Patwin.* 1922.
8. Kroeber, Alfred L. *Elements of Culture in Native California.* 1922.
9. Pope, Saxton, T. *A Study of Bows and Arrows.* 1923.

4014. Volume 14, 1918-1919. Paperbound $25.00

1. Mason, John A. *The Language of the Salinan Indians.* 1918.
2. Gifford, Edward W. *Clans and Moieties in Southern California.* 1918.
3. Loud Llewellyn L. *Ethnogeography and Archaeology of the Wiyot Territory (California).* 1918.
4. Barrett, Samuel A. *The Wintun Hesi Ceremony.* 1919.
5. Radin, Paul. *The Genetic Relationship of the North American Indian Languages.* 1919.

4015. Volumne 15, 1919-1922. Paperbound $25.00

1. Barton, Roy F. *Ifugao Law.* 1919.
2. Moss, Claude R., and A. L. Kroeber. *Nabaloi Songs.* 1919.
3. Moss, Claude R. *Nabaloi Law and Ritual.* 1920.
4. Moss, Claude R. *Kankanay Ceremonies.* 1920.
5. Barton, Roy F. *Ifugao Economics.* 1922.

4016. Volume 16, 1919-1920. Paperbound $25.00

1. Barrett, Samuel A. *Myths of the Southern Sierra Miwok.* 1919.
2. Lowie, Robert H. *The Matrilineal Complex.* 1919.
3. Dixon, Roland B., and A. L. Kroeber. *Linguistic Families of California.* 1919.

4. Cope, Leona. *Calendars of the Indians North of Mexico.* 1919.
5. Waterman, Thomas T. *Yurok Geography.* 1920.
6. Hooper, Lucile. *The Cahuilla Indians.* 1920.
7. Radin, Paul. *The Autobiography of a Winnebago Indian.* 1920.
8. Kroeber, Alfred L. *Yuman Tribes of the Lower Colorado.* 1920.

4017. Volume 17, 1920-1925. Paperbound $25.00

1. Radin, Paul. *The Sources and Authenticity of the History of the Ancient Mexicans.* 1920.
2. Kroeber, Alfred L. *California Culture Provinces.* 1920.
3. Parsons, Elsie C. *Winter and Summer Dance Series in Zuni in 1918.* 1922.
4. Goddard, Pliny E. *Habitat of the Pitch Indians, a Wailaki Division.* 1924.
5. Moss, Claude R. *Nabaloi Tales.* 1924.
6. Loud, Llewellyn L. *The Stege Mounds at Richmond, California.* 1924.
7. Kroeber, Alfred L. *Archaic Culture Horizons in the Valley of Mexico.* 1925.

4018. Volume 18, 1922-1926. Paperbound $25.00

1. Gifford, Edward W. *Californian Kinship Terminologies.* 1922.
2. Gifford, Edward W. *Clear Lake (California) Pomo Society.* 1926.
3. Gifford, Edward W. *Mikwok Cults.* 1926.

4019. Volume 19, 1924-1926. Paperbound $25.00

1. Radin, Paul. *Wappo Texts.* (First series). 1924.
2. Loeb, Edwin M. *Pomo Folkways.* 1926.

4020. Volume 20, 1923. Paperbound $25.00

1. Boas, Franz. *Notes on the Tillamook.*
2. Dolores, Juan. *Papago Nominal Stems.*
3. Faye, Paul-Louis. *Notes on the Southern Maidu.*
4. Freeland, L. S. *Pomo Doctors and Poisoners.*
5. Gifford, Edward W. *Pomo Lands on Clear Lake (California).*
6. Goddard, Pliny E. *The Habitat of the Wailaki.*
7. Jones, Philip M. *Mound Excavations near Stockton (California).*
8. Kroeber, Alfred L. *The History of Native Culture in California.*

9. Lowie, Robert H. *The Cultural Connection of Californian and Plateau Shoshonean Tribes.*
10. McKern, Will C. *Patwin Houses.*
11. Marsden, W. L. *The Northern Paiute Language of Oregon.*
12. Mason, John A. *A Preliminary Sketch of the Yaqui Language.*
13. Merrill, Ruth E. *Plants Used in Basketry by the California Indians.*
14. Natches, Gilbert. *Northern Paiute Verbs.*
15. Sapir, Edward. *Text Analyses of Three Yana Dialects.*
16. Spier, Leslie. *Southern Diegueno Customs.*
17. Stricklen, Edward G. *Notes on Eight Papago Songs.*
18. Waterman, Thomas T. *Yurok Affixes.*

4021. Volume 21, 1924-1927. Paperbound $25.00

1. Kroeber, Alfred L., and W. D. Strong. *The Uhle Collections from Chincha (Peru).* And
2. Uhle, Max (Kroeber, A. L., ed). *Explorations at Chincha (Peru).* 1924.
3. Kroeber, Alfred L. and W. D. Strong.*The Uhle Pottery Collections from Ica (Peru).* 1924.
4. Strong, William D. *The Uhle Pottery Collection from Ancon (Peru).* 1915.
5. Kroeber, Alfred L. *The Uhle Pottery Collections from Moche (Peru).* And
6. Kroeber, Alfred L. *The Uhle Pottery Collections from Supe (Peru).* 1925.
7. Kroeber, Alfred L. *The Uhle Pottery Collections from Chancay (Peru).* 1926.
8. Gayton, Anna H. *The Uhle (Pottery) Collections from Nieveria (Peru).* 1927.

4022. Volume 22, 1925-1927. Paperbound $25.00

1. Reichard, Gladys A. *Wiyot Grammar and Texts.* 1925.
2. Gifford, Edward W. *Californian Anthropometry.* 1926.
3. Dangberg, Grace. *Washo Texts.* 1927.

4023. Volume 23, 1926-1928. Paperbound $25.00

1. Gifford, Edward W., and W. E. Schenck. *Archaeology of Southern San Joaquin Valley, California.* 1926.
2. Schenck, William E. *Historic Aboriginal Groups of the California Delta Region.* 1926.
3. Schenck, William E. *The Emeryville (California) Shellmound (Final report).* 1926.
4. Kroeber, Alfred L. *Arrow Release Distributions.* 1927.
5. Kniffen, Fred B. *Achomawi Geography.* 1928.

6. Goddard, Pliny E. *Pitch Accent in Hupa.* 1928.
7. Gifford, Edward W., and R. H. Lowie. *Notes on the Akwa'ala Indians of Lower California.* 1928.
8. Gifford, Edward W. *Pottery-Making in the Southwest.* 1928.
9. Kroeber, Alfred L. *Native Culture of the Southwest.* 1928.
10. Leigh, Rufus W. *Dental Pathology of Aboriginal California.* 1928.

4024. Volume 24, 1927-1930. Paperbound $25.00

1. Gayton, Anna H., and A. L. Kroeber. *The Uhle Pottery Collection from Nazca (Peru).* 1927.
2. Steward, Julian H. *Petroglyphs of California and Adjoining States.* 1929.
3. Gayton, Anna H. *Yokuts and Western Mono Pottery-Making.* 1929.
4. Kroeber, Alfred L. *The Valley Nisenan.* 1929.
5. Goddard, Pliny E. *The Bear River Dialect of Athapascan.* 1929.
6. Kelly, Isabel T. *Peruvian Cumbrous Bowls.* 1930.
7. Kelly, Isabel T. *The Carver's Art of the Indians of Northwestern California.* 1930.
8. Gayton, Anna H. *Yokuts-Mono Chiefs and Shamans.* 1930.
9. Kelly, Isabel T. *Yuki Basketry.* 1930.

4025. Volume 25, 1929. Paperbound $25.00

1. Loud, Lewellyn L., and M. R. Harrington. *Lovelock Cave (Nevada).* 1929.
2. Loeb, Edwin M. *Mentawei Religious Cult.* 1929.
3. Loeb, Edwin M. *Tribal Initiations and Secret Societies.* 1929.
4. Schenck, William E., and E. J. Dawson. *Archaeology of the Northern San Joaquin Valley (California).* 1929.

4026. Volume 26, 1929. Paperbound $25.00

Strong, William D. *Aboriginal Society in Southern California.* 1929.

4027. Volume 27, 1929. Paperbound $25.00

Radin, Paul. *A Grammar of the Wappo Language.* 1929.

4028. Volume 28, 1930-1931. Paperbound $25.00

1. Olson, Ronald L. *Chumash Prehistory.* 1930.
2. O'Neale, Lila M., and A. L. Kroeber. *Textile Periods in Ancient Peru.* 1930.
3. Gayton, Anna H. *The Ghost Dance of 1870 in South-Central California.* 1930.

4. Forde, Cyril D. *Ethnography of the Yuma Indians.* 1931.
5. Du Bois, Constance, and D. Demetracopoulou. *Wintu Myths.* 1931.

4029. Volume 29, 1930-1932. Paperbound $25.00

1. Strong, William D., W. E. Schenck, and J. H. Steward. *Archaeology of the Dalles-Daschutes Region (Oregon and Washington).* 1930.
2. Lowie, Robert H. *A Crow Text, with Grammatical Notes.* 1930.
3. Gifford, Edward W. *The Southeastern Yavapai.* 1932.
4. Kroeber, Alfred L. *The Patwin and Their Neighbors.* 1932.

4030. Volume 30, 1930. Paperbound $25.00

Spier, Leslie. *Klamath Ethnography.* 1930.

4031. Volume 31, 1931-1933. Paperbound $25.00

1. Radin, Paul. *Mexican Kinship terms.* 1931.
2. Gifford, Edward W. *The Northfork Mono.* 1932.
3. Kelley, Isabel T. *Ethnography of the Surprise Valley Paiute.* 1932.
4. Driver, Harold E., and A. L. Kroeber. *Quantitative Expression of Cultural Relationships.* 1932.
5. Gifford, Edward W. *The Cocopa.* 1933.
6. Beals, Ralph L. *Ethnology of the Nisenan.* 1933.

4032. Volume 32, 1932. Paperbound $25.00

1. O'Neale, Lila M. *Yurok-Karok Basket Weavers.* 1932.
2. Clements, Forrest E. *Primitive Concepts of Disease.* 1932.

4033. Volume 33, 1932-1934. Paperbound $25.00

1. Loeb, Edwin M. *The Western Kuksu Cult.* 1932.
2. Loeb, Edwin M. *The Eastern Kuksu Cult.* 1933.
3. Steward, Julian H. *Ethnography of the Owens Valley Paiute.* 1933.
4. Olson, Ronald L. *Clan and Moiety in Native America.* 1933.
5. Steward, Julian H. *Two Paiute Autobiographies.* 1934.

4034. Volume 34, 1934-1936. Paperbound $25.00

1. Leigh, Rufus W. *Notes on the Somatology and Pathology of Ancient Egypt.* 1934.
2. Voegelin, Charles F. *Tubatulabal Grammar.* 1935.
3. Voegelin, Charles F. *Tubatulabal Texts.* 1935.
4. Gifford, Edward W. *Northeastern and Western Yavapai.* 1936.
5. Steward, Julian H. *Myths of the Owens Valley Paiute.* 1936.

4035. Volume 35, 1934-1943. Paperbound $25.00
   1. Waterman, Thomas T., and A. L. Kroeber. *Yurok Marriages.*
   2. Kroeber, Alfred L. *Yurok and Neighboring Kin Term Systems.* 1934.
   3. Drucker, Phillip. *A Karuk World-Renewal Ceremony at Panaminik.*
   4. Kroeber, Alfred L. *Karok Towns.*
   5. Nomland, Gladys A., and A. L. Kroeber. *Wiyot Towns.* 1936.
   6. Waterman, Thomas T., and A. L. Kroeber. *The Kepel Fish Dam.* 1938.
   7. Drucker, Phillip. *Contributions to Alsea Ethnography.* 1939.
   8. Goldschmidt, Walter R., and H. E. Driver. *The Hupa White Deerskin Dance.* 1940.
   9. Spott, Robert, and A. L. Kroeber. *Yurok Narratives.* 1942.
   10. Erikson, Erik H. *Observations on the Yurok: Childhood and World Image.* 1943.

4036. Volume 36, 1935-1939. Paperbound $25.00
   1. Du Bois, Constance. *Wintu Ethnography.* 1935.
   2. Nomland, Gladys A. *Sinkyone Notes.* 1935.
   3. Driver, Harold E. *Wappo Ethnography.* 1936.
   4. Drucker, Phillip. *The Tolowa and Their Southwest Oregon Kin.* 1937.
   5. Lowie, Robert H. *Ethnographic Notes on the Washo.* 1939.
   6. Kniffen, Fred B. *Pomo Geography.* 1939.

4037. Volume 37, 1935-1937. Paperbound $25.00
   1. Klimek, Stanislaw. *Culture Element Distributions, I: The Structure of California Indian Culture.* 1935.
   2. Gifford Edward W., and S. Klimek. *Culture Element Distributions, II: Yana.* 1936.
   3. Kroeber, Alfred L. *Culture Element Distributions, III: Area and Climax.* 1936.
   4. Gifford, Edward W., and A. L. Kroeber. *Culture Element Distributions, IV: Pomo.* 1937.

4038. Volume 38, 1939. Paperbound $25.00

   Kroeber, Alfred L. *Cultural and Natural Areas of Native North America.* 1939.

4039. Volume 39, 1942-1945. Paperbound $25.00
   1. Lowie, Robert H. *The Crow Language: Grammatical Sketch and Analyzed Text.* 1942.

2. O'Neale, Lila M. *Textile Periods in Ancient Peru, II: Paracas Caverns and the Grand Necropolis.* 1942.
3. Muelle, Jorge C. *Concerning the Middle Chimu Style.* 1943.
4. McCown, Theodore D. *Pre-Incaic Humachuco: Survey and Excavations in the Region of Huamachuco and Cajabamba.* 1945.

4040. Volume 40, 1942-1953. Paperbound $25.00

1. Lowie, Robert H. *Studies in Plains Indian Folklore.* 1942.
2. Stewart, Omer C. *Notes on Pomo Ethnogeography.* 1943.
3. Stewart, Omer C. *Washo-Northern Paiute Peyotism: A Study in Acculturation.* 1944.
4. O'Neale, Lila M., and Bonnie J. Clark. *Textile Periods in Ancient Peru; III: The Gauze Weaves.*
5. Cook, Sherburne F., and A. E. Treganza. *The Quantitative Investigation of Indian Mounds, with Special Reference to the Relation of the Physical Components to the Probable Material Culture.* 1950.
6. Cook, Sherburne F. *The Fossilization of Human Bone: Calcium, Phosphate, and Carbonate.* 1951.
7. Cook, Sherburne F., and R. E. Heizer. *The Physical Analysis of Nine Indian Mounds of the Lower Sacramento Valley.* 1951.
8. Kroeber, Alfred L. *Paracas Cavernas and Chavin.* 1953.

4041. Volume 41, 1946. Paperbound $20.00

Nimuendju, Curt. *The Eastern Timbira.* 1946.

4042. Volume 42, 1945-1951. Paperbound $20.00

1. Beals, Ralph L. *Ethnology of the Western Mixe.* 1945.
2. Foster, George M. *Sierra Popoluca Folklore and Beliefs.* 1945.
3. Heizer, Robert F. *Francis Drake and the California Indians.* 1947.
4. Goldschmidt, Walter. *Nomlaki Ethnography.* 1951.

4043. Volume 43, 1946-1956. Paperbound $20.00

1. Pettitt, George A. *Primitive Education in North America.* 1946.
2. Gifford, Edward W. *Surface Archaeology of Ixtlan del Rio, Nayarit.* 1950.
3. Cook, Sherburne F. *The Epidemic of 1830-1833 in California and Oregon.* 1955.
4. Kroeber, Alfred L. *Toward Definition of the Nazca Style.* 1956.

4044. Volume 44, 1945-1954. Paperbound $20.00

1. Beals, Ralph L., and George W. Brainerd, and Watson Smith. *Archaeological Studies in Northeast Arizona.* 1945.
2. Heizer, Robert F., and Edwin M. Lemert. *Observations on Archaeological Sites in Topanga Canyon, California.* 1947.
3. Dozier, Edward P. *The Hopi-Tewa of Arizona.* 1954.

4045. Volume 45, 1952. Paperbound $20.00

Nimuendaju, Curt. *The Tukuna.* 1952.

4046. Volume 46, 1954, 1963. Paperbound $20.00

1. Rowe, John Howland. *Max Uhle, 1856-1944; A Memoir of the Father of Peruvian Archaeology.* 1954.
2. Lanning, Edward P. *A Ceramic Sequence for the Piura and Chira Coast, North Peru.* 1963.

4047. Volume 47, 1956-1959. Paperbound $20.00

1. Heizer, Robert F., and Alex D. Krieger. *The Archaeology of Humboldt Cave, Churchill County, Nevada.* 1956.
2. Kroeber, Alfred L. *Ethnographic Interpretations 1-6.* 1957.
3. Kroeber, Alfred L. *Ethnographic Interpretations 7-11.* 1959.

4048. Volume 48, 1962-1964. Paperbound $20.00

1. Oliver, Symmes C. *Ecology and Cultural Continuity as Contributing Factors in the Social Organization of the Plains Indians.* 1962.
2. White, Raymond C. *Luiseno Social Organization.* 1963.
3. Nadar, Laura. *Talea and Juquila, A Comparison of Zapotec Social Organization.* 1964.
4. Wilson, H. Clyde. *Jicarilla Apache Political and Economic Structures.* 1964.

4049. Volume 49, 1958-1963. Paperbound $20.00

1. Murphy, Robert F. *Mundurucu Religion.* 1958.
2. Baumhoff, Martin A. *Ecological Determinants of Aboriginal California Populations.* 1963.
3. Lanning, Edward P. *Archaeology of the Rose Spring Site INY-372.* 1963.

4050. Volume 50, 1964. Paperbound $20.00

Menzel, Dorothy; John H. Rowe and Lawrence E. Dawson. *The Paracas Pottery of Ica. A Study in Style and Time.* 1964.